Strangers or Co-Pilgrims?

Strangers or Co-Pilgrims?

The Impact of Interfaith Dialogue on Christian Faith and Practice

S. WESLEY ARIARAJAH

FORTRESS PRESS
MINNEAPOLIS

STRANGERS OR CO-PILGRIMS?
The Impact of Interfaith Dialogue on Christian Faith and Practice

Cover image: Indoor flight. ©iStock/Thinkstock; Polka dot. Geometric hipster seamless pattern with round, dotted circle. ©iStock/Thinkstock.
Cover design: Ivy Palmer Skrade

Print ISBN: 978-1-5064-3367-7
eBook ISBN: 978-1-5064-3368-4

The paper used in this publication meets the minimum requirements of American National Standard for Information Sciences — Permanence of Paper for Printed Library Materials, ANSI Z329.48-1984.

Contents

Part IV. Dialogue and Mission

Part V. Dialogue and Religions

Part VI. Three Relevant Issues to Interfaith Relations

Introduction

DIALOGUE BEGINS AT HOME

One morning I opened the mail to find a number of paper-cuttings in a language I did not understand. Among them was a note from a Sri Lankan friend living in Norway. "You are very much in the news here," it said. "You are under attack for the views you are expressing on Christian relations to people of other faiths." Weeks earlier some from the Norwegian press had been in Geneva and interviewed me on the question of dialogue with people of other faiths, and found what I had to say was rather controversial. The interview was published in a leading newspaper in Norway together with extended critical comments from some of the church leaders in the country. The sharpest criticism came from the head of the Methodist Church of Norway: "Dr Ariarajah represents Methodism neither in Sri Lanka nor in the world," he had said.

The criticism and the overall reaction to dialogue in Norway were understandable. Even though Norway is a highly secularized nation, over 90% of the population is at least nominally Christians mainly of the Lutheran tradition. Until Muslim migrants and asylum seekers moved into Norway in recent years, most Norwegian Christians saw the rest of the world as a vast mission field. They never had to live with people who professed another faith. They have not had the experience of knowing a Muslim or a Hindu as a praying person, a believing person and a person with a spiritual history. The belief system of a Norwegian Christian did not have the "theological space" for what God might have been doing in the lives of millions of people who lived outside the Christian fold.

The call to enter into dialogue and to have a new theological assessment of other religious traditions, therefore, fundamentally questioned the presupposition on which their faith and especially the mission of the Church were based. It was to be expected that dialogue would come under attack. And it was just as well, for it created a lively debate within the Norwegian Church.

I have been involved in interfaith relations and dialogue for nearly forty years, locally, regionally, and then globally, by accepting the invitation of the World Council of Churches in Geneva to become initially the Program Secretary for Buddhist/Hindu–Christian Dialogue, and then for over ten years the Director of the Council's Interfaith Dialogue Program.

The most significant aspect of this long involvement, when I look back, is how I have myself grown and changed in my interfaith understanding. Perhaps more importantly, I have recognized how interfaith relations challenges and affects the way one looks at one's own theology, one's attitude to one's scripture, concept of mission and so on. However, all this began when I was still a high-school student, and it would be useful to the reader to know what influences have shaped my long journey.

THE NEIGHBOUR I COULD NOT DISMISS

I began with the story from Norway because my own childhood was, in many ways, the opposite of that of a Norwegian child. In the northern coastal town of Kankesanthurai (KKS) in Sri Lanka, where I grew up, our family was one of only two Protestant Christian families in the town at that time. All our immediate neighbors were Hindus and the nearest church we attended on Sundays was some three miles away. I recall that the children of our immediate Hindu neighbors often sat with us in our evening family prayers. Equally often, I was at the Hindu home when they sang devotional songs and did their *pooja* in the evenings. During Hindu festivals we received fruits, rice-cakes and Asian cookies as gift from our Hindu neighbors. We reciprocated this at Christmas time with cakes and cookies.

Reflecting now on those early years, I suppose what made the difference to me as a child was that in this shared life something more than mere good social interactions was at work. Some of our Hindu neighbors were true devotees. Their religious life meant much to them. And out of that religious life there also sprung a profoundly loving relationship to us, their Christian neighbors. It was natural to them that their children should learn whatever good Christianity had to offer. The fact that we were Christians made little difference to our level of friendship and shared life. They would be the most surprised, if for some reason, we as a family were not all dressed up to go to church on a Sunday!

Years later, when I studied theology, missiology and the history of religions, I felt that the seminary teaching on these subjects did not do full justice to my experience in the Hindu neighborhood. How could we talk about God as though only we had something to say on the experience of being touched by God's grace? How could we talk about mission, as if it is to a people who have had no relationship at all with God? How could we study the history of religions as if it were an academic subject when, in fact, it was the source of throbbing spiritual life in the hearts and minds of many of our neighbors, shaping their views about the world and giving purpose to their whole life?

Yes, the deepest theological problem I faced as a young adult was to realize that we had no place at all for our neighbours' religious life in our theology; they were part only of our missiology. Their religious life was only studied but was never plugged into our self-understanding. Our approach appeared to emphasize the differences among religious communities, rather than seeing ourselves as one community where people lived by different religious symbol systems, often comparable and sharable. At that time I could not articulate what the theological issues were that influenced the way we thought of our neighbors, but I knew there was something missing.

NON–EXCLUSIVE CHRISTIANITY

When I went to the Christian boarding school in Jaffna, I was among the privileged that had the late D.T. Niles, an internationally celebrated ecumenist and missiologist in the 50s and 60s, as the principal of our school and pastor of our church. Niles was deeply influenced by Karl Barth, who was also his personal friend. But he adapted Barth to the Hindu- Buddhist context. It was from him that I learned that a firm and deep commitment to Jesus Christ and a Christian understanding of the world does not necessarily involve condemnation or

rejection of other religions. He showed that one can be committed
to one's faith, be rooted in the Bible, and be open to others as part of
one's obedience to God.

My academic work at the postgraduate level was related to other
religions. After my basic theological studies in Bangalore and a ThM
at Princeton, I did my MPhil at the London University Kings College, specializing in Indian philosophy. My thesis, "Why we live in
a Body? – The Nature, Purpose and Destiny of the Human Body
in Saiva Siddhanta," helped me to delve deeply into the subtle and
profound depths of the analyses of the human predicament found in
the Hindu tradition. I decided to do my doctoral work at the University of London, on "Hindu–Christian Relations in the Ecumenical
Movement."

My interest in a new relationship with people of other faith was
nurtured further by two leading theologians in Sri Lanka, the late
Dr. Lynn A. de Silva and Fr. Aloysius Pieris, who are both known
in Sri Lanka and within dialogue constituency around the world
as among the pioneers in Buddhist-Christian dialogue. I learnt a
lot from them. I have highlighted their contributions in an article
included in this volume, "Buddhist-Christian Dialogue: In Search of
Common Grounds."

THE GLOBAL SCENE

The invitation in 1981 to join the staff of the World Council of
Churches (WCC) in Geneva, to work first as Program Secretary for
Hindu/Buddhist relations, and then as director of its dialogue program for over ten years opened more avenues. It gave me the opportunity to gain more experience in organizing and participating in
dialogue events, and to speak and write on the many dimensions
of dialogue. The divisive debates over dialogue at WCC Assemblies
in Nairobi and Vancouver and in its World Mission Conferences
showed that there are much deeper issues to be taken into account
within the dialogue journey, namely, some of the Christian doctrines
that make it difficult to accept and relate to religious plurality.

Many Christians are willing to be in dialogical relations with
neighbors of other faiths. However, when it comes to the theological
perceptions of other religions, they find that the traditional interpretation of the Bible and the theological explanation of the person and

work of Christ made it impossible to relate to others as fellow pilgrims on a spiritual journey. Theologically, the only possible option vis-à-vis other faiths seems to be a missionary one. Many may have moved away from this approach at the level of relationships, but their theology has not moved. Moreover, preachers keep up the pressure from the pulpit, calling on Christians to save those others "who would perish if they are not brought to the knowledge of Christ."

Most members in Asian congregations, who are not convinced of the need to somehow convert all others, carry a guilty feeling of not fulfilling a Christian obligation. Others, who have an ongoing and friendly relationship with people of other faiths, fail to recognize the witness that is in fact taking place between them as they live together. There is no awareness of the enrichment and mutual correction that can result from a good relationship with neighbors of other faiths.

While working with the WCC and organizing seminars on interfaith dialogue in churches around the world, I found that if we wanted to enable Christians, especially the Protestant Churches, to come to a new relationship with people of other faiths, we needed to re-read the Bible from the perspective of religious plurality. There wasn't any seminar in which "I am the Way, the Truth and the Life, no one comes to the Father except through me" (John 14:6) and "Go therefore and make disciples of all nations, baptizing them in the name of the Father and of the Son and of the Holy Spirit" (Matt 28:19) were not raised.

Therefore, I began to re-read the Bible to see if dialogical relationship and respect for the spiritual life of our neighbors is biblical. The Bible is, of course, not a book on dialogue, and there are a number of passages that are unfriendly to people of other religious traditions of that time. These passages, of course, need to be understood in their specific contexts. But I was also amazed at the enormous resources there are in it for a life of dialogue. I began to collect these resources, resulting in the book, *The Bible and People of Other Faiths* (WCC Publications, 1985), translated into twelve languages.

We, as Christians, have not been equipped to deal with many issues that arise in the context of living in religiously plural societies, such as interfaith marriages, invitations to pray with others, and how one might deal with religious extremism and violence inspired by religious sentiments. I attempted to address these and other pastoral issues in another volume, *Not without My Neighbour: Issues in Interfaith*

Relations (WCC, 1999). The wide receptions these books continue to receive, many years after they were written, indicate that Christians are, in fact, looking for help on these issues. Writing these volumes has also been a learning experience in my own spiritual journey.

Then I began to look at the theology of the church and found that its explication of the faith left no room for a positive response to religious plurality in the world. Rethinking our theology in the context of other religions has become my major preoccupation today. This interest led me to write my latest volume, *Your God, My God, Our God: Rethinking Christian Theology for Religious Plurality* (WCC, 2012). Without this rethinking, our congregations will have no alternative but to operate in two worlds: the "real world" where they interact with neighbors of other faiths as friends and coworkers, and the "religious world" where the same friends become, at least in theory, the objects of their mission. This appeared to be at the heart of the crisis of faith facing most churches which live in pluralistic situations.

This work cannot be done without being attacked by those who stand within the classical theology handed down from the Middle-Ages and the traditional teachings on mission, which were at the service of the expansion of the Church. Dialogue, they assert, undercuts the rationale and the urgency of mission; it compromises Christian theology; and is overly open to other faiths. Indeed it does, and in doing so it challenges us to rethink our faith for a religiously plural world. For me, dialogue seems to be the gospel imperative for our time. We have to be in dialogue in order to build a community of communities. We cannot do otherwise in a world that in so painfully divided. Dialogue therefore constitutes the basic mission and ministry of the church in a divided world.

A number of years after the controversy over the interview in the Norwegian newspaper, I recently returned to Norway for a conference. While I was there, one of the ministers of the Norwegian church gave me a periodical in Norwegian, which I could not read. But I could make out that one part of the title of the magazine contained the word 'dialogue'. "Yes, this is a periodical in Norwegian on dialogue," he told me. "There are so many Muslims among us these days that people want to know what they believe and how we might relate to them." It was good to know that the winds of change have also begun to blow in that part of the world, and they are beginning to experience what churches in Asia and Africa have experienced for centuries. It is perhaps only a breeze at the present time, but it will not be long before it becomes a strong wind. The winds of change on Christian attitudes to other faiths are evident all over the world.

ABOUT THIS VOLUME

For over thirty-five years, I have had the opportunity to travel to many parts of the world to conduct workshops and seminars in various churches on the meaning and practice of interfaith dialogue. I have also organized and participated in many dialogue encounters between peoples of different religious traditions both locally and at the global level. All these have been great learning experiences. This also means that I have been invited to give lectures in many places and to write a number of books and many articles on the subject of dialogue.

When I recently looked at the large collection of articles and lectures I had with me, I was surprised that they touched many areas related to interfaith relations such as scriptures, theology, mission, spirituality and so on, which would give a comprehensive look at the dialogue concern. I felt that a volume that touches the many dimensions of dialogue and the history of the discussions would be a valuable one. In fact, when I gave regular courses that dealt with religious pluralism and interfaith dialogue at the Drew University School of Theology I found it difficult to come across a volume that touched on the different issues that should be addressed, especially in a seminary setting. I have, therefore, selected fifteen of the articles that touch on six areas related to interfaith dialogue for this volume, and hope this volume will meet a felt need in churches, and especially the need for a comprehensive textbook on the subject for seminaries.

These articles were delivered as lectures at conferences or written for periodicals, mainly in Asia, at different times and in response to a variety of circumstances. The unity of the volume lies in the fact that each of the articles addresses one or another of the issues crucial to interfaith relations.

One of the problems I faced is that since these were originally independent lectures given or articles written at different times and locations, there are repetitions of some issues, concerns, and especially my arguments. After a failed attempt to try to deal with it, I have decided to leave them as they are, because each time they were relevant to the topic discussed in the article. I ask for your understanding. I hope you will find it a useful introduction to issues in interfaith dialogue and help you to further explore the questions they raise for you.

I want to add a special note on the first chapter on "Dialogue of Life." This is the very first article I wrote on dialogue some thirty-five years ago, when I was still a parish minister. It was written at the invitation of the Christian Conference of Asia (CCA) in response to the dialogue controversy at the WCC Assembly in Nairobi (1975), which I had attended as a youth adviser. I was asked to write it in a language and style that is easily accessible to a reader in an Asian congregation. I decided to include it as the first article because it is still a very basic introduction to what dialogue is, and what it is not, for those who begin to show interest in it. It also shows where I began, even as other articles would show how I have grown over the years.

Interfaith dialogue began with the basic goal of improving Christian relationships with people of other religious traditions. Gradually we became aware that this new ministry, when taken seriously, presented many new challenges. We were forced to re-examine our approach to religious plurality and our theology of religions. It also has begun to raise questions on how we read our Bible, how we understand Christian mission, and how we do theological reflections in a multi-faith context. As the title of the volume suggests, the emergence and the growth of interfaith dialogue has been looked upon by some as a threat to the future of Christianity and its mission in the world. Others consider dialogue as a phenomenon that would give new vitality and relevance to Christianity in a religiously plural world.

Wherever one stands on the question, I have no doubt that church historians of the future would look back at our times and would identify the quest for new relationship with other religions as one that major turning points in the theological traditions of the church.

I am grateful for my wife, Shyamala, for the enormous help she gave me in the preparation and organization of these articles. I am indebted to the Ecumenical Institute for Study and Dialogue in Colombo, Sri Lanka, and especially to its Director, Marshal Fernando, for his initiative and support in bringing out an earlier version of this volume for the Sri Lankan readers, which includes some of the

articles in this volume. A special thanks to my friend and a fellow pil-
grim in interfaith dialogue, Jesudas Athyal, for his interest in bringing
out this reworked volume with a number of new articles for a wider
audience, and to Fortress Press for making it a reality.

S. Wesley Ariarajah

PART I

The Theory and Practice of Interfaith Dialogue

1.

Dialogue of Life

DIALOGUE IN THE JAFFNA TRAIN

Colombo is the capital city of Sri Lanka. Jaffna is an important town in the northern part of the country. An express train runs between the two cities. "Express" is perhaps a misleading word; the train takes eight hours to cover the distance of some two hundred miles. In many parts of the world trains are much faster and train services are much more efficient. But here in Sri-Lanka express trains take their time.

There are, of course, people who complain about this; they think it is a terrible waste of time. But most of us are used to it, and resigned to it. Some of us even think that the Colombo-Jaffna train has played an important sociological role through the decades

Before the inhibitions of modern life crept into the Jaffna train, perfect strangers who started on the journey in the same compartment, sitting next to or opposite each other, often ended the journey as good friends. They talked; they exchanged information regarding their jobs and their families; they discovered mutual friends and shared interests. In a country where 'arranged marriages' are still the order, even some marriage proposals originated during these long journeys.

Things have changed. Today people are less open. They do not make friends so easily or so fast. But even today eight hours of enforced togetherness will rarely be eight hours of silence. We are bound to make enquiries, ask questions and offer comments. In human company we are rarely silent in the East. It is here in the Jaffna train, more than in any other place, that I have learned the meaning of the word 'dialogue'.

In Sri Lanka 65 percent of our people are Buddhists, 18 percent are Hindus, and eight percent are Muslims. Christians, almost of the same percentage as Muslims, are a small minority, spread throughout the island. The chances of getting a Christian next to you in the Jaffna train are rather remote. Jaffna has the highest concentration of Hindus, in the country, and normally your neighbors in the compartment are likely to be Hindus.

"When do you think we would reach Jaffna?" That's usually how we begin the conversation. In the Western parts of the world they discuss the weather; not in Sri Lanka. Here, when the train will arrive in Jaffna is far more uncertain than the weather.

We move quickly to personal introductions. Then, in all likelihood, we pass on to politics and education—two of the most common topics of conversation in this part of the world. They are topics on which even the least informed hold strong views. Then, more often than one imagines, we pass on to subjects like family life, the problems of youth, unemployment—even to topics like suffering, death and rebirth.

I am a Christian. In fact, a clergyman, though in short sleeves. Fairly early in the proceedings I admit my Christian and clerical status. In my experience, such admission has never put a break on the gathering process of exchanging news and views. But within myself I must face an important issue. Here I am, discussing with a Hindu or a Buddhist, politics and even the questions of suffering and death. Am I, or am I not, engaged in this discussion as a Christian—that is, as one who has committed his life to Jesus Christ? Can I engage in a conversation on any of these issues from a neutral standpoint?

To me the answer seems obvious. If I am a Christian I am always a Christian. I am no less a Christian in this train, talking to a Hindu, than I am in the church participating in a service of worship with fellow Christians.

DIALOGUE UNDER ATTACK IN NAIROBI

Nairobi is a long way off in Kenya, Africa. The Fifth Assembly of the
World Council of Churches (WCC) met there in 1975. I attended
that Assembly as a youth advisor. One of the programs of World
Council has to do with "Dialogue with people of living faiths and
ideologies." When this programme was discussed at the Assembly,
there was heated controversy. There were those who expressed the
fear that dialogue would dilute our faith; others who argued that dialogue would lead to syncretism; still others were afraid that the dialogue programme might divert us from our commitment to mission.
"Why are some Christians so keen on dialogue?" some of them asked.
"Have they lost their sense of mission? Do they not want to proclaim
the Gospel to the millions of people who have not heard the Good
News?" "What is the purpose of dialogue?" others asked. "Is it to join
'them'? Is it to eliminate the differences between 'them' and 'us'? Is it
to form a 'world religion'?"

DIALOGUE IS A WAY OF LIFE

But dialogue goes on in the Jaffna train. Here we are unaware of the
debate that took place in Nairobi. And dialogues go on in all Asian
countries; in trains and buses and schools and markets and fields and
factories. Millions of Asians are daily in dialogue with their brothers and sisters who profess faiths different from their own, or profess no faith at all. Sometimes they are conscious of their religious
differences; at other times they are not. Sometimes the dialogue is
superficial; at other times it deals with issues at depth and matters
of significance. Dialogue goes on at different levels, in many places.
Dialogue is unavoidable; it is inevitable; it is not planned; it simply
happens. In Asia, it is the way of life.

DIALOGUE IS A WAY OF RELATING TO PEOPLE
OF OTHER FAITHS

But the word 'dialogue' has acquired in recent years a more specialized meaning. It denotes a new approach to relating to peoples other
faiths. The purpose here is to explain what such dialogue means and

what it does. But in order to understand that, we must first recognize and affirm the ongoing dialogue of life in all pluralistic situations—that is, in situations like ours in Sri Lanka, where the nation is made up of people who belong to a variety of religious and cultural backgrounds.

Our interest in dialogue is rooted in the belief that God is creator, and therefore the earth and all its people are in one way or another related to God. At the level of theology, dialogue affirms that this world is God's world; God makes and remakes it, and is involved in its total history—not just in the history of Christian people, but in the history of all people. God does not leave himself without witnesses at any time anywhere.

Christians are the community of people who witness to the coming of God's Reign into the world in Jesus Christ, but even they cannot deny God's abiding concern for and continuing activity in the whole of creation. Nor can they ignore the attempts of his creatures everywhere to know him, to love him and to reach him—however different from theirs, or however feeble and ineffectual such attempts may seem to them.

All religious communities are on a pilgrimage. Are they partners in that pilgrimage or rivals and competitors? Should they make it as friends, comparing notes, or as strangers, unconcerned one with the other?

What has God been doing, it asks, in the lives and with the history of hundreds of millions of men and women whose beliefs are different from ours? How do we evaluate their rich spiritual heritage? How do we understand their life and history in relation to our own mission of communicating the message of the gospel to all people everywhere?

THEN AND NOW

It is true that we did not always ask such questions. There was a time when Christians considered other religions to be 'untrue', and that they must be replaced by Christianity. They looked upon other religious communities as rival communities which have to be 'conquered' for Christ.

Much of this is past history. In our attitude to other religions we are more charitable today, and more realistic. We are more willing to listen and to learn; we are more dialogical. Dialogue, thus is a positive approach to the problem of religious plurality. It is positive theologically. It is also positive in our relations and transactions at the practical level.

GUIDELINES FOR DIALOGUE

Two years after the dialogue controversy at the WCC Nairobi Assembly, a group of Christians from many parts of the world met in Chiang Mai, Thailand, to address the problems raised about dialogue at the Assembly. Their purpose was to clarify the meaning of dialogue and think together regarding the goal of dialogue. The meeting produced an important WCC document, "Guidelines for Dialogue with People of Living Faiths and Ideologies" that helped people to understand the nature and purpose of dialogue.

Dialogue is an attempt to understand people of other faiths not as people opposed to us or competing with us but as partners with us in a pilgrimage. It is in the course of the pilgrimage and in the spirit of partnership that we share the message of Christ with them.

THE GOAL OF DIALOGUE?

But what will dialogue achieve? What is it really for? That was the question most persistently asked in Nairobi. Before we discuss the goal and purpose of dialogue, let me share with you an experience I had a few years ago.

The Ramakrishna Mission, named after a great Hindu saint, is a Hindu mission organization. It has centers in many parts of the world. It runs schools and hostels and hospitals—much in the same way as Christian missions did in the past and still do in many places. In Colombo we have a Ramakrishna Mission. It has been their custom for some years now to invite a Christian minister on Christmas Eve to give a message during their evening devotional meeting.

On one of these occasions I was invited to give the Christmas message. Hundreds of Hindu devotees had gathered together in the pooja (prayer) hall to listen to the Christian preacher. I preached a sermon which contained much of what I would preach the next day to my congregation on Christmas Day, but I began with a quote from the

Hindu scriptures and related the Christmas message at many points to what Hindus also believed.

After I had preached the sermon, a Hindu friend took me to the Swami's (priest's) residence in the same compound. "We were much blessed by your message," my friend said to me. I smiled, feeling a little embarrassed. "You have a large gathering" I said, "and people listen so attentively!"

"Yes," he said. "We can get Christians to come and speak to us more often but. . . ." He paused, and then continued, "Most of them do not preach the way you did tonight. They are so closed. They seem to think they have nothing to learn from others."

I was looking into the hall where the Swami was leading the people in the final acts of the *pooja*. They were now joining him in the last devotional song.

My friend was awaiting my response to what he had said.

"Those Christian are convinced," I said, "that they have a message to preach; they are convinced that the message would bring release to all people. . . ."

"Certainly," he interrupted me. "But you see, we too are a mission. We too have our beliefs. We must all preach what we believe. But how can it be that Christians have nothing whatever to learn from Hinduism? How can one reject Hinduism as a whole? When one rejects the religion, one rejects the people."

The Swami had now joined us for a cup of tea and thanked me with great warmth.

On my way home I kept thinking of my friend's questions and his final comment. Have we nothing to learn from Hinduism? In rejecting the religion are we rejecting the people?

DIALOGUE IS FOR COMMUNITY

By listening and learning we grow into a community with others. The purpose of dialogue is indeed to create community across the religious barriers. Let us try to understand clearly what this statement means.

There is the very simple fact that we live with people of other faiths. In Asia we are surrounded by them; we share our life with them; they are our neighbors; they are our colleagues. Our lives at many levels are intertwined with theirs. When a person accepts

Christ, very often his or her immediate relations—parents, brothers and sisters—continue in their old faiths.

We share our racial, national and linguistic identities with people of other faiths. We join hands with them in our struggles to make human life more truly human. In the search for peace and in the task of building up our nations we work with them.

In actual practice, however, we have not fully understood what this shared life means. Both as churches and as individual Christians we live a kind of double life. We seek community with people of other faiths in many spheres of life, but we won't have anything to do with the faith by which they live. We eat with them and work with them but we won't pray with them. In the sphere of religion we hold ourselves apart. We consider them 'lost' until they believe exactly the way we believe. We are ready to teach them but are unwilling to learn from them. In other words, we go on seeking community and at the same time deny community.

Dialogue seeks to counter and correct this attitude. It points to the need for mutual openness. We cannot have community without communication, but we often forget that true communication is a two way process. It cannot take place if one of the partners involved in it says, "I won't listen; I'll only talk."

Of course we have our identity as Christians and it is important to us, but only as others have their own identities as Buddhists or Hindus or Muslims. These distinct identities need not insulate us from one another. Ours need not be an identity which separates or sets us apart. Rather, it can become the basis of a relationship—a relationship of caring and sharing. Dialogue will help us to grow in that relationship.

DIALOGUE AND WITNESS

But why are people opposed to dialogue? Among people who were opposed to dialogue at Nairobi, many were sincere Christians who fear that the stress on dialogue will blunt the cutting edge of mission. "People are already indifferent in matters of evangelism," they say; "the emphasis on dialogue will make them even more indifferent."

This is a legitimate concern, and we must take it seriously. Will dialogue make us less committed to evangelism? Will it prevent us from proclaiming the good news of Jesus Christ to people around us? There are many words we use as Christians, like witnessing, preaching, proclaiming and confessing. Sometimes we talk of "taking Christ" to a place or a people; sometimes we talk of "presenting Christ."

When we preach the gospel, we do not preach in a complete vacuum. We preach to people with whom God is already present. Long before the preacher came along God was with them. An African theologian once said, "God was not a stranger in Africa before the coming of the missionary." God is not a stranger in Asia either. After all, God created Africa and the Africans, and Asia and the Asians—even as he created the missionary! That's why none of us can 'take' God to a new place. For God, no place can be 'new'.

If God has been with the people to whom we proclaim the Gospel, then should we not find out how God has been active in their life? The Good News needs to be shared in the context of God's ongoing activity among a people. Dialogue is what makes us listen to their account of that activity, which is their experience of God.

Many who have taken part in dialogue testify that it is an educational process. They are deeply impressed by the spirituality and the sincerity of many with whom they had been in dialogue. Their sense of commitment is strengthened and their ideas about God become broader. Often we tend to think of God as a tribal deity—our God and not theirs. Dialogue results in a new experience of being challenged in our faith and convictions. Our proclamation thus becomes both a witness and a discovery.

That was true of Peter's proclamation at the house of Cornelius. He began the sermon saying: "Truly I perceive that God shows no partiality, but in every nation anyone who fears him and does what is right is acceptable to him" (Acts 10:34–35). An important point about that story is that Peter was open to listen and to learn. Through listening he came to have a new experience. That experience had a tremendous impact on the early church's mission to the Gentiles. Peter had been preaching for months about God's gift of Christ to his own Jewish people, but now he discovered a new truth about God's relation with other peoples. We ourselves in Asia are in one sense a product of Peter's discovery.

Perhaps at this point we should ask the question: "What is the purpose of witness?" Is it to make the listener come to the same theological understanding as the person who witnesses? What passed for witness was often not witness to the living Christ. Rather it was witness to a theological position about Christ; it was witness to a dogma and not to a person. But what right do we have to insist that everyone must understand and experience Christ exactly as we do?

Incarnation is the Word becoming flesh. It is God embracing humanity in Jesus. It is God's dialogue with the world. What we proclaim is Jesus Christ; when we proclaim him, we are in fact proclaiming God's dialogue with people.

THE EXAMPLE OF GANDHI

Let us take a concrete and fairly well known example. From the writings of Mahatma Gandhi we know that he had a profound interest in Jesus and his teaching. The missionaries insisted that Gandhi was not a Christian because he did not believe in Christ in the way they did, and because he had not received baptism. Gandhi was troubled by this. He could not understand why the missionaries behaved as though Jesus Christ was their private possession. He felt hurt and let down. Why should the missionaries deny that Jesus could have a profound influence on him and others like him in India in ways that perhaps the missionaries could not discern?

Gandhi saw in Jesus "the greatest source of spiritual strength" ever known to human beings. He was convinced that in Jesus we had "the highest example of one who wished to give everything, asking nothing in return," not caring what particular creed people professed. Gandhi knew that Christians believed in Jesus as God's only begotten Son. "Could the fact that I do or do not accept this belief," he asked, "make Jesus have any more or less influence in my life?"

Gandhi's problem was not with Jesus but with Christian people who appeared to treat Jesus Christ as their private property. They insisted that the only way one could have access to Christ was by believing exactly the way they believed. That was the way they bore witness to Christ. Could it be that they were bearing witness to what they believed about Christ, and not to Christ himself?

Dialogue and witness do not present to us alternative courses of action. We do not have recourse to dialogue because we have decided not to witness. Dialogue points to a way of life with others; witness is what happens within that way of life. Dialogue calls us out of our closed and intolerant ways to mutuality and genuine relationship.

Within that relationship, witness does not 'shout at' others or try to 'win over' people; it becomes sharing of what is most precious in our lives, what, in fact, controls our lives.

A PERSONAL EXPERIENCE

Such witness is demanding. It is far more difficult than preaching to large crowds from the isolation and security of pulpits and platforms. Let me illustrate the relation between witness and dialogue from one of my own experiences.

Once, I was travelling by train to a town in the eastern part of Sri Lanka, which has a large concentration of Muslims. I found myself in the company of three young Muslims. We talked about the cyclone that had laid waste to much of the countryside a few months earlier. My companions were traders. They were surprised to learn that I was a Christian minister. Perhaps they thought a clergyman was not knowledgeable about other subjects, so they started talking about religion.

"There is not much difference between the Bible and the Qur'an," one of them remarked, "Most of the stories you have in the Bible we have also in the Qur'an."

At that point it is tempting for a Christian to protest or to point to the differences in the stories. But I knew that they were offering not a theological statement but a statement to link our two religions as a mark of friendship. I registered neither assent nor dissent. I merely smiled.

"There is a lot about Jesus in the Qur'an," the Muslim friend continued, "We consider him a great prophet."

I warmed up. Not even a well organized inter-religious dialogue would offer such a natural opportunity for mutual sharing. I told my friends that I had read the Qur'an in translation and had once written a paper on the concept of justice in the Qur'an. I wasn't trying to impress them; I was also offering them my hand of friendship.

They were visibly pleased that I, a non-Muslim, had studied the Qur'an. We talked of Islam, of the revival of Islam and the rise of Islamic states. We discussed the punishments meted out to people in some Muslim countries. "Why are these so harsh?" I asked them.

"That's very necessary," one of them said. "Islam wants to bring about a just society and a community of love. These punishments are never given privately. They are always given in public. When you cut off a hand of a thief, it is not so much a punishment as a deterrent. Others will now think twice before embarking on a career of crime. Thus its aim is to bring peace and justice in society."

Another friend took over. He related the story of a lady of some standing who had committed an offence. The Prophet had sympathy for her, but he insisted on punishing her because of his total commitment to the goal of a righteous society. "As Christians are you not committed to the same goal?" he concluded.

So I told them how we also had the same emphasis on the primacy of community. I explained to them our understanding of the relationship of the individual to the community, and spoke briefly of the Christian understanding of forgiveness and love and how it is consistent with what we believed about God.

My Muslim friends did not at anytime assert that their religion was superior to mine. I did not claim that Christianity was superior to Islam. We bore mutual witness, and many in the train compartment followed our conversation with interest. I do not know how we measure witness. But I felt that I had borne witness to what I believed about God and how God deals with us, even as the Muslims did to their beliefs.

STRUCTURED DIALOGUE NOT AN END IN ITSELF

We have seen that dialogue is not a new technique which we have to adopt or a new experiment which we are called upon to try out. It is part of our pattern of life in many countries. The purpose of structured dialogues is to deepen this ongoing dialogue of life. It is to make this natural human interaction the arena where we strive to build community.

In order to help us toward this goal, we have had organized dialogues where two or more partners have come together to share their faith and concerns. Christians have had dialogues of this kind with Jews, Hindus, Muslims, Buddhists, and with people who belong to a few other of the traditional religions of Asia and Africa. They have also had dialogue with Marxists, humanists, and others who follow what are called 'secular ideologies'. Such organized dialogues are not ends in themselves. They are meant to help us in our dialogue of daily life.

LOOKING BACK AND AHEAD

But are people of other religions keen on dialogue? It should be admitted that in the beginning they were suspicious and hesitant to enter into dialogue with Christians. That was natural. The history of Christian people abounds with instances of intolerance. So often we have given the impression that we were out to conquer or displace all other religions. So often we have given the impression of being the religious arm of colonizing powers from the West. It was little wonder that friends of other faiths suspect our motives in the beginning. They were afraid that dialogue was a sort of camouflage, and our real motive was to make them Christians and enlarge the Christian empire.

But this situation has changed to a considerable extent. Leaders of other faiths are increasingly more willing to have dialogue with us. Successful dialogues have taken place at national and international levels. In places where relationships between religions have virtually broken down, it is the people who engage in dialogue who keep the lines of communication open. In many instances bridges of understanding have been built and dialogue has borne tangible fruits of friendship.

Apart from this, dialogue has helped us to re-examine our own faith and practices. It has challenged our traditional understanding of God, of salvation, of the uniqueness of Christ, and of the authority of Scripture. It has changed our self-understanding as Christians.

We cannot at this stage evaluate what dialogue has accomplished. While dialogue itself is as old as religions, the recognition of its significance and potential is relatively new. After many years, perhaps, those who keep track of the developments within Christianity may be able to make some assessment of its impact.

Meanwhile, there is a great deal that we can do. Dialogue challenges us to change and renewal. It beckons us to a whole new world of relationships. It urges us to re-examine our theology. It calls us not to give up our faith but to grow in it by living it with humility. And it challenges us to work together with others to meet human need and for justice and peace for all people.

Of course dialogue also involves risks. But that's nothing new for Christians. Their teacher and Lord risked his life for the sake of what he stood for. And he has told us in so many words that we should not expect more: "He who finds his life will lose it, and he who loses his life for my sake will find it."

2.

Who Is the 'Religious Other' to Me?

Self-awareness is said to be one of the important characteristics that separate humankind from the rest of the animal kingdom. Our capacity to reflect on the nature, purpose, and destiny of our own lives contributes to the complexities that mark human thought and relationships; it has been the driving force of the heights and depths of our civilization. Who are we in relation to our own selves, to our neighbors, and to the reality that is behind the universe? This question has given birth to the philosophical and religious traditions that both unite human communities and separate them from one another.

Therefore, in our attempt to foster dialogue, reconciliation, and peace among religious traditions, we may need to return to some of these fundamental issues at the heart of religious life and its manifestation. The issue we hope to explore here is the concept of the 'other'. Who are we in relation to the religious 'other'?

THE 'OTHER' IN THE CONTEMPORARY WORLD

There is a sense in which human beings have always lived in pluralist societies and have found ways to cope with plurality. The emergence of 'world religions' like Christianity, Islam, and Buddhism that crossed cultural boundaries of their origin, and actively sought to create alternate religious communities around their convictions created considerable pressures on interfaith relations. There have been periods of conflict; and other periods when they have lived in harmony, as long as they were in mutual isolation or in an undeclared peace with each other for specific historical reasons.

What is happening in our day is that human communities are being thrown together in unprecedented ways by population movements and the forces of globalization. Be they races, ethnic groups, cultural entities, or religious communities, they are all challenged to live in close proximity to each other and to participate together in a number of dimensions of life, especially in the economic and political fields. We no longer have apples, oranges, and grapes, but a 'fruit salad' of human communities. One of the fears is whether we are in the process of making them into a 'fruit juice' that retains some of all the flavors but obliterates the distinctions.

Much of the tension between religious communities today may well have to do with this enforced proximity and the need to find social, economic, political, and spiritual spaces to be themselves. It is the attempt to deal with this reality that has brought interfaith dialogue into vogue. It has, therefore, become important for the dialogue enterprise to think more about the ways of conceiving the 'religious other' in order to facilitate life in community.

WAYS OF CONCEIVING THE 'OTHER'

There are two distinct schools of thought within the dialogue discussions on the concept of the 'other'. There are some who argue that the aim of dialogue is to remove the alienation between communities by enabling them to go beyond the concept of the 'other'. In a genuine dialogue, they would argue, there is a fusion of horizons and one sees the 'other' not as a distinct reality but a part of oneself. The goal of interfaith dialogue, they hold, is to move from 'us' and 'them' to a common 'we' in which we see ourselves as part of the one human community. In this view we embrace the 'other' and see the 'other' as part of ourselves. This involves the search of a 'spirituality of inclusion' that stands above distinctions and differences.

Others see such a close embrace of the 'other' as both unrealistic and perhaps unwarranted. In their view, what we need to develop is a spirituality that respects the 'otherness' of the 'other'. In other words, in this perspective the distinctions, plurality, and differences among communities need not be superseded or undermined. Dialogue, for this group, is a way in which communities can learn to appreciate differences, respect the distinctiveness of each community, and still search for foundations that would help them to live as a 'community of communities'.

The ultimate goals of the two views, however, point in the same direction, namely, to find ways and means to enable human communities to live together in peace and harmony. It would, therefore, be more useful to go beyond and look at the ways in which the concept of the 'other' can be articulated and related to in ways that build community.

WAYS OF RESPONDING TO THE 'OTHER'

The human response to the 'other' is also a complex phenomenon that needs to be studied in depth from sociological and psychological perspectives. History and memory as well as social identities and psychological needs play significant role in a community's responses to the 'other'. They are further complicated by economic and political realities. One cannot separate out the 'religious' dimensions from the complexities involved in being a segment of the human community. Therefore, what one can hope to do is to point to some of the possible typologies of the responses to the 'other' and examine their role in a religiously plural world.

THE 'OTHER' AS A THREAT

One of the problems that bedevil human communities is the perception of the 'other' as a threat. One need not elaborate the extent to which this reality plays out today in the Middle East. The perception of threat may be real or imagined, but it is often based on historical memories and claims that mutually exclude communities. These perceptions are aggravated by economic and political realities. The perceptions of threat can be dealt with only when the communities are enabled to have a 'new experience' of the 'other'. Providing such a new experience of the 'other' is indeed the goal of dialogue, but the initiation of dialogue becomes an uphill task because of mutual suspicions that are very much a part of the experience of threat. For instance, the divergent views and claims about the land on which both Jewish and Palestinians communities had lived for centuries add to the problem in the Middle East. In such situations, both in the Middle East and elsewhere, the 'other' soon deteriorates into the 'enemy'.

THE 'OTHER' AS DIFFERENT

Where there is no experience of threat, relationships can also be made difficult by the overemphasis of the differences between religious communities. Christian-Muslim relations, for instance, have been corrupted from the beginning by the overemphasis of the differences between them. The long history of accentuating the differences has resulted in an inability to listen to each other with understanding and sympathy. Thus, even though Christians readily accept several characters, including many who seemed to have played minor roles in the Hebrew Bible as prophets, they have had considerable difficulty in affirming Prophet Muhammad, who brought a religious revolution among his people, as a prophet. Theoretically there is nothing in Christianity that should rule out prophets after the time of Jesus. Prophecy is one of the gifts emphasized in the early church.

Similarly, the overemphasis on differences has made it impossible for the Muslims to understand the Christian insistence on the oneness of God and the adherence to the doctrine of the Trinity. I am not suggesting that there are no real issues here that need to be tackled, but the overemphasis of differences has made the listening process a difficult one.

Perceiving differences is not a bad thing. In fact it is important to see differences and it would be less than honest to paper over our differences in search for some facile unity. However, interfaith dialogue is about the art of dealing with our differences. "Different does not mean wrong; it simply means different," I catch myself saying to my World Religions class every year. There are many possible approaches to differences and the plurality that goes with it. Plurality can be experienced as a blessing or a curse, a danger or an opportunity, the reality or its distortion. In a real sense interfaith dialogue has to do with a spirituality that enables us to deal with plurality and the differences that go with it.

THE 'OTHER' AS THE ALTERNATIVE

Many of us are aware of the ongoing difficulties in India between the Christians and Muslims on the one hand and sections within Hinduism on the other. Again, the issues here are enormously complex, defying any simple analysis. However, I would like to isolate one aspect of the problem, the debate over conversion, to illustrate the issue being raised in this discussion. Christians and Muslims see the issue of conversion as a matter of human and religious rights, and all communities, including most of the Hindus, condemn the violence that has attended the conflict.

Some of the Hindus accuse Christians and Muslims of using unethical methods, inducements, and coercion in order to increase their numbers. Muslims and Christians deny these allegations and see legislation against conversions as denial of fundamental human rights. They see the opposition to conversion as the Hindu attempt to preserve the entrenched caste system in India, conversion being the only way in which a low caste or an outcaste person could step out of the system in this life.

But it is important to deal with the deeper issue that troubles the informed Hindu constituency. India has of course seen the rise of many religious impulses in its long spiritual history, and what is loosely called 'Hinduism' is a league of religious strands that embrace such diverse positions about the Ultimate Reality as atheism, monotheism, polytheism, pantheism, panentheism, monism and so on. Religious diversity and the possibility of persons choosing what is the most appropriate religious mode for their own search is generally accepted within Hinduism. The possibility of moving from one commitment to another is also within the Hindu understanding of spiritual life. But they are all seen as part of the common search for a relationship between human beings and the Reality that is behind the universe.

In this context, Christianity and Islam are the two religious traditions within India that strike a discordant note in so far as they present their religious tradition as strict alternatives to other ways of being and believing. The Christian claim to have the 'only' way to salvation, and the Islamic claim to have had the 'final' revelation from God runs against the grain of Indian religiosity. In other words, Hindus are not invited to deal with Christianity and Islam as realities that can enhance and enrich Hindu spirituality (and if necessary reform the Hindu social traditions) but as 'alternatives' to their tradition. The Hindu therefore asks, *Should we be asked to support that which is out to destroy us?*

This is of course a difficult issue because it deals with the self-understandings of religious traditions. But both Christianity and Islam need to come to terms with this reality in an in-depth dialogue with the Hindus and followers of other traditions that have reservations about missions and their goals. Is there a place for the sharing of religious truths in interfaith relations? If so, on what basis, with what intentions, and with what anticipated results?

THE 'OTHER' AS PART OF MY OWN REALITY

Within the Christian tradition there has been, over the past twenty years, an intense search to deal with religious reality in ways that take plurality with the seriousness it deserves. Much of this discussion has taken place under the search for a new Theology of Religions and in attempts to develop Christological formulations that move away from presenting the Christian message as the 'only' alternative to other forms of belief. In the early period of discussions this search was classified under the broad concepts of 'exclusivism', 'inclusivism', and 'pluralism'. Today these categories have been rejected as unhelpful in dealing with the highly nuanced positions that have been developed.

One of the temptations within this debate, however, is to include other religious traditions into one's own perception of reality in one's own terms. There is some legitimacy to this exercise as long as it is an internal religious reflection of a community that seeks to take the total reality seriously in its self-expression. But in the interfaith context, respecting the 'otherness' of the other and allowing the other to define itself are important disciplines. Dialogue is not about dissecting or digesting the other. Rather, it is a truth-seeking and community-building conversation.

THE 'OTHER' AS MY PARTNER AND CO-PILGRIM

It has been said that one needs three attributes to be a true dialogue person: "Humility, more humility, and much more humility." This statement must be seen not as a pietistic sentiment but a theological, spiritual, and pragmatic basis for interfaith relations.

There are three reasons that call for humility on our part:

First, even those whose religions are based on 'revelations' would agree that they do not know the 'whole truth' about the Ultimate Reality. Certainly many religious persons may claim to have, on the basis of their religious tradition, sufficient knowledge about reality and human destiny to be able to make ultimate commitments. Yet no religious tradition can claim to have exhausted the mystery of existence as a whole.

Second, and this is perhaps the most important for our discussion, we do not have direct involvement, knowledge, or experience of the religious experience of the 'other'. Even though in the past some of the religious traditions have drawn negative conclusions about the others based on their positive affirmations, we are increasingly aware of the impropriety of this exercise. My neighbor's religious experience and the ultimate commitments he or she makes on that basis can only remain a mystery to me.

Third, persistent plurality appears to be the stuff of reality. All human attempts at social, political and spiritual levels to enforce uniformity and to bring all of reality into a manageable unity have been frustrated from the beginnings of history. If plurality is the essence of reality, realism demands that we deal with it in creative and proactive ways.

The considerations above challenge us to find new ways of dealing with the other that would contribute to the creation of human community within which religious traditions might play a creative role. I would like to make five points on this issue:

Neighbors Not Strangers

Globalization has made the human community neighbors to each other with the human community having little or no say on the matter. Many of the cities of the world have become a collection of interfaith neighborhoods. People who had been strangers have come to live next door to us, and we are thrown together in having to deal with neighborhood issues.

It is of course possible to still treat neighbors as strangers and to isolate ourselves as religious communities from others. This has been the case with communities that have lived for centuries in multi-religious societies. Today it has become difficult to protect our children from making friends with the 'strangers' at school and the playground, and our young adults from falling in love across the boundaries. The refusal to accept the reality of the neighborhood can lead to much pain and suffering. Dialogue enables us to go beyond living in a state of denial.

Partners and Co-Pilgrims

Those who accept the reality and begin to deal with it gradually begin to realize that at the spiritual level their neighbors are not simply neighbors but also partners and co-pilgrims on a spiritual journey. One of the amazing realities of our day is the way people of religious traditions are discovering each other as praying and believing people with spiritual histories of their own. Never before has there been so much knowledge of each other's faith traditions; never before has there been so much sharing of spiritual practices and resources; never before have there been so many interfaith initiatives and groups. At the heart of the religious consciousness of our day is an interfaith revolution that would bring about remarkable changes to the understanding and practice of religion as we know it. Wilfred Cantwell Smith is right in proclaiming that the "World has gone irreversibly interfaith."

Mutual Correction and Enrichment

The proximity and interaction between religious communities is also resulting in mutual correction, enrichment, and self-criticism. Human interactions can never remain neutral. All the engagements between religious traditions have a way of holding up a mirror to each of the religious traditions involved. Many issues (for example exclusive claims about 'truth', the place of women in religion and society, the balance between individual and community rights, the relationship between religion and state, the meaning and practice of mission, religion and violence, religion and ecology, religious freedom, etc.) have come under scrutiny not only in multi-religious gatherings but within each of the religious communities. There is no doubt that the impetus for these explorations has come from the encounters between religious traditions. Dialogue takes us into unfamiliar territories and forces us to probe unexplored issues within our respective traditions. Dialogue and transformation are deeply interrelated.

Identity in Relationship

This reality calls on all religious communities to rethink the issue of identity. Much of the religious identity is formed in isolation from our neighbors. In that formation there is often an implied exclusion of the 'other'. At times they are formed even as rival identities. Christian theological formation is often accompanied by a missionary formation that builds in a particular perception of the 'other'. While some communities work hard on healing memories, others consciously work on perpetuating memory. This is an important issue because formation of religious identity is central to the future of multi-religious societies. If we do not take steps to build in our children identities founded in relationship—the capacity to see neighbors as an inalienable part of our own lives—we would condemn our future generations to the same vicissitudes we have suffered in our own.

To Ourselves through the 'Other'

In fact, it has become difficult to define our religious traditions or ourselves *without* the other. The boundaries that separated us from the other have begun to erode, and we can no longer pretend to be the only ones that have something to say about life and its destiny. Nor can we ignore the reality that our destinies are closely tied up in social, economic, and political life. Interdependence has become the key word to describe the world we live in.

At the religious level much has changed as well. The interreligious reality has become so prominent that Wilfred Cantwell Smith observes that we already see the emergence of an understanding of religious traditions as nothing more than 'strands' of the "common religious history of humankind." Soon religious traditions would not only need to know each other, but would need each other for their own renewal and advance. As has been said, "We not only need to know the other but also need the other to know ourselves."[1] The path to us runs through the highways and byways of other lives.

This does not of course mean that we will not have our own religious identities or that religious traditions would cease to remain as distinct entities. Rather, we are challenged to explore the other traditions so that we may arrive at a new sense of who we are and how we stand in relationship to others. T. S. Eliot's much-quoted saying rings so true to the interfaith experience in our day:

> We shall not cease from exploration,
> and the end of all our exploring
> will be to arrive where we started
> and know the place for the first time.[2]

1. Diana L. Eck in an address to the Dialogue Working Group of the WCC. Quoted in: S. Wesley Ariarajah, *Power, Politics and Plurality* (Colombo: EISDA, 2016), 35.
2. T. S. Eliot, "Little Gidding," in *Collected Poems* (London: Faber and Faber, 1963).

PART II
Dialogue and Scriptures

3.

The Role of Sacred Texts
in Religious Traditions

When the Sixth Assembly of the World Council of Churches met in August 1983 in Vancouver, Canada, the aboriginal inmates of the Vancouver area penitentiary decided to give a gift "on behalf of the first nations of Canada" to the "Christian peoples gathered from all corners of the earth." The gift was a fifteen meter high totem pole, carved out of a single Cedar wood, given as a "labor of love" by the "marginalized peoples of the land."[1] Although a gift could not be turned down, some sections within the assembly had grave misgivings about formally erecting a totem pole in the middle of a Christian assembly-site. A similar, but a more open and divisive controversy broke out when the aboriginal people of Australia performed traditional rituals and danced around the altar to begin the Opening Worship of the Seventh Assembly in Canberra.

I recall these two incidents not only to lift up the abiding prejudice of the peoples with religious 'texts' about those who do not have written texts, but to recount one of the statements made by a young man from the first nations of Canada during one of several conversations that took place at Vancouver on the significance of totem poles: "The totem pole" he said, "is like your Bible; it talks to us about our origins, our peoples, our connections to the Great Spirit and to the

---

1. Based on the talk given by the leader of the Indigenous People on the occasion of erecting a totem pole at the site of the WCC Assembly in Vancouver, Canada, and the conversations that followed on 25th July 1983. (The author was present on the occasion. No written source.)

creatures of the earth." I was struck at that time by the effortless connection he was able to make between the Bible and the totem pole, but only now, after so many years, I have an opportunity to reflect a little further on the significance of that statement.

RELIGIONS WITHOUT A TEXT

Recent a volume was brought out to mark the hundredth birth anniversary of M. M. Thomas, a celebrated ecumenist from India. In it, David C. Scott, who had worked very closely with Thomas, and had been professor of Religion and Culture at the United Theological College, Bangalore, has contributed a perceptive article on how even liberal, progressive scholars have a troubling blind-spot when dealing with religious traditions. "The first working assumption" says Scott, "is that it is sufficient to be concerned with elite, classical, canonical manifestations of human religion," based on the notion "That by examining the world religions, the so-called great traditions accessible through a dominant classical scriptural tradition, one can adequately understand human religious aspirations and values. Popular, folk, usually pre-literate, regional religious expressions found in myths, stories, and related ritual and shrines are ignored, and even dismissed as peripheral, primitive, unsophisticated and illiterate."[2]

While recognizing the increasing interest among scholars of religion in aboriginal and tribal spiritualities, and acknowledging that the traditions of literacy embody a great deal of the content, form, and style of the more common oral tradition, which are absorbed and sanctified in the text, Scott maintains that "Prior to the universalization of modes of literacy in many cultures, the prestige of literacy was to be found in the belief in and regard for sacred text, which itself was considered to have a supernatural, authoritative meaning in addition to the content of its particular writing." He also notes that within this view, "the written word of the god or gods resided with, and under the control of, elites within the society."[3]

Those who identify religion with written 'sacred texts' too quickly have considerable difficulties in recognizing the aboriginal, native,

2. David C. Scott, "M. M. Thomas in the Multiverse of Religious Traditions," in *The Life, Legacy, and Theology of M. M. Thomas*, ed. Jesudas Athyal, George Zachariah, and Monica Melanchthon (London and New York: Routledge, 2016), 237.
3. Ibid.

tribal and traditional indigenous religions as authentic religious expressions. Year after year, at the first session of my course on Religions at Drew University School of Theology, I asked the students to reflect for a few minutes, and then put down some of the words that came to their minds when they thought of the word 'religion'. The most common words they put down, and repeated to the class, were 'God', 'prayer', 'ethical life', and 'scriptures'. I had given up the hope of hearing the words, 'myths', 'stories', 'rituals', 'land', 'spirit', 'people', and so on. Most Christians in the class cannot imagine a religious tradition without scriptures and their own particular understanding of God, and it comes as a surprise to them that there are, in fact, so many spiritual traditions without any sacred texts right there in their own country.

As we continue to explore the issue in the class, we begin to discover that many of the functions that sacred texts play in the major world religions, and much more, are covered for the indigenous traditions by the myths, stories, traditions and rituals that are handed down from generation to generation, within an unwavering commitment to the land and to the community. Wati Longchar, professor of Christian Theology at the Senate of Serampore College, says that "for many indigenous communities, the land is not just a source of life, but it is also a symbol of unity and identity. The land holds family, clan and tribe together. It is also a symbol of unity of all living creatures, the spirit(s) and the Creator. Therefore the preservation of land is not an issue of utility, but life itself."[4]

One begins to discover that there are religious traditions where the land takes the place of a founder or a sacred text. And when one begins to reflect on this in some depth, one also begins to see the wisdom couched in the words of the young man from the first nations of Canada that the totem pole is like the Bible to Christians. He appears to say that the spiritual heritage of a religious tradition need not always be expressed in a written text but can even be carved into a fifteen meter high totem pole!

It is estimated that there are over three hundred seventy million indigenous peoples on the earth, constituting some five thousand distinct Peoples and Nations, and speaking about four thousand

---

4. Wati Longchar, *Return to Mother Earth: Theology, Christian Witness and Theological Education—An Indigenous Perspective* (Kolkata: Program for Theology and Culture in Asia and Sceptre, 2012), 30–31.

of the seven thousand languages prevalent in our day.[5] It comes as staggering news to my students that so many millions can have meaningful spiritual lives without having to depend on sacred texts.

And yet, when the class moves on, we discover that texts do play a significant role in many of the major religious traditions of the world. So we need to ask questions like, "Why a text?", "How does it emerge?" "What role does it play?" and "How religions differ in their approach to the text?"

DIFFERENT APPROACHES TO THE TEXT

When seen from an inter-faith perspective, what is fascinating is the array of reasons why the text occupies the center of some of the major religious traditions of the world. These religious traditions exhibit a number of different beliefs about the nature and authority of their sacred texts which are instructive for our discussion on the 'text'.

Perhaps four of the world religions—Judaism, Christianity, Islam, and Sikhism—can be called 'religions of the book' because of the central role their scriptures play in shaping their theologies, practices, spiritualities, and understandings of community. But different circumstances led to the emergence of the text in each of these religions. Further, in some of them the finalized text, which assumed scriptural status, emerged through long and complex processes. It is difficult to give an exhaustive account of the struggles and conflicts and the historical and non-theological factors that attended the emergence of sacred texts. What I hope to do is to give the broad outlines of how the text received prominence in each of them in order to draw some general conclusions on the importance texts assumes in religious traditions.

CENTRALITY OF THE TEXT WITHIN JUDAISM

In the case of Judaism, Jews generally hold the view that God 'revealed' or 'gave' the Torah to Moses on Mount Sinai, making it the basis of a covenant relationship between God and the Hebrew people. However, from the time the Hebrews settled down in Canaan and especially after the building of the first Temple, much of Jewish reli-

---

5. https://intercontinentalcry.org/indigenous-peoples/.

gious life was centered on the temple, dominated by the ritual where the produce from the land and animals were offered as sacrifices.

Although the tradition holds that the first five books of the Torah were written by Moses himself, the Book of Leviticus, for instance, is primarily on the temple and the sacrificial system, pointing to the reality that what are considered 'Books of Moses' were, in fact, gradually put together long after people had settled down in Palestine and temple worship had become a reality. The tension between the Torah and the temple, between the prophet and the priest, is evident in many parts of the Hebrew Bible.

Unfortunately, for most of the first millennium BCE the land occupied by the Hebrews was under constant pressure from the super powers of that time like Egypt, Assyria and Babylon. This reality affected all dimensions of Jewish life, but had a lasting impact on the place of the Torah in Judaism. The worship life of the Jewish people, centered on the temple and the sacrificial system, underwent a radical change when around 597 BCE the Babylonians invaded Jerusalem, and as part of the practice at that time, deported a significant part of the population of Judah to Babylon and re-settled peoples from other areas of the Babylonian Empire in Palestine. This dislocation of a substantial part of the Jewish community, called the "Babylonian exile," lasted until around 538 BCE, when Cyrus, the Persian king, allowed the Jews, who wanted to do so, to return to Palestine.

The deportation resulted in the Jewish people in exile having no access to temple-worship and the sacrificial system, aggravated by the Jewish belief that the temple for Yahweh can exist only in Jerusalem. Unlike Hindus, Buddhists, Sikhs, Christians and others who built places for ritualized worship wherever they moved to, Jews looked upon Jerusalem as the only earthly abode of God. Deprived of the home-land, the temple, and the sacrificial system, the only powerful religious symbol to which the Jews in exile turned was the Torah.

Thus, when the Jews in exile retuned to Palestine, and with subsequent developments (not discussed here), there emerged a number of sects within Judaism, some still holding on to the re-built temple as the center of Jewish life, while others gave more importance to the synagogue, where worship was rooted in the Torah. The tension between the two came to an end when the Romans besieged Jerusalem and destroyed the temple in 70 CE, and the eventual dispersal of the Jewish people from Palestine to escape Roman persecution. Torah now became the sole religious symbol for the scattered Jewish community. A religious tradition with the synagogue, where the scripture is interpreted and studied, and rabbis who facilitated this process emerged and established itself; the Judaism we have today is Rabbinic Judaism. Thus, the text moved to the center of Jewish identity and spiritual life and Judaism became almost exclusively a 'religion of the book,' where practices, observances, ceremonies and festivals that sustained the community were drawn from the text.

THE EMERGENCE OF THE CHRISTIAN 'TEXT'

Unlike the Jews and the Muslims, Christians do not believe that God revealed God's will or teachings in a form that had to be committed to a text. Christian belief is that God's revelation took place in the person of Jesus Christ; even Jesus's own teachings are not considered revelations from God. In fact, although the early Christian community, coming from the Jewish tradition, continued to own the Torah, they were without any scriptures of their own for the first two centuries.

Even when the New Testament eventually emerged, it is significant that none of the authors (with the possible exception of the writer of the Book of Revelation) of the Christian Scriptures claim to pass on what has been 'revealed' to them. They do not even contend that the texts produced were written under the inspiration of the Holy Spirit. In fact, the texts that constitute the Christian scriptures had very mundane origins. The initial kernel of what became Christian Scriptures was a collection of Paul's letters, written to congregations he had established to strengthen their faith and to deal with specific questions they had directed to him on pastoral and theological matters.

The writers of the synoptic gospels too had no inkling that what they were writing would become scriptures. Since those who had been Jesus's immediate disciples were gradually passing away, there was the need to preserve the story of Jesus and his teachings. The synoptic gospels were written to meet this need, and in the course of doing so, to interpret the meaning of Jesus's life, death and resurrection to their respective readers. Even the Gospel of John, while dwelling at greater length and depth on the theological and spiritual significance of Jesus and his life, refrains from calling its contents as revealed or inspired by the Spirit.

Most of the books of the New Testament, apart from an early collection made of Pauline letters, would have, under normal circumstances, remained as distinct and isolated pieces in the possession of different early Christian communities. However, as Jesus emerged as a significant religious figure, many others, who had no direct knowledge of Jesus and his life, also began to write 'gospel' narratives (Gospel of Thomas, Gospel of Barnabas, Gospel of Mary and so on) and 'Epistles' which, in the view of the Christian community, were distorting Jesus's life and teachings and the emerging beliefs about him in the early church.

It is this reality that forced the church to develop a 'canon', a list of authoritative writings that represent Jesus's life and teachings and what Christians believed about him at that time. The finalization of the canon, because of deep disagreements over what should be included or left out, lasted for a couple of centuries. The canon was eventually finalized and closed only in 397 CE. It is important to note that the early church developed the canon of texts only to mark the boundaries of the tradition. They never claimed, at that time, that they were sacred, revealed or inspired. They did not even consider them specifically as 'scripture'. All these attributions to the Christian text came much later.

THE SIKH SCRIPTURE

It is of interest that the Sikh scripture, the Guru Granth, also came into being in response to an existential need. Guru Nanak, the founder, was succeeded by his important disciple he had chosen, and initially transition from one guru to the next appears to have gone smoothly, mainly through hereditary lines. However, with the passage of time, serious conflicts began to emerge over succession, threatening to tear the community apart.

Faced with this intractable problem, the tenth guru, Guru Gobind Singh, decided to resolve the issue by declaring that a book containing the available collection of the teachings of Guru Nanak and some of the other Gurus would become the new Guru for the community, and that there would be no more human Gurus in Sikhism. Guru Granth, the Sikh Scripture, has forty-two authors, including

Guru Nanak and six other gurus. It also includes sayings and poems of Islamic Sufis and Hindu holy men.

Thus the text became the center of Sikh life and worship through a historical necessity. Each day it is brought to a podium in the Gurudwara in a procession. When worshippers enter the Gurudwara they would go forward and pay their respects to the Guru Granth before sitting down for worship. The whole worship constitutes an accomplished set of musicians singing the contents of the Granth set to music, followed by a brief mediation on a passage from it. At the end of worship, the Granth is again taken back to its resting place in procession, the leader carrying it on his head, and devotees chanting prayers in great devotion as they followed him.

And yet, the Sikhs do not attribute any divine power to Guru Granth and do not claim that the text was given by or inspired by God. Rather it is seen as a deposit of the wisdom and teachings of the Sikh Gurus and others that would help them to direct their thoughts toward God and their lives toward justice, compassion, and righteousness.

THE ISLAMIC TEXT

A discussion of the origins and development of the Qur'an, the religious text of the Muslims, is a difficult one because of the prevalent view among most Muslims that the Qur'an was given to Prophet Mohammad by God, through the agency of angel Gabriel, word by word, and that it was remembered, memorized and eventually put down in writing without any distortions. It is not important here to discuss this faith-conviction of the Muslim community.

However, at the scholarly level, both Islamic and other Qur'anic scholars point to a much more difficult, contested, and long process that resulted in the text of the Qur'an we have today. The difficulty had to do with the reality that the revelations to the Prophet came over a long period of time, beginning in Mecca in 610 CE and continuing in Medina, to which the prophet had to flee in 621 CE. The preservation of what was recited by the Prophet was difficult, except through memory, because there were no reliable materials to write on at that time. It is said that:

Muhammad was in the habit of asking his scribes to add new verses to different texts. However, this procedure did not apply to all the Qur'anic passages. What he had left before his death (AH 11/AD 632) were merely scattered fragments written on primitive materials, like leather, clay, and palm leaves. These pieces were not kept with Muhammad or anyone in particular. When the compiling of the Qur'an was initiated, the compilation committee did not designate any specific person to collect these pieces but asked everyone who held any portion of the Qur'an to bring it forth. It seems clear that Muhammad had never sought to collect the Qur'an.[6]

It is generally believed that Abu Bakr, the prophet's immediate successor, is instrumental in the effort to collect the scattered sayings, with the help of Zayard B. Thabit, who had served as prophet Mohammad's own scribe. A detailed study of the process of the compilation of the Qur'an in its written form would show that there were parallel collections and conflicting views over the authenticity of a number of passages.

The main point here is that initially the revelations to the Prophet was not intended to be written down as a text. The word 'Qur'an' in Arabic means 'recite'. The Qur'an was to be recited, memorized, remembered and recited again and again. The reciting of the Qur'an itself was the spiritual goal. Even today, at the popular level, recitation of the Qur'an takes precedence over its study. Muslims are expected to obey the will of God that they 'hear' through its recitation. The written text was a secondary necessity so that parts of it may not be forgotten, altered, or distorted with the passage of time.

The religions that have founders like Moses, Jesus and the Prophet Muhammad, carry the burden of having to preserve the story and teachings of the founders, and this has invariably led to the emergence of the texts. This reality is seen also in Buddhism, although it does not necessarily fit the description of a 'religion of the book'.

THE BUDDHIST TEXT(S)

Since Buddhism is also a founded religion, sometime after the Buddha's death, there arose the need to preserve an authentic account of his life and teachings. Ulrich Pagel gives an account of what the tradition says about it:

6. Cf. www.thequran.com/ArticleComments/Details/163.

For this purpose, Mahakasyapa, a prominent disciple of the Buddha, reportedly convened a council in Rajagraha, the capital of Magadha. He appointed five-hundred *arahants* (accomplished monks free of all attachments) to check the authenticity of the teachings submitted to the council. For the doctrine he called on Ananda, the Buddha's personal attendant known to have heard most sermons, to recite all the discourses (*sutta*) he remembered. . . .

For the monastic code, Mahakasyapa summoned Upali, great expert in the *Vinaya,* and asked him to relate all monastic rules he heard from the Buddha's lips. Before a discourse or a precept was formally authenticated, it was subjected to careful scrutiny and required unanimous approval by all five hundred *arahants.* Whenever in doubt, the assembly refused admission out of fear that they unwittingly might alter the Buddha's teaching.[7]

THE HINDU TEXTS: A RELIGION WITH AND WITHOUT FOUNDERS

We had begun with a discussion of traditional, tribal and aboriginal religions that have no specific founders or scriptures, and followed it with the discussion of religions founded by spiritual leaders that invariably resulted in texts. This neat distinction breaks down when one come to the Hindu tradition, which is a mix of a traditional religion, without a known beginning or founders, as well as a number of steams of founded traditions embedded within it.

There is a plentitude of texts that come under the general notion of Hindu Scriptures. Although the *Vedas, Upanishad,* and the *Bhagavad Gita* enjoy special authority within classical Hinduism, a vast corpus of mythology (*puranas*), *agamic,* and *tantric* literature, and great epics (*itihasas*) like *Mahabharata* and *Ramayana* are also considered scriptures. In addition, a considerable body of materials in the many regional languages of India, is also considered authoritative sacred text to specific sections of the Hindu society. The devotional songs of *Alvars* (devotees of Vishnu) and *Nayanmar* (devotees of Shiva), and the devotional songs of saints, like Manikkavasagar (*Tiruvasagam*) and Vallalar (*Tiruvatudpa*), are also considered sacred texts by sections within the Hindu community.

---

7. Jean Holm and John Bowker, *Sacred Scriptures* (London: Printer Publisher Ltd., 1994), 12–13.

The *Vedas* and *Upanishads* are considered 'revealed'scriptures. However, the word 'reveal' in the Hindu tradition does not imply what is meant in the Jewish and Islamic traditions. The word used is *sruti*, which means 'that which was seen', as against all other scriptures, considered *smriti*– 'that which was heard'. It is difficult for those outside the Hindu tradition to understand why the scriptures that are 'seen' are not simply called 'revealed'. Further, since the Qur'an, which is considered a revelation, was all 'heard' by the Prophet, it is also difficult to understand why what was 'heard' cannot be considered to have been 'revealed'. The distinction could be explained this way:

Suppose I *see* a car accident as I walk along the read, I have one kind of knowledge of it. When I return home and tell my wife about the accident, she also gains knowledge of it, but there is a qualitative difference between the two types of knowledge. That which came from my *seeing* is more direct, more authoritative. What my wife *heard* also participates in the same knowledge on the same subject, but is not so direct and therefore cannot be as authoritative as the knowledge that came from the act of *seeing*. The word *seen* in this context denotes knowledge that arises from immediacy of spiritual experiences that the ancient *rishis* have had in their attempts to be in communion with the Divine.

But does this mean that the Vaishnava and Saiva saints, who sang songs of such great devotion of their experience of God's love and grace, did not have the same immediacy of communion with the Divine? When this question is put to the Orthodox Hindus, they would say that the authority of the *Vedas* arise not only from their status as *seen* but also because they are the oldest scriptures and have been remembered and passed down for nearly three thousand years. The predominance of the *Vedas* is argued further with the claim that the *Vedas* existed even before the sages came to know it.

It is also of interest that the *Bhagavad Gita,* which is of much later origin (probably between 400 BCE and 200 CE), is elevated almost to the level of the *Vedas*, and is considered, along with the *Upanishads*, as part of the informal "triple Canon" of Hindu orthodoxy. This meant that the requirement for scriptures to be considered "authoritative" depended more on its inner authority to elicit acceptance than on some external proof that it was 'given' or 'descended' from heaven.

DIVERSE APPROACHES TO THE TEXTS
WITHIN HINDUISM

Most Hindus do not know the text of the *Vedas*, nor are expected to know them in order to be considered Hindus. Neither do they look to the *Vedas* and the *Upanishads* for guidance for their ethical and moral lives. Much of the Vedic texts are memorized in their original language of Sanskrit by priests who use them in rituals. The Upanishadic parts of the *Vedas* provide the basis or the starting point of much of the Classical Hindu philosophic reflections, and the *Bhagavad Gita*, along with the epics, provide the inspiration for Hindu conduct.

Thus, even though *Vedas*, *Upanishads*, and the *Bhagavad Gita* carry greater weight of authority within classical Hinduism in comparison to other scriptures, they do not nullify others. Further, there are vast numbers of Hindus who look to the non-Classical parts of the scriptural tradition as authoritative to them. Much later teachings, like those of Ramakrishna Paramahamsa, Vallalar, and others, are raised by sections of the Hindu community to scriptural status because of the spiritual authority they carry in themselves. And most Hindus who live deeply devout lives may never have read a single page of any of what are considered scriptures within their tradition.

This expansive attitude to the text, and even a lack of any attitude to it, has not undermined Hinduism as a religion, or the authentic spirituality of many who live within that tradition. The phenomenon stares at the face of those who hold that the truth of their religion would stand or fall on the authority given or not given to their scriptural texts.

Further, in India, many millions who adhere to the religious traditions of their particular tribes, like the Dalits, with their own local religious expressions, reject the caste-ridden texts of the Classical/Brahminic Hinduism as oppressive, having no relevance to their religious lives.

To sum up, the discussions we have had so far show that there is a plurality of attitudes to the text in different religious traditions. Islam looks at the Qur'an as God-given revelation—unalterable and binding through time and space. Judaism holds that the Torah was 'revealed' and unalterable, but since it was given centuries ago, one needs to argue over its meaning, interpret it, and re-interpret again and again to arrive at what it can mean for us day. This approach, within Judaism, has meant that the many interpretations given to the original text through the centuries are as important as the text itself. In fact, serious study of the written Torah is always done alongside the two major collections of interpretations (Talmud), which are called the Oral Torah, said to be equally important as the original written text.

In the Christian tradition the text was intended as a witness to the "word made flesh" and as marking the boundaries of the original teachings of Jesus and the early church. In subsequent history the Christian approach to the text underwent many changes to which we will return shortly.

Buddhism, as seen above, began with the intention of having a definitive text and a fixed canon. However, when Buddhism began to move into other parts of Asia, like Tibet, China, Korea, Japan etc., in the true spirit of Buddhism, it 'let go' of both the Buddha and the Canon. The Buddha of the Theravada school of Buddhism of Sri Lanka, Thailand and other parts of South Asia has only little in common with the Bodhisattvas of the Mahayana Buddhism of Tibet and China. Even more radical changes took place when it reached Japan, especially in its expression as Pure Land Buddhism.

What is of interest from the perspective of the 'text' in Buddhism is that India, Tibet, and China also developed their own canons in Pali, Tibetan, and Chinese. While the core of the Buddha's teachings is preserved in these cannons, the Tibetan and Chinese cannons include many texts that would have been firmly rejected at the first Buddhist Council called by Mahakasyapa. In Buddhism, canon came to mean nothing more than a list of texts accepted in different contexts.

ACCRETIONS TO THE ORIGINAL UNDERSTANDINGS OF THE TEXT

In many of the religious traditions, the original intensions of the text underwent significant changes with the passage of time and historical circumstances. This is particularly true of religious traditions like Buddhism, Christianity, and Islam, which began missions to carry the messages of their founders beyond the geographical and cultural contexts in which they were given. The problem lies in the reality that in a new geographical, cultural and linguistic context the original message is likely to be assimilated, syncretized, or distorted.

Buddhism, Islam, and Christianity have responded to this problem in different ways.

In the case of Buddhism, as discussed above, although a canon was produced to preserve the Buddha's original teachings, no special attempts were undertaken to monitor and control the 'purity' of the message and the text that carried it, resulting in a multiplicity of scriptural canons and Buddha figures. As Buddhism moved into Tibet, China and Japan it got heavily syncretized, almost losing its moorings in the Buddhism that emerged in North India.

Although some equate the Buddhist traditions in these countries to Christian confessions and denominations, it is more appropriate to speak of them as different forms of Buddhism that emerged from the original Buddhist movement in India. Some would rightly ask, "What, if any, does the Buddha of the Pure Land tradition in Japan has to do with the Buddha who received enlightenment under the Bodhi tree at Budh Gaya?" Such was the price Buddhism had to pay for letting go of its text!

Islam, for its part, responded to this problem by solidifying its position that the Qur'an was given word by word by God and cannot be changed or altered for any reason and anywhere in the world to which the message was taken. Further, it insisted that the Arabic language in which it was revealed was intrinsic to the Qur'an. Translations of the Qur'an were eventually allowed out of necessity, but Qur'an essentially exists only in the Arabic language. Therefore, Muslims in all parts of the world memorize and recite the Qur'an only in Arabic, even if they do not always understand the meaning of the Arabic words.

Although Christianity had a canon, as mentioned before, originally its contents were not considered to have been revealed. This resulted in any authority the text might have had being subsumed within the authority of the church. When the church, as an institution, grew in power, the text served the purpose mainly of propping up the teachings of the church, which were not necessarily drawn from the scriptures. It is this reality that led Martin Luther to protest, resulting in the Protestant Reformation.

In the course of the polemics against the church's inordinate levels of authority on matters of faith, Luther enunciated the principle, *sola scriptura*, 'scripture alone', as one of the three cardinal pillars of Protestant Christianity. In subsequent developments many accretions were made to fortify the authority of the scripture. Now the Christian text was claimed to have been 'revealed', 'inspired', and said to contain 'everything necessary for salvation'. Some sections within Christianity went even further to claim that the Christian scriptures are 'inerrant' and 'infallible'. In fact, within some sectors of Christianity, the attitude to the Christian scriptures mirror that of the conservative Muslims' approach to the Qur'an, both insisting that the texts are not the Word of God but the *Words* of God, and that only a literal reading of the text is permissible.

Attributing divine authority to the text created many problems to the Christian community, leading to new divisions over the question of the nature of the authority of scripture. In what sense is the Bible authoritative? Do the teachings in Book of Leviticus and in the Sermon on the Mount have the same authority to a Christian because the whole Bible is believed to be 'revealed'? Or do we, unofficially, live with our own 'canons within the Canon'? On what basis is Bible authoritative? Is it because it was revealed by the God? Is it because it comes out of an immediacy of experience on the part of those who wrote it? Is it because it has an intrinsic power to elicit authority? If it is inspired, inerrant, and infallible, can the text be submitted to historical critical studies? Christian tradition, by spinning new attributes to its text, got caught in a web that it had spun, with very few options to move out of it. The very text that could have been the center of unity turned out to be the source of dissention.

THE ADVANTAGES OF HAVING A RELIGIOUS TEXT

Since we are aware that a text is not a necessity to be a religious tradition, and that vibrant religious/spiritual traditions exist in all parts of the world without sacred texts, one might ask the question: What are some of the advantages and problems in having a text to define one's religion? In terms of advantages, we have already seen the role texts play in preserving the teachings of the founders and in setting the boundaries of tradition to prevent excessive dilution and distortions of its central message that might occur in the course of time.

This is especially useful when a religious tradition, unlike the tribal, aboriginal and traditional religious that remain indigenous, move or are forced to move from the place of its origin into different cultures. Judaism is a compelling example of how a persecuted, scattered and beleaguered community, at a particular period of history, survived by clinging on to the text as the predominant provider of its identity and hope.

The common owning of an agreed text as the spiritual source helps the communities to hold together: joint study, reflection, and meditations on the text play a significant role in some branches of Christianity and Buddhism. Further, in all religious traditions with written texts, the texts play a significant role in community worship. In fact, in Judaism, Islam, Protestant forms of Christianity and Sikhism, the reading, expounding and application of the message of the text for life situations constitute the main acts of worship. In Hinduism and Buddhism, chanting of the text plays a central role in worship. Most of the religious traditions also look to the texts for directions for ethical and moral lives.

THE PROBLEMS RELATED TO THE TEXT

The religious texts that are embraced as 'scriptures' present a serious problem in that they belong to a particular period of time, pertinent to the cultural ethos of that time, and in most cases, address issues and concerns that were relevant to the people of that time. In most cases, thousands of years stand between the text and those who use it today. It is, of course, true that some enduring spiritual and ethical values and teachings transcend time and space. But it is also the case that much of the teachings in the texts are contextual and become obsolete with the passage of time.

The Latin American liberation theologians go further to point out that many ignore the reality that most of the texts that assume sacred status have particular social contexts as well. Therefore, they refuse to take the text as its face value; they are suspicious of everything that involves ideas, including theology. Juan Luis Segundo says that "anything and everything involving ideas, including theology, is intimately bound up with the existing social situation in at least an unconscious way."[8]

Reading of the Jewish and Hindu scriptures would show that, in fact, conscious social biases have also dictated the shape of some of the texts. Some parts of the Hebrew Scriptures are clearly intended to

8. Juan Luis Segundo, *The Liberation of Theology*, trans. John Drury (Maryknoll, NY: Orbis, 1976), 8.

elevate and privilege the priestly class within the Jewish society. And much of the texts of Brahminic Hinduism—including those that are said to have been revealed ('seen')—justify the caste-based ordering of society, giving divine sanction to caste hierarchy. Although the Hindu dharma is claimed to be *sanathana dharma* (eternal and ever-lasting dharma) it is clear that it is very much bound up with societal organization, dictated by those in power to do so. Closer examination would show that while in some situations the text shapes the nature of the society, in others, the powerful within the society produce and shape the text so that it would serve their purposes.

This brings us to the second problem closely related to the first. At the time when most of the texts were put down in writing, education and literacy was the privilege only to the elite in society, who were also mostly of the priestly class or caste. In the case of Western Christianity, which used Latin for its text and its liturgy, the scriptural text could be read only by theologians and priests and who knew Latin. It meant that they were also the only interpreters and commentators of the text. With such power over the text, which was declared to be the Word of God, the text turned out to be the primary tool of manipulation of the people.

The Protestant Reformation, thus, was about redeeming the text from its captivity to ecclesial power. The full impact of the ecclesial revolution that Martin Luther initiated did not actually begin when he refused to take back his ninety-five theses at the Imperial Diet of Worms (1521), but by his clandestine act of translating the Bible into the German language, so that ordinary people would know what the text actually said and compare it with the Church's teachings and actions.

In other words, the question about the text is: "Who owns it?" In the wrong hands the text can become the instrument of oppression. In the Christian tradition, for instance, the Bible was used to justify slavery, wars, suppression of women, unethical missions, Apartheid etc. In Judaism the text is used to justify the occupation of the Palestinian lands, and in Hinduism it is used to perpetrate the unjust status quo of the social structure.

In the scholarly world within the Christian tradition much work is also being done on the relationship of the text to the empires at the time they were written and read, the impact of the empire on the text itself, and the role the text has played in the colonial enterprises and the missions that went with them. In his volume, *The Bible and Empire – Post colonial Explorations*, R. S. Sugirtharajah, for instance, gives revealing accounts of the use and abuse of the biblical text in the context of colonialism in India.[9]

In all traditions, the formation of the text, the status it assumes, and its use have been influenced by the balance of the social, economic and political power within the community, which needs to be examined. At the same time, the very text has also provided the impetus for liberation movements and movements that struggle for justice, peace, and human rights. Plurality of functions of the text and its positive and negative impact on the community are based on 'who', 'why', and the 'how' of its use. This can be illustrated in all traditions.

THE TEXT AND RELIGIOUS EXTREMISM

Treating the text as in some sense the 'Word of God', or literally as the 'Words of God', and claiming that it is inspired, inerrant, infallible, etc. creates considerable problems to religious communities. We see this problem illustrated both in Islam and Christianity. Born into the context of Judaism and Christianity, Islam sought to establish the supremacy of the Qur'an with two claims: In the first instance, it claimed that the Jews and Christians had corrupted the revelations given to them through the series of prophets in the Hebrew Scripture and through the prophet Jesus, making it necessary for God to reveal his message for the third and final time. Second, that it was directly dictated to the Prophet (through angel Gabriel) so that it would not be distorted by any human agency.

Although Islam had to find some creative ways to deal with matters not addressed in the Qur'an and with contemporary challenges, the absolute claims made for the text has created a number of problems for Islam. Religious fanatics, extremists and fundamentalist could lift up isolated verses of the Qur'an as reflecting God's will, even when the sentiment expressed in the selected text is in conflict with other verses or the overall message of the Qur'an. If the whole text was declared to have been dictated by God, it is difficult to argue that any part of it was not from God.

The Christians who insist that the Bible should be read literally and

9. R. S. Sugirtharajah, *The Bible and Empire – Postcolonial Explorations* (Cambridge: Cambridge University Press, 2005).

attribute inerrancy and infallibility to it, have considerable difficulties with responding to contemporary advances in scientific knowledge about the universe, to changing cultural trends within society, religious plurality and so on. In other words, the texts, when approached with certain assumptions, present the danger of becoming prison houses in which people languish.

It is important to note that while giving spiritual authority to their texts most religious traditions have also developed ways to deal with the temporal and cultural remoteness of the text and its inability to adequately address contemporary questions. The strong and elaborate interpretative and preaching traditions of Judaism were built to address this problem. Islam preserved the utterances of Prophet Muhammad (as distinct from the Qur'an) and his actions as additional guides on matters not touched in the Qur'an. It also developed elaborate schools of jurisprudence based on the Qur'an to assist the fulfillment of the intentions of the Qur'an in the organization and implementation of the many dimensions of life in society.

The Christian tradition, following Judaism, also developed a strong preaching tradition so that the text would be interpreted and applied for today. The intention, it is claimed, is to "take the words once spoken and make them speak again." The existence of innumerable commentaries on the text is witness to the belief that the remoteness of the text demands props to make it relevant in new situations.

This sense is articulated within Liberation Theology in the sentiment that the text always comes to today's readers accompanied by three deaths: The author, the people to whom the text was addressed, and the contexts in which it was written and received are all no more. In this sense the text is dead, or at least is orphaned. And they developed the concept of the 'hermeneutical circle'—a movement from the text to the context and back to the text—so that new life might be infused into the text to make it speak meaningfully again today.

FUTURE OF THE TEXT

It is no secret that all religious traditions have begun to lose not only the influence they have had on society as a whole but also on their own followers. The decline of religious authority is accompanied by the weakening of the hold texts have had on religious communities.

The decline of the influence of the text itself, among other things, has to do with three realities.

The first is the insistence on the part of a number of religious communities that their texts have been 'revealed', 'given by God', or that they are the result of 'divine inspiration'. Given the wide variety of the nature of the biblical material, today, any intelligent reader of the Bible would find the assertion that it is the inspired word of God a difficult claim to accept.

Pastors and teachers learn about the actual nature of the text and its ambiguities in the seminaries. But they assume that the people in the pews would not be able to handle it. What the people really cannot handle is the deception that comes out of the pulpit on this matter, for they suspect that even the pastor ought to know better. It is an insult to the intelligence of the people in the congregations to assume that telling the truth about the text will destroy their faith. It is this unwarranted fear that leads the people to eventually lose faith in the pastor, the Bible, and the church.

But the problem is not new. Here is what Gandhi had to say about his experience when, as a Hindu, he attempted to read the Bible:

> I began reading it, but I could not possibly read through the Old Testament. I read the book of Genesis, and the chapters that followed invariably sent me to sleep. But just for the sake of being able to say that I had read it, I plodded through the other books with much difficulty and without the least interest or understanding. I disliked reading the Book of Numbers. But the New Testament produced a different impression, especially the Sermon on the Mount which went straight to my heart. I compared it with the *Gita*.[10]

And yet, Christians insist that the Bible as a whole is the Word of God. In the famous public debate, Panadura Vada, between Buddhists and Christians in Sri Lanka (1873), the Buddhist debater kept insisting, based on passages in the Book of Joshua and other passages in the Bible that the Christian God is a bloodthirsty God. The Christian debater had a terrible time because he felt that he had to defend the Bible.

This is not a complaint specifically aimed at the Old Testament, or to claim that the New Testament is better than the Old. We

---

10. M. K. Gandhi, *Christian Missions: Their Place in India* (Ahmedabad: Navajeevan Press, 1941), 15. Quoted in R. S. Sugirtharajah, *The Bible and Empire*, 145.

are aware of the beautiful passages and sentiments about God in the Hebrew Scriptures. Rather, it is an insistence that we learn to treat the biblical text for what it is. The reification of the text in all traditions has led not only to their rejection but also to the questioning of the validity and relevance of the religious traditions themselves.

The second problem is that many religious traditions use their texts to nullify the validity of other religious traditions, to support aggressive missions aimed at others, and to prove the superiority of their tradition over others. In so doing, religious traditions pitch one text against the other. In Judaism the text is used to claim that they are the chosen people among the nations of the world, and that God has promised a particular geographic area as their possession. Islam quotes the Qur'an to prove that it has the last and final revelation of God. Christians use the text to justify missions that target other religions and even claim that their evangelistic approach has been mandated by God. It also cites verses from its text to claim that the Christian way is the only way to salvation.

I am aware that not everyone in each of these religious traditions holds these views. In fact, there is considerable internal plurality within religions in their attitude to the text, to missions, and approach to other religions. Many religious traditions are also re-examining their assumptions about their texts and how they are used. However, the picture I have painted is still a major trend of thinking within these religious traditions. In other words, historically, the religious texts have been one another's enemies.

In the contemporary context, as people live closer to each other and get to know one another's religious traditions, they find it difficult to accept the prevailing understandings of their religion about the texts of other religious tradition. When I was a lecturer in the Theological College of Lanka in Sri Lanka, I had to also teach Tamil literature to the students. When I taught one of the songs of the Saiva saint, Manikkavasagar, students were simply amazed at the intensity of devotion to God expressed in beautiful poetry, and the depth of understanding of the wholeness that results from truly loving God. I have myself found the devotional literature in Hinduism profoundly moving and helpful in deepening my Christian spirituality.

As people get to know other religions, there is a clamour to lower the boundaries between religious traditions so the spiritual heritage of all religions becomes the common property of all humankind. This requires a revolution in some of the religions on their understanding of their text and how it might be used in religiously plural societies. Where the text originated should not necessarily stand in the way of its ownership. It is interesting that Gandhi not only felt that the Sermon on the Mount 'went straight to his heart,' but was able to discern in it some of the cardinal principles for the nature of the independence struggle he fought. For him 'truth' is universal; no religion can treat it as private property.

Third, is the problem of using the text to assert hegemony over those religious expressions that do not have texts as part of their tradition. Historically, religions based on the text claimed some kind of superiority over those who did not have them, primarily because most of the texts were assumed to have been 'revealed'. The metacosmic religions, which build a spiritual hierarchy by placing humans above the rest of creation and introduce transcendence between God and the created order, fail to appreciate the spirituality of religious traditions that see a continuum between God, humans and creation. It is only now, partly because of the ecological crisis, that metacosmic religious traditions have begun to understand and appreciate the cosmic religions, which respect the earth as the 'mother' and all beings as part of an interconnected whole.

The following is a well known saying attributed to Chief Seattle, one of the prominent Native American Chiefs, with whom Washington had to negotiate on buying the lands of the Native Peoples:

> How can you buy or sell the sky, the warmth of the land? The idea is strange to us. If we do not own the freshness of the air and the sparkle of the water, how can you buy them? . . . Every part of the Earth is sacred to my people. Every shining pine needle, every sandy shore, every mist in the dark woods, every clear and humming insect is holy in the memory and experience of my people. . . . Teach your children what we have taught our children that the Earth is our mother. Whatever befalls the Earth befalls the sons of the Earth. If men spit upon the ground, they spit upon themselves. . . . This we know – the Earth does not belong to man; man belongs to the Earth. This we know- all things are connected like the blood which unites one family. All things are connected.[11]

There is dispute among scholars on whether these were, in fact, the words that Chief Seattle actually spoke or wrote. My intention,

11. http://www.ascensionnow.co.uk/chief-seattles-letter-to-the-american-president-1852.html.

however, is not to deal with authorship issues but with the content. The words express a spirituality that would easily rise to 'scriptural' status in the context of the widespread concern for the earth. There are, in fact, numerous stories, myths, reflections, and practices in religious traditions without texts which can match, and even supersede, the prevalent texts in responding to many issues we face today as a human community. We need not romanticize these traditions, but the long-standing prejudice about these traditions, based on the absence of 'texts', needs to come to an end.

Thus in closer examination we discover that some of the widely celebrated sacred texts can also be troubling and ambiguous. We also discover that spiritual resources and treasures need not always take the form of texts. They can be expressed in many other forms, and even be carved out into a fifteen-meter high totem pole.

4.

Interpreting John 14:6 in a
Religiously Plural Society
"I am the way, the truth, and the life"

"I am the way, and the truth, and the life. No one comes to the Father except through me." This well-known and easily remembered verse in John's gospel has played a significant role in Christian spirituality, theology, and missiology over many centuries. This text, along with Matthew 28:18–19, provided the biblical inspiration of the eighteenth- and nineteenth-century missionary expansions into Asia, Africa, and Latin America. Even today, many Christians are convinced that these biblical passages provide the rationale and the mandate for the evangelistic task of the church.

At the same time, there is new interest among Christians on questions of religious plurality, of dialogue among peoples of different religious traditions, and on ways in which persons and communities can work together on the many issues that cut across all communities. The experience of living in closer proximity with others has also brought in new appreciation of the religious life of others. Many are reluctant to dismiss or stand in judgment on other ways of being and believing.

This reality presents us with a difficult question: What can we do with such a clear and unequivocal assertion in the Bible that Jesus is the way, the truth and the life, and that no one can come to God except through him? Are we to disregard the Bible and its teachings?

The Bible is at the center of the spiritual and liturgical life of all Christians. Much of Protestant theology also draws its primary inspiration from the scriptures. The Protestant movement itself began with Luther's insistence on 'sola scriptura'; other reformers followed his lead, taking the Bible as the primary source of theology. Karl Barth, whose writings still have great impact on Protestant theology, fortified the place of scripture with his 'Theology of the Word of God'. Methodism was built on studying the scriptures in small groups and on spreading 'scriptural holiness' in all the land.

Scripture has also been at the heart of the Missionary Movement. Translating, printing, and distributing of the whole or parts of the Bible constitute the biggest missionary endeavor to this day. At the third World Mission Conference at Tambaram, Madras, in 1938, Hendrik Kreamer, the Dutch missiologist, developed the concept of 'Biblical Realism' about the nature of human predicament, which held that as 'fallen' creatures human beings can do nothing that can help them to save themselves. He made this the basis for the negative evaluation of all religious traditions and of the need of all human beings to directly hear and respond to the challenge of the Gospel. Much of the congregational faith is rooted in the Bible.

Therefore, any effort to bring about a change in people's attitude to other religious traditions should also take the Bible seriously and seek to face those passages in the Bible that do teach, or have been interpreted as teachings, attitudes that are dismissive of other religious traditions. The passage related to John 14:6 is perhaps the most well known of these passages. It is important to look at this passage from the perspective of our new awareness of plurality and the new dimensions of our life with peoples of other religious traditions.

THE PROBLEMS IN DEALING WITH JOHN 14:6

The fundamental problem in dealing with John 14:6, however, is that there is no agreement among Christians on how to read and interpret the scriptures. Many Christians treat the Bible as the 'words' of God with a variety of theories of inspiration of scripture. In some circles these theories of inspiration have been further elaborated into theories of 'inerrancy' and 'infallibility' of scriptures. Therefore, some strands within Christian tradition would resist historical and other critical hermeneutical principles being applied to the reading of the scriptures. Despite the many contradictions and errors in the Bible, they would insist that a literal way of reading the scriptures is the only valid way of understanding its message.

One of the helpful ways of approaching this issue is to enable Christians to become more familiar with the way the scriptures are read and interpreted within the Jewish tradition. Jesus himself belonged to this tradition. Within Judaism, arguments, disagreements, and plurality of interpretations are deemed absolutely necessary to understand the words spoken and written many centuries ago. Therefore, the 'Written Torah' (the five Books of Moses) and the 'Oral Torah' (their interpretation through the centuries, preserved in the Talmud) are part and parcel of the one scripture.

While some Christians are troubled by the possibility of more than one interpretation of a scriptural verse, the Jews are delighted by it because plurality of interpretations of a verse, in their thinking, would throw so much more light on that verse. This attitude to scripture is also built on the belief that no one can ever hope to have the full and final understanding of a scriptural text because the human mind can never exhaust the fullness of the meaning of scriptures. They believed, that the generations to come would find even more treasures as they seek to interpret the scriptures for their own times and contexts.

Therefore, even though some would frown at the idea of holding a whole conference to delve into the depths of John 14:6, one must insist that such an endeavor is very much in the spirit in which the scriptures were searched in the tradition of those who wrote them.

EXPLORING THE TEXT

We are in the process of exploring this text for a specific reason: What has this text to say about Christian understanding and approach to peoples of other religious traditions? Today we have a new awareness of many of our neighbors as peoples who pray, believe, and have long spiritual histories of their own. We are often moved by their intense devotion to God and exemplary ethical lives. We have also become aware that the proclamation of the gospel does not always lead to people choosing to become part of our community. Many have listened to the gospel and have not chosen to become Christians because they find a life in God in their own traditions that already gives them meaning and purpose.

More importantly, we are aware today that we need to work and live in a pluralistic society in which mutual trust and understanding among religions has become a necessary ingredient of our search for peace and harmony. There is, for example, a growing awareness of how different religions speak about humanity's relationship to the natural world. Conversation among religions is seen as one of the essential steps in facing the impending ecological crisis.

It is in this context that we are faced with Biblical texts like Matthew 28:18–19 that calls us to go out into the world and preach the gospel. John 14:6 appears to give the rationale for this activity. "I am the way, the truth, and the life. No one comes to the Father except through me." At first sight, it appears to be unambiguous and clear. If Jesus is the Way, the Truth, and the Life, and if no one can indeed come to the Father except through him, Christians have the obligation to open this 'only way' to neighbors of other faith traditions. By implication this would also mean that all other ways that humankind has used to reach God are defective or inadequate.

How does one deal with the dilemma presented by this text? I think we need to look at this text from several angles—hermeneutical, exegetical, theological, missiological, and spiritual. What follows are brief indications of the points of entry that might be made from each of these angles. In so doing I have chosen not so much to address biblical scholars and theologians but Christians in our pews who are caught in the middle of a genuine search for a new relationship with their neighbors and biblical verses that appear to be uncompromising in their missionary fervor.

PRINCIPLES OF INTERPRETING A BIBLICAL TEXT

Much of the material in the New Testament was written some two thousand years ago. And they were written by a number of authors, living in different life situations and holding a variety of views on how to understand the great mystery of the life and death of Jesus of Nazareth and especially of their experience of him as the Risen One. It should come as no surprise that the eyes of faith and the lenses of cultures and traditions influenced the responses to the risen reality of Christ. It is also known that the gospels, and especially John's Gospel, were written several decades after the events. It is no wonder, therefore, that if they were to be treated as strictly historical accounts there are considerable discrepancies in the gospels.

To take only one example, the Synoptic Gospels place the 'cleansing of the temple' as one of the last public acts in Jesus's ministry, as the one that precipitated the plot to put Jesus to death. John, on the contrary, places the 'cleansing of the temple' right at the beginning of Jesus's ministry and introduces the raising of Lazarus as the event that troubled Jesus's adversaries.

Centuries of biblical scholarship has used numerous tools to seek to arrive at a definitive text from among the many manuscripts with variant readings (textual criticism), to determine the character and nature of the material in the gospels (source, form and literary criticism) and to seek to understand the intension of the authors in the way they have written up, arranged and interpreted that material that were available (redaction criticism). Several additional tools of criticism have been used to get at the meaning of the message of the gospel writers.[1]

Much light has also been thrown on the study of the gospels by the examination of extra canonical writings about Jesus (including other 'gospels' that were excluded from the canon), of historical accounts by other contemporary writers, and what we know from archeological discoveries from that period. There is much, in fact, too much material to be considered for a full interpretation of John's Gospel and its background. I would lift up here few factors that should guide us as we look at this text.

THE PURPOSE AND SCOPE OF ST. JOHN'S GOSPEL

The first, and perhaps the most important, fact is that the gospels were not written to inform people who did not know the story of Jesus, or as evangelical tools to spread the gospel message to people of other religious traditions. On the contrary, the gospels were written to believing communities who already knew the story of Jesus. The gospel narratives are, therefore, by nature, attempts to both recount

---

1. In more recent times the New Testament field has seen additional types of criticism (Canonical Criticism, Rhetorical Criticism, Social-Scientific Criticism, Structural Criticism, Narrative Criticism, Reader-Response Criticism, Poststructuralist Criticism, Psychoanalytic Criticism, Feminist/Womanist Criticism, Ideological Criticism, etc.) all attempting to get to the meaning of the text from a great variety of points of approach. See Steven L. McKenzie and Stephen R. Haynes, eds., *To Each Its Own Meaning* (Louisville: Westminster John Knox, 1999).

events as well as to *interpret* them to the readers. John does not set out to give only a historical account of what Jesus did and said. His interest in *interpreting* Jesus for his readers is clearly and unambiguously seen in the way he begins the Gospel: "In the beginning was the Word, the Word was with God, and the Word was God . . . and the Word became flesh and lived among us." Here John is surely not making a historical statement but an interpretation of who Jesus was in his perception. His interpretation of Jesus is both profound and fascinating and would enable his readers to celebrate and enrich their faith in Jesus Christ. This goal of using a version of the story of Jesus's earthly life to interpret the *meaning* of Jesus as the Christ to his Christian readers permeates the whole of the Gospel.

In so doing, John appears to take considerable liberty in the way he casts Jesus as a teacher. All three Synoptic Gospels present Jesus as a rabbi, a teacher, who used parables, sayings and stories that were intended to reach the ordinary people ('the crowds') who followed him.[2] Jesus's stories and illustrations are drawn from nature ("Look at the birds of the air . . . "), ordinary events in daily life ("A man went out to hire laborers for his vineyard . . . "), and from experiences in human relationships ("And the younger son said to his father . . . "). In fact, the synoptic writers present him as someone who expected people to draw their own conclusions on the stories he was telling them. "Those who have ears to hear let them hear"—this seems to be the overall portrayal of Jesus in Matthew, Mark, and Luke, even though each of them also had their own biases in the way they present his life.

But Jesus in John goes into long theological discourses about himself. While Mark gives the story of the feeding of the multitude, John would follow it with a discourse on the Bread of Life, where Jesus would claim himself to be the Bread of Life that has come down from heaven to supersede the manna that Moses had given them in the desert. At every turn of events John presents Jesus as making discourses about himself as the Bread of Life, Water of Life, the True Vine, the Good Shepherd, the Resurrection and the Life, etc. John also liberally uses the "I AM," which God uses in the encounter with Moses in the burning bush, to fortify his conviction that the "Word was with God, and the Word was God."

2. There are also many portrayals of Jesus today as a reformer, prophet, a wandering cynic type of teacher, miracle worker, and so on showing how the same body of material can be looked at from a variety of angles.

Who was Jesus? Was he a Galilean teacher, or one who expounded theological discourses on who he was in relation to God? No intelligent reader of the Bible would miss the dramatic differences in the portrayal of Jesus between the Synoptic Gospels and John. One cannot expect Jesus of Mark's Gospel who (in Mark's presentation) insists on calling himself the 'Son of Man', and restrains those who recognized him as Messiah to silence ('Messianic Secret'), to make the declaration: "I am the Bread of Life that came down from heaven." It would be completely out of character with the Jesus that Mark presents.

It is perhaps reasonable to assume that the synoptic gospels (while each giving their own *interpretation* of who Jesus is) appear to give a more reliable picture of the kind of teacher Jesus was. We have to assume then that John, while building on a historical account of Jesus, is more interested in celebrating with the believing readers his understanding of who Jesus was. This does not make John's gospel any less interesting or valuable. In fact it is one of the richest treasures of the Christian tradition.

In this context John 14:6, where Jesus is presented as saying, "I am the Way, the Truth and the Life. No one comes to the Father except through me," must also be seen as the Johannine celebration of the Christian faith. No Christian should have any difficulty with such celebration of faith of the one who had in fact become for them the Way, the Truth and the Life. But what relevance and place would such a celebration of faith have in our witness to Jesus Christ in a pluralistic society? This is a question to which we would return.

We need to hold this question for a while because the considerations above would raise an important issue to many Christians about the nature of the saying itself, namely, whether Jesus actually said these words or not. "If Jesus has said it, who are we to question it?" some would ask, "And if he has not actually said it, how reliable are the Gospels; on what basis can we hold them as scriptures?"

DID JESUS ACTUALLY SAY THE WORDS OF JOHN 14:6?

To many Christians the very question would create difficulty; they would say that such questions undermine the authority of the scripture. But would intelligent study of scriptures undermine its authority? Part of the problem here lies in the gulf that still exists in most places between the seminary and the pulpit, and our failure to find appropriate and creative ways of integrating New Testament scholarship into the teaching and preaching ministry of the church. Surely, God does not expect Christians to be 'blind believers'.

Any intelligent reader of the Bible would realize that the Bible is full of creative literary approaches in the way it presents the story of the Jewish people and of the Christian community that emerged from it. In the Genesis 3 story of the 'fall' of humankind, there are many detailed conversations between Adam, Eve, the serpent, and God. Even though the story gives exact conversations with very precise words, there was no one there in the beginning of creation to listen and record them. It is obvious that a literary tool is being used here that includes full-blooded conversations to tell an important truth about the human condition.

The fact that the narrative style presents it as an 'event', with characters and conversations, does not mean that the 'event' actually took place. Every Jewish reader of Genesis 3 understands that he or she is here not dealing with history. At the same time, the literary form (story, saga, or myth) that is used enables him or her to understand the truth about the human condition that an essay of a thousand words would not do.

In the same manner, much of what the prophets had to say to the nation begins with "Thus says the Lord God of Israel." A closer examination would show that it is the prophet who is speaking in the name of the Lord. The Jewish reader understands that it is the prophet's voice. For them it is not a problem that he speaks as if the Lord were speaking because everyone understands the convention. Thus, within the literary styles used in the Hebrew tradition, it is permissible to put words even into God's mouth. There is no deception here, and the same convention is present in the Johannine narratives as well.

In John's story of the meeting between Jesus and the Samaritan woman, the text says that the two of them were by themselves at the well because the disciples had gone into the village to buy bread. Yet, detailed account of conversations mark the encounter between Jesus and the woman. Unless Jesus himself or the woman had given all the details of their conversation (including Jesus's discourse on the Water of Life) to someone, and that had been faithfully preserved and handed down to John many decades later, John would have no way of knowing exactly what conversation took place between Jesus and the woman. And yet, for John's readers it is a 'true' story, and all the conversation that is written up has rich meaning at another level of understanding.

Historical accuracy of events and conversations is a modern problem. Ancient people looked for *meaning*. In the Hindu tradition, whether the Bhagavad Gita was given in an actual historical situation would be a moot question; it has little significance to the value of the Gita. In the African and Native American traditions the question is not whether the stories are true, but whether the stories are telling the truth.

What does all this amount to? Are we to consider biblical material to be completely fictitious and devoid of any reliable information?

THE QUEST FOR THE HISTORICAL JESUS

What we can actually know about the Jesus of history has preoccupied New Testament scholarship for many centuries. The 'quest' for the 'Historical Jesus' itself is a long story and is said to have gone through four or five phases.[3] Today the search for the historical Jesus takes place in a widely known process called the 'Jesus Seminar.' The crux of the problem is this: If the New Testament writers are writing to believing communities and are motivated primarily to give shape to the 'Christ of Faith', how far can we expect them to be presenting the 'Jesus of History'? In other words, if the evangelists are primarily interested not to write history but statements of faith, how much freedom did they take in the way they presented the story of Jesus?

No doubt, there are a great variety of opinions on the historicity of the materials in the four Gospels. Some have argued that we have hardly any sayings that can be directly attributed to Jesus himself. Others have tried to build up a historical profile of Jesus based on the passages that are most likely to include actual events and teachings. I would venture to suggest three principles that have guided my own approach to this problem:

---

3. According to Gerd Theissen and Annette Mertz they include the initial impulses toward the question by H. S. Reimarus (1694–1768) and D. F. Strauss (1808–1874), the attempt to break out of the imprisonment of Christ in dogma by H. J. Holtzmann (1832–1910), the counter movement to theological liberalism by A. Schweitzer, R. Bultmann, M. Dibelius and those who followed this line of thinking, the 'new quest' led by Kasemann, Bornkamm and others and the 'third quest' led by Sanders, Vermes, Theissen, and others. See *The Historical Jesus – A Comprehensive Guide* (Minneapolis: Fortress Press, 1998), 1–15.

First, it is reasonable to believe that because of the distance in time between the events and the writings, and because the gospels were written by the four evangelists to make their own input into the significance of Jesus for our faith, the evangelists do not give us an *exact* historical account of what Jesus did and said, even when they attribute words directly to him. This is natural and normal within the tradition, and it would not have in any way devalued their accounts in the eyes of their readers.

Second, even though the evangelists took such freedom, there is reason to believe that between the three Synoptic Gospels we have a reasonably reliable account of the life of Jesus, the primary foci of his teachings and ministry, and in many places close approximations to the actual words he might have used in his teaching ministry. The ancient peoples, both in the Middle East as also in other parts of the world, un-spoilt by the modern recourse to committing everything to writing, had remarkable capacity to remember, to recall, and to repeat.

Third, while John also seeks to build on the major historical events in the life of Jesus, he attempts a more radical reinterpretation of the Jesus tradition that is known to his readers. He takes much more liberty than others in the drawing of a theological portrayal of Jesus, and in so doing attributes to Jesus passages and sayings that are more of a reflection of the faith of the community than words actually said by Jesus himself.

Once we approach John's Gospel with this understanding we would be able to better enter into the mystical faith in John's Gospel that has inspired and enriched Christian piety, mysticism and theological explorations through the past many centuries.

The words, "I am the way, the truth and the life. No one comes to the Father except through me" has to be understood in this context. They are 'true' in the most profound sense to the faith community to which John was writing. But precisely for that reason the words hold no value as proof that Jesus is the 'only' way or to claim that there is 'no salvation outside Christ'. Streams within the Christian tradition may well hold such convictions, but John 14:6 is certainly not the best support to prove such claims.

EXEGESIS OF THE TEXT

The issue does not end there. We need to go further and ask how we might interpret and understand the text of John 14:6. Throughout the Christian history there has been the practice of interpreting the scripture to get at the meaning of the text and to apply it to the context of the people. This practice comes from the Jewish belief that God, having given the Torah to humankind, expects human beings to explore its meaning and significance for their life. The Jewish tradition argues that this is the reason why God created human beings with freedom and intelligence.

This understanding of the relationship between the 'given revelation' and the 'challenge to the human mind to grasp it' is at the heart of the great exegetical traditions within Judaism and Christianity. Even in church traditions that hold theories of inspiration and inerrancy of scriptures, there is preaching that follows the reading of the scripture. The practice of preaching on the word read is an implicit admission that a scriptural text needs to be interpreted so that the 'words once spoken might be enabled to speak to us again'. Therefore, whatever position one holds on John 14:6 from the perspective of historical criticism, one still needs to ask how we might *interpret* the saying attributed to Jesus in this passage.

The text in John 14:6 can be interpreted in many ways:

- The first is of course to take it at it stands, as an isolated verse, and to argue that Jesus here claims himself to be the way, the truth and the life, and that no one can come to God except through faith in him. This is the most common use of this verse especially for missionary purposes.

- It is also possible to interpret this verse to imply, as some have done, that while there are many possible ways to understand and relate to the Reality we call God, one comes to an understanding of God as Abba, a loving parent (Father), through the life and witness that Jesus has offered to God. In other words, in Jesus we come to a dimension of understanding of God, not simply as a personal God, but also as the intimate Abba.

- Still another interpretation centers on how we might understand the words "I am." Even if one were to overlook the Johannine use of I AM from the Hebrew Scriptures to give his own

Christological assumptions about Jesus, "I am" can have a much richer meaning. Jesus had lived a life that was totally turned toward God and was in solidarity with the poor, the oppressed and the marginalized in his society. He went about with little or no care for material things. He saw wealth and power (Mammon) as the greatest enemy of God and challenged us to live a life that is God-centered rather than Mammon-centered. He refused to compromise the principle of loving God and of loving one's neighbour as though the neighbour was oneself. In his effort to witness to God's universal love for all people, he was willing to take rejection and to be crucified.

In so doing, Jesus, in his person, life and ministry, shows us the way, the truth, and the life. It is in following his Way of love and self-denial, and in accepting the Truth that he has told us about our life with God and our neighbors that we come to grasp the meaning and truth about Life and are awoken to a new vision of who God is.

This interpretation links the verse to discipleship. It moves us away from a simple dogmatic assertion about Jesus to a profound spiritual understanding of the text as it relates to his whole life and teachings.

Even though such meditative interpretations of the verse are legitimate, we need to read the verse in context of the whole passage that relates to Jesus's last moments with his disciples and in the wider context of John's Gospel. When we take the whole text together it does appear that John intends to speak of Jesus himself as the way, the truth and the life; the one who leads people to the 'Father'.[4]

How then can we understand the text in the context of religious plurality?

THEOLOGICAL INTERPRETATION OF THE TEXT

As said earlier it is common to use John 14:6 to draw the conclusion that God's saving will for the humankind has been revealed only in Jesus Christ and that it is in him alone that all humankind finds its salvation. Such a belief has led to the missiological conclusion that it is the duty of Christians to convert all of humankind to acknowledge Jesus as their Lord and Saviour.

4. Cf. Raymond E. Brown, *The Gospel According to John: John XIII–XXI –Introduction, Translation and Notes to the Anchor Bible* (New York: Doubleday, 1970), 637–57.

How far are we justified in building such a theological and missiological edifice on the foundation of John 14:6? One should immediately admit that John 14.6 is not the only verse that calls for an exclusive understanding of the Christian faith. There are other verses in the New Testament, both in John and elsewhere, which support the position found in this verse:

"For God so loved the world that he gave his only Son . . . Those who believe in him are not condemned; but those who do not believe in him are condemned already." (John 3:16–18)

Peter and John, taken before the High Priest to answer questions about the healing of the man born lame, proclaim: "There is salvation in no one else, for there is no other name under heaven given among mortals by which we must be saved." (Acts 4:12)

The first letter to Timothy (1 Tim 2:3–6) shares the same sentiments of John 14:6. Here Christ is presented as the 'only mediator between God and humankind'. How are we to understand such clear exclusive sayings of which John 14:6 is a part?

THE CONTEXT OF THE SAYINGS

Much of the New Testament material was written in the context of much controversy over the significance of Jesus, whom the early disciples, based on the resurrection experience, claimed to be the long expected Messiah of the Jewish people. Even though Jesus was crucified, building on the experience of the risen Christ and the expectation of his immediate Second Coming, Christians argued that he was indeed the Messiah. But large sections of the Jewish leadership not only disagreed but were also vehemently opposed to this teaching (also to this day). Soon, active persecution of the Christians followed (the stoning of Stephen, Paul's journey to Damascus to arrest Christians, and others). The controversy deepened with the passage of time. In addition, Christians also came under pressure to choose between following Jesus and paying homage to Caesar at the threat of the sword.

It is not surprising that communities under such pressure fortify their faith and counter the opposition with exclusive claims. Almost all the exclusive sayings in the New Testament takes place either in the context of a polemical situation or in the context of writing to prove the validity of a particular theological position over against another. Paul, faced with the opposition of the 'circumcision party', always overstated his case. John, in his attempts to claim Jesus as the Messiah, builds in overt and covert anti-Jewish polemics and exclusive sayings about the significance of Jesus.

THE CONTEXT OF POWER AND PRIVILEGE

We should remember that much of these controversies are in some sense 'internal controversies' because they were taking place within the Jewish community, some of which had become Christian. New Testament writings were written by persons in minority situations to peoples in minority communities that often were under pressure and persecution. This gives a particular character and context to its exclusivism.

However, with the conversion of Emperor Constantine, the church soon became part of the Roman Empire. Thus, the texts that were once written for the comfort and self-affirmation of suffering minority communities became texts of a powerful majority community. The change of context gave to these texts a new role and meaning. They are now to become verses that defend Colonial hegemony, Christian superiority and intolerance of other ways of believing.

Today, there is a stream of scholarship that advocates a 'Postcolonial' reading of the Bible. This reading of the Bible seeks to expose how the Bible and its interpretation became a tool in the hands of the colonial powers. During the eighteenth- and nineteenth-century missionary expansion the Bible was used to characterize other religions as 'pagan' and 'false'. Isolated verses from the Bible were quoted to justify apartheid, slavery, subjugation of women, control of the environment, and rejection of other religions and cultures.[5] In other words, in the hands of the powerful the same verses that gave life to suffering communities became verses that worked against the liberating power of the gospel.

Given this history, how useful are exclusive verses to build Christian theology and missiology for our day?

---

5. R. S. Sugirtharajah, *The Bible and the Third World: Precolonial, Colonial and Postcolonial Encounters* (Cambridge: Cambridge University Press, 2001), 244–82.

NATURE OF RELIGIOUS LANGUAGE

There is also a more fundamental issue at stake here, which has to do with the nature of religious language. In all religious traditions faith is born out of intense religious experiences that give some notion of decisiveness and finality to that faith experience. It is, therefore, only natural that all religious traditions make ultimate claims for the founding experience on which the religious tradition is built. The Buddha was convinced that the four Noble Truths to which he was awakened under the Bo tree was indeed the true nature of reality, and that devoid of such a realization humankind would not free itself from suffering (dukka). Muslims are convinced that God was revealing to Prophet Muhammad, for the last and final time, God's will on how personal, family and societal life ought to be organized. Jewish people believe God's covenant with Abraham and Moses makes them the 'chosen people' to this day.

Many Christians forget that exclusive and ultimate claims are made not only by them but also by other well-meaning and deeply religious people. People of other religious traditions are annoyed and even amused to learn that on the basis of statements in our scripture we have concluded that they would not be 'saved' unless they believe as we do. The Bible belongs to the faith community. It has no authority to people who have not submitted themselves to its authority.

In other words, scriptures are *confessional material*; they are written by people of faith to a community of faith in the language of faith; they witness to our love and commitment to the primary religious experience that has gripped our life; they are internal to the community; they enable us to elevate our faith experience, to celebrate it, and to own it as our precious possession. Within this *internal language of faith* there is a place for exclusivism and claims to decisiveness and finality. Such claims, however, hold validity only within that specific faith community.[6]

But when we use such confessional material to judge the faith of others, to make claims of superiority, or to undermine the religious experiences of others we violate not only other religious experiences but also our own scriptures.

---

6. George A. Lindbeck, *The Nature of Doctrine, Religion, and Theology in a Post-Liberal Age* (Philadelphia: The Westminster Press, 1984), 16ff.

We undervalue and abuse scriptures when we use them in ways that they were not intended to be used.

NATURE OF THE THEOLOGICAL TASK

But the theological issue raised by the traditional use of the text raises more fundamental questions about our theological task; namely, about the practice of building theological positions based on sections of scripture. Here again, there has been a long debate within church traditions on the 'resources' or 'principles' or 'criteria' for doing theology. Reformation churches often present this issue as the tension between 'scripture' on the one hand and 'tradition' on the other. Methodist tradition speaks about the 'Wesleyan Quadrilateral', arguing that one has to bring together scripture, tradition, reason, and experience in our theological task. The theologians of the 'third' world have introduced yet another resource, the 'context'.

The Latin American theologians also brought into biblical exploration the concept of the 'hermeneutical cycle', calling for a movement that takes us from the text to the context and back again to the text. Such a cycle, they contend, would help us to see the text from a new perspective. Juan Segundo argues that each biblical text is accompanied by three 'deaths': the writer, the people to whom it was written, and the context that it sought to address are all no more. Therefore, the text can become alive again only when it is related to the current context and made to speak to the present reality.

What does all this amount to? It means that theology must arise not from isolated verses but from the total biblical message. And it has to relate to our present experience and context and help us discern the challenge of the Gospel for our day. We would distort the biblical message when we build Christological or Missiological positions from isolated verses. For example, Peter's words, "I truly understand that God shows no partiality, but in every nation anyone who fears him and does what is right is acceptable to him" (Acts 10:34–35), taken in isolation, could be used to argue for an exactly opposite position from John 14:6.

But, does theology has to do with proof-texting or with searching the depths of God's love and purpose for all creation?

MISSIOLOGICAL USE OF JOHN 14:6

The most common use of John 14:6 is of course in popular missiology. I have been involved in the ministry of interfaith dialogue for over 30 years, and I have never managed to come away from a congregational discussion on interfaith dialogue without being challenged with John 14:6. It is as if people are programmed to raise this verse if there is a discussion on dialogue. Some raise the issue out of genuine perplexity. They have been trained to consider the Bible as the word of God. If the Bible is so clear on the issue, we have no alternative, they would say, but to hold the position that those who do not believe in him are 'lost'. Some others quote the verse to argue and justify their own pre-conceived understanding of what constitutes mission, and use the verse to prop up their position.

I find three basic problems with this almost instinctive reaction to use John 14:6 as a text to invalidate the reality of other religions.

First is the larger theological question about God and God's relationship to the world. People of Israel began with their belief in Yahweh as a tribal God who was only concerned with affairs of Israel. But soon they found that such a limited understanding of God did not do justice to God. Gradually Yahweh was proclaimed the creator and provider of the whole universe.

The confession "The earth is the Lord's and all that is in it, the world, and those who live in it" (Ps 24:1) is the reflection of the maturing of Israel's conception about God. Very soon Israel had to also think of Yahweh's relationship to other nations and develop the concept of God as the 'Lord of the nations'. It is out of this tradition that Amos is able to address the people of Israel in the name of God with the question: "Are you not like the Ethiopians to me, O people of Israel?" says the Lord. "Did I not bring Israel up from the land of Egypt, the Philistines from Caphtor and the Arameans from Kir?" (Amos 9:7).

In a similar development, missionary movement moved away from seeing salvation as a possession of the church and the task of mission as the sole activity of the church. At the World Mission Conference in Willingen (1952) the missionary movement developed the concept of the *missio Dei*, the 'Mission of God', in which the church's mission was seen as participation in a wider mission of God in the world. Gradually it was recognized that God's world is made up also of peoples who seek God in ways other than our own, and that we have no reason to exclude God's presence and activity in the world of religious traditions.

Even though some within the missionary movement disagreed with this line of thinking, these currents of thought that recognized God's freedom in God's work of salvation led the World Mission Conference, meeting in San Antonio, Texas (1989), to incorporate the following words into its official report: As Christians, "We cannot point to any other way of salvation than Jesus Christ; at the same time we cannot set limits to the saving power of God." It also added that our conviction that God offers salvation to all humankind in Jesus Christ "stands in tension with what we have affirmed about God being present in and at work in people of other faiths; we appreciate this tension, and we do not attempt to resolve it."[7]

Christian exclusivism based on texts like John 14.6 presents an image of God that is too small, too limited, and does not do justice to the biblical image of God as one in whom all beings live, move, and have their being

Second, those who adopt this as the primary verse of their missionary understanding fail to recognize the breadth and depth of the understanding of mission in the Bible, especially in Jesus's own teaching and ministry. Jesus own understanding of mission constituted the announcement of the in-breaking of the Reign of God over all life, of solidarity with the poor and the marginalized, of bringing healing and wholeness to the community, of driving out the forces of evil, of challenging people to resist the temptations that come with wealth and power, of resisting false, ceremonial and hypocritical religion, of challenging the abuse of the Scriptures and the Temple, and of proclaiming God's love and forgiveness to all who seek to end their alienation from God and their neighbors. At the heart of Jesus's own mission is the challenge of calling people to self-denial and to life of loving relationship to God and one's neighbour.

Jesus's disciples, however, following the resurrection experience, gave considerable significance to the life and death of Jesus and were convinced that God was present and active in his life, death and resurrection. It is, therefore, only natural that Christological convictions became part of the message, with the call to 'believe in him'.

7. Frederick R. Wilson, *The San Antonio Report – Your Will be Done: Mission in Christ's Way* (Geneva: WCC Publications, 1990), 32–33.

However, reducing mission primarily to Christological beliefs does violence to Jesus's own understanding and practice of mission.

Third, those of us who have been in close relationships with peoples of other faiths would be aware that John 14:6, however precious it is to the Christians, is the least suitable verse as a rationale for Christian witness to others. Its exclusivism alienates people when used as a mission text. Used in relation to other faiths it would be seen as further proof of Christian arrogance and intolerance of others. Hindus would see it as depicting a defective vision of God and a cheap method of promoting one's religion.

"If Jesus is indeed the Way, the Truth, and the Life," Hindus would say, "it must be borne out in one's inner spiritual experience." It is not an issue for theoretical argument, doctrinal claim, or for judging the spiritual life of other believers.

THE SPIRITUAL DIMENSIONS OF THE USE OF JOHN 14:6

At the end of one of my presentations calling for a new relationship with people of other religious traditions, one of the participants stood and challenged me with John 14:6, insisting that the text clearly states how one might be saved. "No one comes to the Father," says Jesus, "except through me."

"Let us hold that text for a moment," I pleaded, "and go to Mark 10 where we have the story of the man who came to Jesus with the question, 'What must I do to inherit eternal life?'" Certainly this is a question related to salvation, and Jesus's answer was that he should sell everything he has and give to the poor, and then come and follow him. Here we have a direct question, "What must I do to inherit eternal life?", and a direct answer, "You must sell everything you have and give to the poor."

Predictably, the person objected to making the Marian text the primary salvation verse, claiming that this was a one-to-one conversation between Jesus and a rich man.

"But so was also John 14:6," I insisted. "It is presented as an intimate conversation between Jesus and one of his disciples, Thomas, who was troubled by some things Jesus was saying to his disciples as he prepared them for his impending death. In many ways the Johannine text has a much more intimate, confidential and private context than the open and public question that the rich man had with Jesus on how one might inherit eternal life. On what basis do we choose one and not the other as having greater importance to our understanding of salvation?"

My intention was not to win an argument but to make all of us gathered there to realize that all of us, in our human frailty, have learnt to excel in the art of 'selective reading' of the Bible. We mute the challenges that the Bible brings to our own discipleship and tend to use it selectively to suit our purposes.

If we truly intend to give witness to who Jesus is, what he has taught us about God and about God's loving and compassionate relationship to the world, what are passages of the Bible we would choose? The biblical verses we choose and the uses we make of them are intimately related to our own spirituality. For mission is not just activity, but spiritual activity. In the way we talk about Jesus we also say something about who we are and what rules our hearts.

PART III

Dialogue and Theology

5.

Toward a Theology of Dialogue

Theology can be defined in many ways but one of the definitions is: "A systematic discourse concerning God and God's relationship to human beings and the world." It arises in the first instance on the basis of a specific religious experience, which takes place in a particular context. Here the phrases "specific religious experience" and "particular context" are important.

For Christian theology, the point of departure is the experience of Jesus Christ, faith in him, and commitment to his message. The shape of theology that arises out of this experience, however, depends on the particular context within which Christ is experienced and the nature of the commitment and discipleship such context demands. This is why Christian theology in Asia, Africa, and Latin America, when rightly done, can never be the same. Even though the point of departure for all is their experience of Christ, the vastly different contexts make it impossible to say the same things about him and the challenge he brings. Commitment to him can never be the same thing in different cultures and in different centuries.

For the same reason theology, rightly understood, is also done in the context of the life of the believing community. One needs not labor this point, because the New Testament and the early church provide compelling examples of the nature of the theological task and the way to do it. One cannot read the Acts of the Apostles without being struck by the tremendous amount of searching and groping of the significance of the Gospel and what it meant. Acts 15 relates how the theological perspectives of the church, which was predominantly

Jewish at the beginning, had to undergo a radical change when Gentiles joined the community.

Today, there are many reasons why we need to turn toward a "theology of dialogue." I would point to three of them as points of departure for the thoughts that are to follow.

COMMITMENT TO ALL HUMAN LIFE

First, there is a growing recognition of something that has been grudgingly admitted but kept at bay in the theological task, namely, that *all human life*—not just an artificially isolated segment called 'religious life', and that all human beings, not just Christians—are part of God's concern, and share a common future. Christian theology has, in varying degrees, either refused to face the issue or has given it marginal treatment. This can no longer be done. Today, it is generally agreed that all human life and all human beings have to be at the centre of any theological reflection. This new attitude and agenda for theology requires new tools and methods of working.[1]

THE NEED FOR NEW WINESKINS

Second, a theology of dialogue has become essential because of the apparent *impasse* to which the practice of dialogue has come within traditional theology. Over the past few decades, many have entered into dialogue with people of other faiths and their encounters have led them to new theological understandings about people of other religious traditions. However, very little of this new experience is able to find expression within the traditional theological framework. There is much new wine that cannot be put into the old wineskins without the wineskins bursting and the wine being wasted: 'New wine needs new wineskins.'

1. This is argued by S. J. Samartha, "The Holy Spirit and Peoples of Various Faiths, Cultures and Ideologies," in *The Holy Spirit*, ed. Dow Kirkpatrick (Lake Junaluska, NC: World Methodist Council, 1974).

BREAKING OUT OF THE 'TEUTONIC CAPTIVITY'

Third, and most important, Christians of Asia, Africa, and Latin America have come to realize the meaning of what C. S. Song has described as the 'Teutonic captivity' of Christian theology. They have not been able to break out of the Western philosophical, historical-cultural framework to which both the Bible and theology have become captive.[2] In his view, the intellectual framework provided by Greek philosophy, institutions, and law as fashioned by the Roman Empire, Germanic temperament, and the major cultural revolutions of the Western Hemisphere have become so much the heart of the Christian religion that the churches of Asia and Africa are in virtual intellectual and institutional bondage to them.

Happily, from the stage of blaming all and sundry for this bondage, Christians in other parts of the world have now come to the stage of breaking loose so that they can struggle with their own experience of Christ in their own contexts. Asian and African theologies have been in the process of emerging, and they can move to the centre of the life of the community only as they enter into deeper and fuller dialogue with their contexts, as the early church did.

What then, is the theological basis for dialogue and what aspects of our faith compel us to enter into dialogue? It is to these questions we turn now.

TOWARD A NEW ATTITUDE
TO RELIGION AND THEOLOGY

A theology of dialogue must have, in the first instance, a new understanding of the nature of religion and theology. One of our sins in the past has been to absolutize the Christian religion and theology, implying that other religions were 'false,' or at any rate 'not true.' Two hundred years ago Fielding's Parson Thwackum could say, "When I mention religion I mean the Christian religion; and not only the Christian religion but the Protestant religion; and not only the Protestant religion but the Church of England."[3] Today, although

---

2. Choan-seng Song, "New China and Salvation History: A Methodological Enquiry," *South East Asia Journal of Theology* 15, no. 2 (1974): 55–56.

3. Quoted in "A Lesson for Thwackum in Religion and Community" in: https://www.timeshighereducation.com/books/a-lesson-for-Thwackum/160236.article.

none of us would be naive enough to say so, a close examination of our attitudes, theological affirmations and evangelistic methods would confirm that not many churches in Asia and Africa have moved from a similar position.

We must emphasize that what we call a religion, whatever religion it may be, is a human phenomenon, all too human for any one of them to make exclusive claims over others. The biggest confusion in the mind of average church goers in Asia today is reflected in his or her refusal to distinguish between the church and the kingdom and between religion and faith.

Of course the Christian faith has its distinctive character in that it is about Jesus Christ and that it announces the in-breaking of the reign or the rule of God over all life, but this gives no additional validity to what can be historically traced as the Christian religion. Religion is the manifestation of the faith of a people in history at a particular time and space, and by virtue of necessity, it expresses itself in the thought-forms, symbols, and rites that are prevalent in the culture, religion and culture thereby exerting mutual influence on each other. There can be nothing sacrosanct, therefore, about its form, or the mode of life that arises from it.[4]

This is also true of theology. Rightly understood, all theology is 'story telling'. It is a framework within which one seeks to give expression to one's experience and faith. All religions seek to tell their religious experience within the framework of a story about the nature of the world, of human beings, of God, and the destiny of life, a necessary framework to hold together different aspects of its experience. For example, the Hindu may speak of his or her religious experience within a 'story', which includes a particular view of history, the law of karma and rebirth and an understanding of the essential unity of human beings and God.

The Buddhist may express his or her experience with an analysis of the nature of human life and the universe that does not necessarily correspond to the Hindu view. A Christian may speak of his or her experience within the context of the 'creation-fall-redemption' story. The point is to realize that all stories have no enduring value in themselves, except to give a framework within which the community celebrates its faith and experience.

4. Wilfred Cantwell Smith, *The Meaning and End of Religion* (New York: Mentor, 1962), 109–10.

THE SIGNIFICANCE OF THIS UNDERSTANDING

Why, one might ask, is this understanding of religion and theology important for a theology of dialogue? There are many answers.

First, the biggest obstacle to genuine theological exploration is an inordinate fear of syncretism. This arises only when one absolutizes a religion, a doctrine or a theological system as the ultimate truth. When it is understood as a human phenomenon, it would be possible to break away from bondage to dogmatism to the freedom of the Spirit.

Second, in a dialogue one has to take one's partner seriously, and seek to learn from his or her experience. Anyone who approaches another with an *a priori* assumption that his or her story is the 'only true story' kills the dialogue before it begins.

Third, and most important, this approach to theology will leave the door open for a more ecumenical and universal understanding of the significance of the gospel. Traditional Christian theology simply ignores the greater part of the human race; it has only after-thoughts to offer concerning God's purposes for all those hundreds of millions of people outside the Christian fold.

The history of Christian missions is an outstanding example of the theological void created by the stubborn refusal of the church to accept the religious experience of others. Aloysius Pieris, in his article, "The church, the Kingdom and the other Religions," says that there have been four distinctive Missiological moods in Christian history: the conquest theory, the adaption theory, the fulfillment theory, and the sacramental theory. A close examination of all these theories shows a willful rejection on the part of Christian theologians to accept the religious experience of others outside their fold, and more seriously, a denial that human religious experience can be expressed and conveyed within thought forms other than that of traditional Christian theology.

THE HUMAN PREDICAMENT IN OTHER FAITHS

What is the human predicament in specific terms and how does it relate to the theology of dialogue? Let us take an example:

The human predicament is described in different ways in each of the different religious traditions. In the Christian theology one speaks about the 'fall' (or rather the 'fallenness') of the human being or the state of 'sin'. The actual words, 'fall' or 'sin' may not be used in modern theology, but words like 'estrangement', or 'alienation' eventually boil down to a particular idea of sin. It is within this predicament that we understand Christ as Saviour—one that gives us new humanity.

The *advaita* thinking within Hinduism, on the other hand, describes the predicament as *avidya* or ignorance that stands in the way of the realization of one's unity with the Ultimate Reality, *Brahman*. Buddhism analyses that situation in terms of *anicca* (impermanence), *anatta* (no-soul), and *dukkha* (experience of existence as suffering).

Is it not willful blindness to insist that the 'creation-fall-redemption' story or its modern counterparts are the only true description of the human predicament? Can we say that the idea of sin exhausts all descriptions of the state of humankind? After all, no one today believes that there was an actual historical 'fall' and that a man called Adam fell from the grace of God, affecting all human beings. Nevertheless we believe in the 'fall' because it speaks about our present human situation and gives us a framework within which we can speak about the significance of Christ.

What is essential to theology of dialogue is to take with absolute seriousness the analysis of human predicament within other faiths. They are no more or no less valid than the concept of the doctrine of sin, with which traditional Christian theology is done. The tragedy of our past is that we have always compared the understanding, say, of *avidya* (spiritual ignorance) with the Christian concept of sin and passed judgment of their suitability or otherwise to express the human predicament. Some have gone a step further to adapt these words, but only to pack them with Christian ideas. This is not dialogue, nor is it responsible way of proclaiming Christ. Rather we must get behind the Hindu and Buddhist stories to comprehend what is conveyed in their 'story telling'. We must listen patiently, and then, we might discover even a much fuller and sharper analysis of the human predicament within which the reality of Christ can have profound meaning.

Up to now the Christian proclamation meant that we first break down their 'story' and present our 'story' as an alternative; and then, having given them a new analysis, we present Christ as the solution. Is this the right way forward?

TELLING OUR STORY WITHIN ALL STORIES

Theology of dialogue has to do with telling our religious faith and experience within all stories, within all different thought forms. For instance, as mentioned earlier, Buddhism has analyzed the human predicament in terms of the three marks of existence, *anicca* (impermanence) *annata* (no-soul) and *dukkha* (the resulting experience of suffering). Lynn de Silva claims that there is no point in attempting to impose the Christian conceptual framework on Buddhists. Rather, Christian dialogue involves not only listening to the Buddhists but also being able to express the Christian experience within that conceptual framework. He says:

> The essence of Buddha's teachings is summed up in the *Tilakkana,* and this forms the conceptual framework of Buddhists. *Anicca* affirms that all conditional things change and are in perpetual state of flux; *annata* affirms that, because of this flux, there is no soul or any permanent entity in human beings; *dukkha* affirms that the conditional nature, being transient and 'soul'-less, is the source of conflict, pain and anxiety. At first glance this *Tilakkana* concept appears to conflict with Christian belief, but closer examination will show that it offers an analysis of the human predicament which can provide a theological framework for an expression of Christian faith in the context of Buddhist thought.[5]

This in fact is the true meaning of religious dialogue. Unless we, coming from different cultures, can tell our faith in our own cultures and in our own languages to our own peoples, there will be serious doubts about its validity, and its power to change the human predicament. This does not of course mean that all 'stories' are equally useful and faiths can be expressed within any framework. The faith itself is always much larger than all thought forms. S. J. Samartha, in his *The Hindu Response to the Unbound Christ,* for example, points out some of the problems and advantages of telling our faith within *advaita:*

The quest for the ground of being culminating in *Brahman* results in minimizing the significance of the world of *history.* Secondly, in its search for the essential nature of man culminating in *atman,* there is a devaluation of human *personality.* These two together in their mutual influence and interaction have contributed to the

5. Lynn de Silva, "Theological Construction in a Buddhist Context," in *Asian Voices in Christian Theology,* ed. Gerald Anderson (Maryknoll, NY: Orbis, 1976) 40.

shaping of a particular outlook of classical *advaita* which has a tendency to ignore the social dimension of human life. It is suggested that here the insights of the Christian faith in Jesus Christ as Lord and Saviour would help in recovering the personal, the historical and the social in the structure of Hindu spirituality. At the same time, however, a narrow view of God's revelation in Christianity as being almost exclusively confined to the historical, thus isolating it from nature on the one hand and human consciousness on the other, must be corrected by the Hindu insight into the larger unity of all life.[6]

TOWARD A NEW UNDERSTANDING
OF THE SCRIPTURES

What we have discussed so far raises many important questions but the one major question will be on the authority of the scriptures. Many new attempts to do theology have fallen by the wayside because they failed in the first instance to see more clearly and state more definitely the relationship between scripture and theology. Much has happened in New Testament Scholarship to undo the belief that the Bible has the unchangeable beliefs and practices which are valid for Christians and others at all times and all places. But is it not true that in all our churches in Asia and Africa, Barth and Kraemer are still the abiding saints on the question of scriptural authority? Is it not true that we still hold to the scripture as containing 'all the doctrines that are necessary for our salvation'? Do we not seek scriptural authority for all statements and judge all new thoughts from the 'point of view of the scripture'? Of all the bondages of the church in Asia the bondage to a *particular attitude and approach* to the scripture seems to be the most difficult to break away from.

SCRIPTURE—NOT A DIVIDING WALL

As early as 1938 the Indian theologian Chenchiah challenged Kraemer on this question and refused to accept scriptures as the only unfailing authority of the faith. "Was there a New Testament at all for Jesus (at his time) to speak of its authority?" he asked. Some Asians

---

6. S. J. Samartha, *The Hindu Response to the Unbound Christ* (Madras: Christian Literature Society, 1974), 171.

speak of getting at the 'core' of the scripture to which one must try to be faithful, but this proves to be another vain attempt. For recent scholarship has shown that there is not one Jesus in the New Testament, but at least five, the Markan, Matthean, Lukan, Johannine, Pauline, etc. and that all the scriptural material we have can only be understood as 'faith statements' by the writers based on the story of Jesus's life, death, and resurrection.

This does not mean, of course, that the scriptures have no historical value or that they are to be totally set aside. What must be insisted on, however, is that we must develop a truer understanding of the nature of scripture and its authority. At best, all scriptures, including the Bible, are confessional material and they reflect the faith and belief of the people who composed them at a given time. It is of course important to understand and appreciate the way in which faith was held at a given time.

For a religion rooted in history like Christianity it may even be indispensable as a source of faith in Jesus Christ. But it does not mean, therefore, that the present understandings of Christ must be judged entirely by the scriptural authority. In other words, scriptures should not become the walls that limit theological reflection and divide one community from another, but the lamp post that shed light and illumination on the religious experience of the community.

This also implies that we need to have a different attitude to the scriptures of other faiths which express and sustain their own faiths. No scripture is more valid or true than another. Each religious scripture provides inspiration and lays bare the basis on which the faith was founded. There is no reason why the Hindu scriptures should not be meaningful and provide the context of faith in Jesus Christ for an Indian Christian. One realizes that there are many questions that remain unanswered here. But a theology of dialogue and dialogue itself will need to take a much more serious and closer look at the nature and authority of the scriptures for Christian faith and practice.

In the Indian context, for instance, scriptures are important sources of authority, but they are to be confirmed by the *anubhava* of the faithful. *Anubhava*, inadequately translated as 'experience' in English, does not denote emotional experience, but an 'inner certainty' that grows and grips a person as he or she enters into a direct encounter with Reality. This inner certainty is confirmed by scripture and tradition but is never dependent on them for validity.

Again, a theology of dialogue will need to take into serious consideration the dynamic aspect of authority. Scripture and tradition as authorities are too static and refer only to the past. In other words, theology of dialogue needs a new cluster of criteria in which scripture and tradition will have to take an important but a proportional share of authority. We need to develop criteria that will hold together the historical and the experiential, the individual and the corporate, the traditional and the immediate aspects of the faith within which theology is done. This is by no means an easy task but must engage our attention.

TOWARD A NEW UNDERSTANDING OF COMMUNITY

Over the years a growing link has developed between the words 'dialogue' and 'community'. Dialogue is never undertaken for its own sake. It can only be meaningfully entered into by those who have a theological understanding of the community we seek. Ultimately, dialogue is the question of the relationship between the Christian community and the human community of which it is a part. The distinctiveness of the Christian community lies not simply in the faith that Jesus Christ is the Lord of our lives, but primarily in our faith-affirmation that God through Jesus Christ is the Lord of the whole created order. Therefore, the ultimate community we seek can never be the narrow group of Christians but a whole new world in which all human beings share a common destiny and God will be 'all in all'.

Russell Chandran points out that "it is significant that in the New Testament the frontier for Christian religion is not between Christianity as a religion and other religions. The Jewish Christians never gave up their Judaism and the Council of Jerusalem (Acts 15) decided that the Gentiles need not leave their religion either. All that was required was to refrain from what would be considered evil in relation to one's commitment to Christ. Neither Jesus nor the Apostles seemed to pay much attention to the problem of religious frontiers as such. Peter sums up his own experience on this question by saying, "God has no favorites, but that in every nation the man who is God-fearing and does what is right is accepted by him" (Acts 10:34–35). The frontier of mission, as the early church sees it, is between good and evil, between righteousness and wickedness, between the Kingdom of God and the powers of evil, not between one community and another."[7]

Again, does not the understanding so prevalent in the churches that the Christian community is the only true community of God move away from all that we know and believe about God in Jesus Christ? Does not the divine love for all humankind, and God's divine Lordship over all life, completely exclude any idea that salvation occurs only in one stream of human history, which is limited in time to the last nineteen centuries and in space to those areas to which missionaries went? The scope, the power, and the means of the love of God can never be determined by any. If God is the God of the whole world, we must presume, whatever its implications for the understanding of the Christian religion, that the whole of humankind is in a continuous and universal relationship to God.

Such a theological understanding of the relationship between God and all people makes dialogue not another option but an imperative for the church. The most unfortunate aspect of human life, John Hick says, is that "most religions have divided themselves into rival ideological communities,"[8] sometimes at each other's throats. Theology in this context has taken the place of some unalterable, divinely inspired truth to protect an ideology, and not the continuous process of reflection on the nature and activity of God in his world, which it rightly should be.

DISCERNING GOD'S ACTIVITY EVERYWHERE

A theology of dialogue thus should take the human community as the locus of God's activity. There is nothing particular about the Christian community except that it has come to accept the event of Jesus Christ as a decisively significant event in the whole history of humankind; this is their belief, but the message is about and for the whole community. The self-realization of the Christian community as one called to proclaim this message does not exclude God's purposeful activity in and through other faith communities. Thus the Christian community must not only proclaim the reign of God, but must also seek to discern it everywhere, by entering into dialogue.

7. J. Russell Chandran, "Christian Approach to Other Faiths." Paper read at a refresher course on evangelization, United Theological College, Bangalore, India, 1974.

8. John Hick, "The Reconstruction of Christian Belief for Today and Tomorrow," *Theology* vol. LXXIII (1970): 400.

CHALLENGING THE THEORY
OF 'SALVATION HISTORY'

By this token the whole concept of 'salvation history', understood as the history of the Jewish nation and the church, is to be seriously challenged by the theologians of Asia and Africa. Without denying the importance of history itself, one must affirm that salvation history is the history of the whole humankind. Dialogue cannot take place in the true spirit of discernment if the parties involved exclude each other's history from the main stream of salvation that God offers to all people.

Herein lays the greatest challenge and opportunity in relation to the theology of dialogue. If the Christian community is not the community that God intends but is the provisional community, the sign-community, the leaven, the salt, the light, the servant, then what in fact is the community we seek? What are the marks of the true community that God intends and how do we arrive at it?

If the whole realm of human history is the arena of God's saving purpose, what are the criteria by which we seek to discern God's actions in history? Here, one must admit, we are in infancy, taking the first few faltering steps: we must fall many times before we can even stand erect. But there is no other way to mature adulthood- to a genuine theology of community.

For how can we speak about community and the struggle to achieve it, without taking seriously what God has been doing with the millions of people of China? Or how can we seek to live in community with people of other faiths without understanding, in the first instance, the community they seek? Here dialogue becomes desperately urgent.

NOT A FORTRESS BUT A GARDEN

A theology of dialogue does not surrender the particularity of Christian faith, Jesus Christ and the community that confesses him and is committed to him. Such commitment, however, must lead us to a more open, generous and inclusive understanding of God and God's ways. It must not separate us from other human beings but must place us in the midst of their struggles and hopes so that we can together seek the community that God intends for all God's people. It must not be an impenetrable fortress but a garden where there are many trees, flowers, colors and scents, above all a garden where there is light and fresh air and where you feel free to be one with the whole creation of God.

6.

Wider Ecumenism: A Promise or a Threat?

'ECUMENICAL'—WHO OWNS THE TERM?

Shortly before the World Council of Churches assembly in Harare (1998) I was invited to write an article on 'Wider Ecumenism' for the *Ecumenical Review*. In Harare, one of the veterans of the ecumenical movement stopped me to say how much he had appreciated my contribution in the Review. Then he added, with clear mark of disapproval, that he only wished that I had not used the phrase 'Wider Ecumenism' for what I had to say in that article. "It creates unnecessary confusion," he claimed, "I would reserve the word 'ecumenism' to the search for the unity of churches."

A similar sentiment was expressed by Visser't Hooft, the first General Secretary of the WCC, when he once participated in a seminar at the Ecumenical Institute in Bossey, during which he heard me mention the phrase "the new, wider, mega, or interfaith ecumenism." He expressed his disapproval in no uncertain terms claiming that "flirting with this idea" would prove to be "a danger to the Ecumenical Movement."

We are, of course, aware that the Greek word 'oikoumene' means, 'the whole inhabited earth'. As Christians, we confess that the world is God's 'first love'; God created it, loves it ("God so loved the world . . . ") and intends to bring it to perfection; we confess that God is in the world and that we are partners with God in God's healing mission in the world; we have spoken of the unity of the church as the 'sign' of the unity and renewal of whole humankind. And yet, the concept of 'wider ecumenism' creates some disquiet among many in the Christian ecumenical movement. Wilfred Cantwell Smith, claiming that the word 'ecumenical' should, in fact, point to the wider movements that are bringing humankind together, complained that it is "unfortunate" that "the word 'ecumenical' has been appropriated lately to designate rather an internal development within the ongoing church."[1]

Happily, like many other words and concepts that meet initial resistance but eventual acceptance, 'wider ecumenism' has also begun to have currency in ecumenical discussions. But, "Why a 'wider' ecumenism?" some would ask, "What does it involve? What relationship does it have to Christian ecumenism? What is its place within goals of the Christian ecumenical movement?"

The question often asked, however, is whether 'wider ecumenism' is consistent with our faith. Such a question often confuses Christian faith in God and the challenge of the gospel to love God and one's neighbour with the theological constructs that had been built around that faith. While doctrines, theological traditions, liturgies, and practices are necessary to give 'form' to the exercise of faith, these are very much conditioned by the culture, historical circumstances, and the philosophical atmosphere in which they are developed. When the life of the church moves into radically new situations they can become inadequate vehicles to inspire a living faith. In fact, they can become a hindrance to the exercise of obedience to the gospel in the new context.

The ecumenical movement was built on the theological foundations laid at the time of the eighteenth or nineteenth century missionary movement. It must be said that from the perspective of challenges of our own day, its God is too small; its perception of the gospel too narrow; its understanding of mission too limited; its theology too tribal; and its concept of community sectarian.

Let me elaborate what lies behind that which appears to be a rather harsh and over generalized criticism of mission theology of the missionary movement that fed its theological basis into the ecumenical movement as a whole.

---

1. Wilfred Cantwell Smith, "The Christian in a Religiously Plural World," in *Christianity and Other Religions*, ed. John Hick and Brian Hebblethwaite (Glasgow: Collins, 1980), 87.

IS OUR GOD TOO SMALL?

The Missionary Movement, and its predominantly Protestant leader-ship of the early twentieth century, gave to the modern ecumenical movement an exclusively Christological focus. This Christological focus eventually inspired all the streams of the ecumenical movement. This is very evident in the original basis of the WCC that spoke of itself as 'a fellowship of churches that confess Jesus Christ as God and saviour according to the scriptures.' Unfortunately, the Ortho-dox insistence, at a later stage, for a Trinitarian basis did not result in a radical re-thinking of the basis. Rather, the phrase ' . . . for the glory of God, the Father, the Son and the Holy Spirit' was tagged on to the original basis to satisfy the Orthodox constituency. But in so doing, the doctrine of God was shortchanged and this deficiency continues to plague our perception of what is 'ecumenical'.

To believe in God as the Creator, Sustainer, and Redeemer of the *whole creation*, of necessity, demands that we take the activity of God in the world with the seriousness it deserves. Such a belief means that all religious quests, all movements that bring about healing and wholeness to the world, all efforts that set up the signs of the reign of God, etc., *despite the ambiguities*, in spite of their not being part of our own community, etc., are of interest to us.

The Jewish people were first tempted to consider Yahweh as 'their' God, as against other gods. But soon they came to the realization that such a belief amounted to apostasy, for it allowed for, and believed in, the existence of other gods. It made nonsense of their claim that the "Earth is the Lord's and all that is in it, the world and those who live in it" (Ps 24:1). They had to develop the doctrine that Yahweh, despite the fact of challenging them to enter into a covenant relation-ship, was still the "God of the nations." Nothing less would do justice to what they believed God to be. Once this was allowed for, the logi-cal next step was to allow for Yahweh to have relationship with other nations both in judgment and in mercy.

The opening chapters of Amos was a striking reminder to the peo-ple of both Israel and Judah that God will deal in judgment both with them and with all the surrounding Gentile nations for their transgres-sions (Amos 1–3). Once Amos had made this claim, he also had to affirm God's ongoing life with other nations, and the other nations' life with God: "Are you not like the Ethiopians to me, O People of

Israel?" says the Lord. "Did I not bring Israel up from the land of Egypt, and the Philistines from Caphtor and the Arameans from Kir?" (9:7). In all eschatological visions in the Hebrew Scriptures the primary emphasis is the restoration of the whole creation and reconciliation between nations: "On that day Israel will be the third with Egypt and Assyria, a blessing in the midst of the earth, whom the Lord of hosts has blessed, saying, 'Blessed be Egypt, my people, and Assyria the work of my hands, and Israel my heritage.'" (Isa 19:24–25).

The Bible can, of course, be quoted selectively to support any argument. I can myself quote many other parts of the Bible to argue an exclusive view that appear to reject all other ways of believing. But then, what of our theology of God? Was not God active in the world before our experience of God in Christ? Does our affirmation of the reality of the risen Christ require us to believe that God has abrogated God's ongoing relationship with the world? The church developed the doctrine the Trinity precisely to guard against Christomonism and to affirm God's presence and activity in the world at all times, in all places, and in manifold ways. If God's concern is to gather up the whole creation, without everyone being required to become part of the covenant community, should the ecumenical movement have lesser goals? If we believe God to be active in the world, can we refuse to cooperate with God or refuse to discern God's activity in the lives of people, despite the different ways in which they respond to God's presence with them? Wider Ecumenism militates against the 'tribal' conception of God and recognizes God for who God is. The case for a wider ecumenism is not just sociological it is profoundly theological.

IS OUR PERCEPTION OF THE GOSPEL TOO NARROW?

Here we have a difficult problem because there is no agreement among Christians on what we mean by the word 'gospel'. For some, the gospel is the story of the life, death and resurrection of Jesus Christ. For others, the gospel is what they believe God to have done through the life, death, and resurrection of Christ, namely the forgiveness of sins and our acceptance as the children of God. To still others, the gospel is what Jesus himself announced as the gospel (good news): That the reign of God has broken into human life, challenging people to a radically new orientation to themselves, to their neighbours, and to God. In his sermon at Nazareth, Jesus, appearing to apply the Isaiah passage to himself, reads it with the implication that he has been anointed to bring good news (gospel) to the poor, which is spelt out in terms of release to the captive, recovery of sight to the blind, letting the oppressed go free, and announcing the acceptable year of the Lord (Luke 4:18–19). Some of the divisions in the church persist because of what we choose to emphasize within this variety of perceptions of the gospel.

Within the missionary movement a theologically narrow understanding of the gospel was introduced primarily by two concepts. First, the concept of 'salvation history', which isolated the history of Israel as an exclusive preserve of God's salvific action. Later, Israel too was abandoned and the church was seen as both the locus and the servant of that history.

The second impetus for narrowness came from Karl Barth's disenchantment with cultures and religions. By relegating cultures and religions to the realm of 'unbelief' and by characterizing them as part of 'the human rebellion against God', Barth managed to marginalize whole civilizations, cultural heritages, religious traditions, and spiritual histories as having little or no significance before God. By marginalizing religion and culture, that had hopelessly failed Europe during the two devastating Wars in Europe, and by isolating the gospel from the Christian religion, Barth gave new purpose and meaning to the Christian faith to the European Christians. In so doing he made an enormous theological impact on the church as a whole. European Protestant Christianity is in debt to Barth for the recovery of faith.

Even though Barth's theology, that universalized the European experience to judge all other cultures and religions, was both unjust and unsound, many of the pioneers of the ecumenical movement (Visser't Hooft and Lesslie Newbigin for instance), and many 'third world' ecumenical leaders of that time remained unrepentant Barthians to the end. Hendrik Kraemer, at Tambaram (1938), interpreted Barth for missiology through his concept of 'Biblical Realism', and in so doing ruled out any meaningful presence of God in the religious experience of others.

Thus, God was made prisoner of God's own actions in Jesus Christ. The result was the division of the world into the 'saved' and the 'unsaved'. Christian missions became the only channel for God's salvific relation to the world. God's love for and identification with the world through incarnation was reduced to propositions and belief statements. Roman Catholic theology, building on natural theology, attempted after Vatican II to come up with a more inclusive theology of religions (Karl Rahner, Raimundo Panikkar, Paul Knitter, Jacques Dupuis, Michael Amaladoss, and others), but is yet to translate such inclusivism, which is still ecclesiocentric, for committed wider ecumenism.

Wider ecumenism takes the doctrine of the immanence of God and the belief in the incarnation with the seriousness it deserves. It is based on the conviction that God's unconditional and generous love has embraced all of human life; that the Spirit of God is active in the entire world. In this view, the historic event of the cross is both a participation in and illustration of God's continuous solidarity and identity with the sufferings of the world. It is based on the confidence that the reign of God has, in fact, broken into human life and that we, along with all others, should participate in setting up the signs of the kingdom.

IS OUR MISSION TOO LIMITED, AND OUR COMMUNITY TOO SECTARIAN?

The original vision of the missionary movement, which resulted in the worldwide outreach to make Christians of other religious traditions, saw the proclamation of the gospel and the invitation to become part of the church as the core of the missionary enterprise. This was also considered the 'evangelization' aspect of the broader mission of bringing healing and wholeness to life. Combining of the broader understanding of mission as humanization of life with efforts at evangelization sent mixed messages to peoples of other religious traditions. And the fact that Christians, as a religious community, were unwilling to collaborate with others in the humanization of life confirmed such suspicions. The church, in the view of others, was 'sectarian' in that it defined itself, in theology and in life, as an exclusive community. One might join the church only through an elaborate process of intellectual assent to certain beliefs and through the ritual of the right kind of baptism. Christians inherited this from the mainline Jewish tradition, where the keeping of the Law and circumcision went with being Jewish.

When one reads the gospel accounts, it appears that Jesus was in profound disagreement with his own tradition on some of these matters. If keeping of the Torah (the Law), in their details, was the hallmark of being a Jew, Jesus insisted on universalizing it by highlighting only its essence—the love of God and of one's neighbour. The Golden Rule, like the Lord's Prayer, removed the exclusive dimensions of being religious. There is nothing particularly Jewish or Christian about them.

In the same manner, the temple was a protected sacred space; no Gentile was allowed to get in, and it had become primarily the place for the religious ritual of offering animal sacrifices to God. Jesus appears to suggest that privatization of sacred space is to make it into a 'den of robbers': "Is it not written that my house shall be called a house of prayer for *all nations*?" (Mark 11:17).

'Closeness', for his religious tradition, had come to mean that they have to be separated from the larger community. Jesus used images of salt, the leaven in the dough, the light on the candle stand, and the seed that is sown as images for those that are to become partners with him in healing the world.

These dimensions of Jesus's own teaching and ministry undergirds the call to a wider ecumenism. It is an attempt to define a place for the Christian community within the human community, not as 'outsiders' bringing in a message or rendering a service, but as 'insiders' who are well aware of their own specific identity, but see themselves as partners and coworkers with all others in seeking the reconciliation and renewal of the whole human community. It seeks to establish the meaning of Christian witness not as an isolated activity but as something that happens in our common life as we seek to build with others a more humane, just, and peaceful world for all.

It is for this reason that our theology also needs to move away from its tribal moorings. Wilfred Cantwell Smith reminds us that if theology is 'speaking the truth about God', then we should speak the 'whole truth.'[2] In Smith's view when our Hindu, Muslim and other neighbours talk about God, or their difficulty in conceiving a personal God, what we have is additional and *new data* about God and God's dealings with humankind. A Theology that takes no account of it leaves too much of the data out and is not speaking the whole

2. See the chapter, "Theology is Speaking the Truth about God," in *Wilfred Cantwell Smith – A Reader*, ed. Kenneth Cracknell (Oxford: One World Publications, 2001), 220–21.

truth about God. Our own 'window' into God in the life, death and resurrection of Jesus Christ is a unique experience that we celebrate. Our knowledge of other 'windows' into the unfathomable mystery of the Divine can only enrich and enhance our understanding, and what we have to say about God. It can also be the basis for a legitimate wider ecumenism. Thus, dialogue and collaboration, which are at the heart of wider ecumenism, are not only to know others, but also to know more about ourselves and the One in whom we have put our trust. For we may know where God is; but we do not know where God is not.

AT THE BRINK OF AN OPPORTUNITY

The ecumenical movement today is faced with an unprecedented challenge. Thanks to the forces at work in the world, we are faced with the opportunity and the challenge to rethink the theological bases of our ecumenical commitment. Would we see ourselves as a separated community or an inalienable part of the human community, but with our own insights in Christ on how God relates to the world, and what God requires of us all? Would we see mission simply as a message that we bring to, or activities we do in the world, or mission as participation with God *and all others* in bringing healing and wholeness, justice and peace, and reconciliation and renewal in the world? Would the unity and reconciliation that we strive for only be about the church and its divisions, or mainly about the brokenness of the world around us? Would we continue to build only a community that is internal to the life and mission of the churches, however turned toward the world it might be, or would we participate along with others in striving for a human community?

As difficult, complex, ambiguous, and even alienating as much of the world and its affairs are, the ecumenical movement is supposed to be about the oikoumene—the whole inhabited earth. Wider ecumenism is both a biblical and theological vision as it is also a calling. What is perhaps more important is to recognize that wider ecumenism is already in process with and without us. The signs are all around us. The only question is whether we have the courage and faith to include it also as our agenda.

D. T. Niles, my compatriot, and one of my mentors, was chosen to preach the opening sermon at the first and founding assembly of the WCC in Amsterdam (1948). It was a momentous occasion; the ecumenical task ahead held out so much promise and yet looked so complex and difficult, fraught with many problems and uncertainties. Could we ever hope that the churches, which had been divided so deeply over the centuries, could be truly gathered into an ecumenical fellowship?

Which biblical text would he choose for a sermon on such an occasion? Niles chose Exodus 3:11, which wrapped up all the impossibilities, ambiguities, fears, and doubts that went with that calling: "Who am I that I should go unto Pharaoh?"

"Sorry, wrong person for the wrong job," was Moses's answer to God. As one who had killed an Egyptian and fled Egypt, as one who was slow in speech, Moses thought he was not the appropriate person to go back into Egypt and bring out the Hebrew slaves. God disagreed. Moses wanted God to at least reveal God's true name so that he might go forward with confidence. But all that God would say was, "I am who I am" or "I will be to you who I will be to you!"

It was not much to go by, but Moses decided to go. Such is the nature of the new ecumenical adventure to which we are being called.

PART IV

Dialogue and Mission

7.

Mission Impossible? Toward a Credible Mission for Our Day

WHAT IS MISSION?

There are number of difficulties in speaking about mission. First, it is a word that means different things to different persons, mission agencies, and churches. The three familiar words, 'mission', 'evangelism', and 'Christian Witness' are sometimes used interchangeably and at other times with very specific meaning and connotations.

The second difficulty has to do with the complexity of what passes as 'mission history'. In Latin America, for instance, Christian missions got mixed up with conquests of peoples and territories leaving a history of mission that is marked by power, domination and subjugation.

In other situations, as in Asia and Africa, it was affected by the unholy alliance between Evangelization, Colonization and Westernization. This was attended by cultural insensitivities and total disregard of the other religious traditions.

However, missions have also been at the forefront to bring about healing and wholeness in many situations.

Missions have been responsible to bring about the liberation of people who have been oppressed in some of the cultures, through advocacy and calling upon the colonial government to legislate against unjust practices. To take only one example, missions played a major role in the liberation of the Dalit, the so called depressed or outcaste communities in India.

Missions have been responsible to introduce education and health-care in places where they were not available or denied to groups of people.

Most significantly, missions had been in the forefront in initiating the liberation of women and the girl-child. In India missions played a major role in issues like the abolition of *Sati*—the practice of widow-burning—the education of the girl-child, and in lifting up the dignity of women and upholding their rights.

For instance, in Korea, the missionary of the Episcopal Methodist Church, Mary F. Scranton, with the support of Ella Appenzeller, began the first formal school for girls with only one student. A few years ago, I went to Korea on a faculty exchange program to teach for a semester at the Ewha Womans University in Seoul. What began as the one-student girl's school grew and eventually became the Ewha Womans University, which was not only the first govern-ment accredited private university to be established in Korea but is now also the largest women's university in the world. There were more than ten thousand women students on the undergraduate cam-pus, where I taught at the faculty of theology. But when you add the eleven colleges, fifteen graduate schools, and sixty-six research institutes attached to it, there are today some twenty-five thousand women students studying in all fields of education with over nine hundred on the faculty. When one looks at this success one cannot help thinking of Jesus's parable of "some seeds falling on good soil, growing up and increasing and yielding thirty, sixty and a hundred-fold" (Mark 4:8).

What we learn from the history of missions is that missions have been a mixed blessing to the world. For all the criticism we have for the colonial, domineering, and insensitive missions, we also have examples of individual missionaries and mission couples that have given all their lives in selfless service to others at tremendous cost to themselves.

Each generation seeks to be faithful to its own vision at the times in which it lived. Our task is to ask, "What is the vision of mission that is appropriate for today?"

WHY CHARACTERIZE CHRISTIAN MISSIONS AS 'MISSION IMPOSSIBLE'?

Historically the world missions undertaken, especially into Africa and Asia, are the result of the revival movements of pietism and Puritanism in Europe, the Methodist Revival movement in the United Kingdom, and what was called the Great Awakening in the United States in the latter half of the eighteenth and nineteenth centuries. They were based on genuine spiritual revival rooted in the study of the Bible and the desire to share the good news with others.

However, soon this changed into a missionary program of 'converting the whole world to Christ'. In 1910, the well known evangelist and ecumenist, John R. Mott, a Methodist layman from the USA, convened the First World Missionary Conference in Edinburgh, Scotland. Mott had convinced most of the Protestant Missionary Societies and agencies in Europe and North America to come together in this twelve-hundred-delegate meeting with the primary agenda of evangelization of the world in that generation. The belief was that if the missionary movement gets its act together, pools its resources and plans a common strategy they would be able to win the whole world for Christ in that generation. This was what was attempted. The plan was supported by the reality that most of the parts of the world to which mission was to be taken were under colonial rule. The hope was that, like Europe and the Americas at that time, Asia and Africa would also become 'Christian continents'.

I do not want go into the many reasons why this dream, in terms of what it hoped to achieve, was a failure. The missions in Asia, for instance, concentrated on China and India in the hope that if these two Asian giants were brought to Christ, others would follow. But today, even though missions did make a big difference to sections of the Indian community, not even 3% of India is Christian. There are disputes over the percentage of Christians in China, but of China's more than one billion people, only 3–10 percent might have become Christian. Not even one percent of Thailand is Christian, and not even one-tenth of one percent of Japan is Christian. With the exception of the Philippines, which was ruled by the Spanish, and to some extent South Korea, Asia remains predominantly a Buddhist, Hindu, and Confucian continent. The mission as conceived in 1910, of converting the peoples of Africa and Asia to become Christians, was impossible at that time and remains impossible today.

Any discussion on mission in our day must begin by asking why this mission failed. And it is on accepting the failure of the kind of mission that was attempted that we should ask, "How can a credible mission be imagined in our day." This leads to the obvious question: What do we make of the growth of Christianity today in Asia and Africa?

GROWTH OF CHRISTIANITY IN THE SOUTH

There is considerable excitement today about the growth of Christianity in the non-Western world. It is common for people to speak about 'the center of gravity of Christianity moving to the South'. There is some truth to this in that there is a measurable increase in the number of Christians in some parts of the world, especially in Africa.

However, what is deeply disappointing about not all, but much, of what passes for mission today is a repeat of the failed missions of the eighteenth and nineteenth centuries that attempted to build an alternate community within the existing human community.

It is also based on the deeply questionable understanding of sin, which saw all human beings as ontologically sinful, needing to be saved by accepting a particular interpretation of the significance of the death of Christ. While all other religions recognize that there is a fault line running through human existence that needs to be addressed, they do not see it as 'ontological sin' about which human beings can do nothing. It is also based on rejecting the validity of other religious traditions and the salvific religious experiences that others find in them.

Christian mission understood within this context is exclusive, colonial, and insensitive, and appeals to a small section of the population. It is the response of this small section of the population within some of the nations that we celebrate as the growth of Christianity in Asia and Africa.

The painful tensions and conflicts that are happening, especially in Asia, as the result of the renewal of the old types of mission, are often not mentioned. In India and Sri Lanka, conversion has become a deeply divisive subject and a number of Indian states have moved to bring legislation against conversion. In Myanmar there are active clashes between Christians and Buddhists. In Malaysia there are not only laws against conversion, but also a ban on the use of the word 'Allah' for God, which is simply the word for God in Arabic language and has been used for centuries by Christians in the Arabic-speaking world. All conflicts result from complex set of factors, but the reintroduction of the nineteenth century missions into Asia is a major factor fueling these conflicts.

HISTORICAL ADJUSTMENTS DONE
IN MISSION THINKING

Mission constituency has been aware of these problems. There had been some major rethinking in mission theology within the missionary movement. In 1952 at the World Mission Conference in Willingen, Germany, the concept of *missio Dei,* 'mission of God', was introduced to remove the emphasis that was entirely focused on church growth in mission thinking. Rather, it held that God is in mission in the world to bring the world unto Godself and we are only partners and coworkers in that mission of God.

This was an important breakthrough, but the mainline missionary movement did only lip service to the concept. Further, this radical move to re-conceive mission around this concept and what it implied led to the major division within the missionary movement, resulting in the 'ecumenical' and 'evangelical' divide, broadly represented by the World Council of Churches and the World Evangelical Fellowship.

Recently, at the WCC Assembly in Busan, South Korea (2013), there has been an attempt to move to an understanding of mission as the work of the Holy Spirit with a much more open understanding of God's presence and work among peoples of other faiths and in the world. But reading the documents closely would show that there has been no serious questioning of the very basic assumptions of the eighteenth and nineteenth century understandings of mission.

WHAT, THEN, CONSTITUTES REIMAGINING A CREDIBLE MISSION FOR OUR DAY?

Much needs to be said but let me put forward some theses on the subject.[1] I do not think that what is needed is an adjustment to our concept of mission as has been done in the latest statement on mission released at the WCC Assembly in Busan. Nor are the joint statements made by the WCC, WEF and others on ethical practices in the conduct of mission sufficient to meet the need.

Rather, what is needed is a complete rethinking and reimagining of the purpose and scope of mission, what it hopes to achieve, and how it goes about it. In other words, we need to ask, "What is mission? Why are we in mission? And when is mission accomplished?" And we should be genuinely open to new answers. In the radically changed world of our day we cannot live with the answers given in the past centuries based on entirely different contexts.

Since much can be said on the topic, let me put forward my reflections in four theses which lay out what needs to be set aside and what needs to be affirmed:

THESIS ONE

We need to move away from an understanding of mission that divides the world into the 'saved' and the 'unsaved'; from an understanding among some of the mission constituency that there are 'perishing millions' that would be 'lost' unless they are reached with the Gospel message. Although this view can be supported by quoting isolated verses of the Bible, I am convinced that there is no real biblical basis for this position.

We should recover the biblical message that God intends to bring the whole creation unto Godself. Christians are not a saved community in a perishing world, but a community that is called to be witnesses and coworkers with God in healing the world of all its brokenness, so that it would become what God intends it to be.

---

1. I have given this discussion in greater detail in my latest volume, *Your God, My God, Our God: Rethinking Christian Theology for Religious Plurality* (WCC Publications, 2012).

THESIS TWO

We need to move away from the traditional anthropology on which the traditional concept of mission is built. It is grounded on an ontological understanding of sin as something that has corrupted human beings. Based on this assumption, it holds that human beings can do nothing for their salvation and are in need of a Saviour. This belief has been the main hindrance to the gospel message being understood in Asia. Although all religions are aware of the imperfections of human existence and are aware of the reality of sin and evil, they do not understand human beings as totally corrupted by some form of original sin. The concept of original sin is not accepted within Hinduism and Buddhism (The Jews and Muslims also do not interpret Genesis 3 as Augustine did). Swami Vivekananda, the highly acclaimed Hindu teacher and philosopher, said that it is a sin to call human beings (ontologically) sinners.

This is further complicated by the insistence that acceptance of a particular interpretation of the death of Christ is the only way to salvation. Any mission that continues to build on this profoundly ambiguous anthropology and Christology is bound to fail, because having rejected our analysis of the human predicament they also turn down the solution we offer. Hindus simply cannot understand why Christians do not lift up the high spiritual values Jesus stood for, lived out, and was willing to die for.

But unfortunately the alternatives to the classical missiology, which is firmly rooted in the concept of original sin and the theory of atonement, are too quickly dismissed as 'liberalism' that puts excessive confidence in human beings to get it right. When one reads the Gospel narratives, it would appear that Jesus was neither pessimistic about human beings nor overly optimistic about them. What Jesus demanded was a radical change of orientation, espousal of new values of the Reign of God, and a move away from self-centeredness to a life centered in God and one's neighbour. In other words, discipleship to new values and relationships is at the heart of the fullness of life. His was a call to follow him; not a call to a belief in the merits of his death on the cross.

This is the hardest part in reimagining mission for today, because a theology of mission based on substitutionary atonement is etched into Christian consciousness. And I assume there would be a large

section of the church that would want to stay with it and carry out
a mission on that basis. There should always be room in the church
for plurality of understandings of the cross and its place in mission.
By advocating the position to move away from the theory of atonement, I do not undervalue the significance of the cross for the Christian faith, or attempt to undermine the way it has influenced Christian
faith and piety. Rather, we need to embrace challenging new interpretations of the significance of cross and resurrection for the faith.[2]

THESIS THREE

We ought to move away from mission that targets other religious
communities for conversion. Religious traditions are responses to the
profound mystery of life; they are attempts to discover and deal with
the fault line in human existence that results in so much sin, evil, violence, and hatred. They seek to help people rise from the mundane to
grasp higher values and nobler goals of life. This does not mean that
all religions are the same, or that we accept everything that goes on
in the name of religion, or that we refrain from saying "yes" and "no"
to dimensions of religious beliefs and practices, including our own,
that militate against the values of the gospel.

However, our struggle is not with other religions. They are not
our enemies, and we have no reason to target them in our mission.
Jesus did his mission in the context of many 'mystery' religions,
Greco-Roman religions, and Gnostic sects. None of them were the
targets of his mission. Rather, the only 'religion' for which he had
harsh words, and challenged people to move away from, was the 'religion of Mammon'.

For Jesus, Mammon, or the confidence and attachment to wealth
and power, was the false God that can make one stray from God and
God's ways. "You cannot serve God and Mammon," he said unequiv-
ocally, "You will love the one and hate the other."[3] However, while
targeting other religions, Christians and churches have made compromises with Mammon, the religion of wealth and power.

2. This is also discussed in detail in my last volume, *Your God, My God, Our God*.
3. Matt 6:24.

THESIS FOUR

This means that Christian mission is not something only Christians do. The word 'Christian' should be treated not only as a noun but more importantly as an adjective. For me the word 'Christian', in the missionary context, has to do with those things that relate to the values that Jesus stood for; those values that embrace the reign of God. Therefore we can collaborate, and in fact, should seek to collaborate, with all groups, including other religious groups and groups with no religious labels, in promoting the life-centered values of the reign of God.

In other words, the Christian message is for the transformation of society as a whole and not to make converts to our camp. On this question I am deeply impressed with the differences in approach between Buddhists and Christians. When a group of Buddhist priests go into a village to spread the Buddha dharma (the message of the Buddha) the group stays in a small hut and is supported by the community around it. The priests do not carry money, nor do they do any cooking in the hut. They are fully supported by the people around. All that they give in return is the preaching of the message. There is nothing equivalent to baptism in Buddhism. You do not leave your religion, culture, or family in order to become Buddhist.

On the contrary, when a group of missionaries goes to a village in Africa or Asia, they are the richest in the village and are by no means at the mercy of the villagers to support them. Rather they begin to do activities that economically support the villagers. The gospel message gets buried in the process and a number of people respond to the material support and not to the spiritual message. In the case of Buddhism, gradually the whole village had become Buddhist in their values and spirituality; and in the Christian case, a couple of families have become an alternate Christian community, continuing to depend on the missionaries to support them economically.

This is a rather oversimplified picture of more a complex phenomenon, because there have been good and bad mission practices in both religions. But the overall picture is clear. The Christian mission to convert Asia remains an unfulfilled dream, whereas Buddhism, without a colonizing force behind it, has made Asia a predominantly Buddhist continent. What lessons do we draw from this for missions in our day?

MISSION IS MORE URGENT TODAY
THAN EVER BEFORE

All this does not mean that we are at the end of missions. Rather, many urgent missionary issues are crying out for our attention today, but we do not understand them as missionary issues. Once, when I went to my home country of Sri Lanka for a conference, one of the ministers of my church said that they are having great success in mission because over three years, fifteen Buddhist families had become Christians. In the meantime, we have had thirty-five years of ethnic conflict in Sri Lanka in which thousands have been killed and tens of thousands have become refugees in countries around the world. Recently it was reported that there are about 80 thousand war-widows in Sri Lanka with small children.

What difference does it make to the reign of God if we convince 15 families to move from one religion to another while we are killing each other? What would constitute mission in this context?

MISSION ISSUES TODAY

We live in a world polluted with a culture of violence at every level of society, also expressed in the violent conflicts and wars that have made over sixteen million people, half of whom are children, into refugees and displaced persons; a world dominated by greed that has resulted in unacceptable levels of economic inequality within and between nations; a world where unconscionable exploitation of natural resources and the abuse of the earth threatens life itself; a world in which people are in search of a spirituality that would give meaning and purpose for their lives.

The list is not new nor is exhaustive, but the problem is that sadly we do not necessarily recognize them as issues that should totally occupy our mission thinking and programs. We have so neatly compartmentalized our theological concern into biblical studies, theology, social ethics, mission etc. that we fail to discern that most of the problems that we encounter today, which cry out for healing and wholeness, are indeed mission issues. We need to divert the millions of dollars that are spent today in the attempts to convert people to the Christian religious fold to these real mission issues of our time.

This is not an easy task because our current understanding of mission is based on power, a sense of superiority and an expectation that everyone else should become part of our group.

The real question we need to ask is "What will mission in 'Christ's spirit' and in 'Christ's way' look like?" When we begin with that question we would be able to discern the urgency of having to completely re-imagine mission for our day.

8.

Rethinking Christian Witness in Our Day

Some years back I taught a seminar course called 'Ecumenical Perspectives on Mission and Evangelism' at the Drew University School of Theology, where I teach Ecumenical Theology. The course had three main components: Biblical perspectives on mission, a brief look at the history of missions, and an in-depth study of the understanding and practice of mission within the Orthodox, Roman Catholic and Protestant branches of the Church (with their own documents). Within the Protestant discussions we take a closer look at the so-called 'ecumenical' and 'evangelical' perspectives on mission.

The seminar had a healthy mix of students. Some were deeply committed to mission and had been actively engaged in evangelism before joining Drew for their theological grounding. Among them were also students from Korea and Korean Americans, some of whom would eventually become missionaries. There were others taking the course to get a deeper understanding of the issues, and still others who were critical of traditional understandings of mission and some of its manifestations today.

The main text we used in the class was David Bosch's *Transforming Mission: Paradigm Shifts in Theology of Mission* (Orbis, 1994). It is a comprehensive and handy statement on the history of missions and of the stages through which missiological discussions have moved over the past centuries. It served as a good basic text for the seminar.

At the end of the seminar, one of the most keen and perceptive of the students asked to see me after the class. "I want to talk to you privately" she told me, "because I am wondering whether I have missed something others were able to see. Bosch was talking about 'transforming mission' and 'paradigm shifts,' but at the end I don't see him pointing to any new paradigm. I was looking for something new; I feel let down!"

This was an interesting observation because she echoed precisely the same feeling I had experienced when I first read Bosch. Admitting that I shared her feelings, I had to make a rather weak defense for Bosch, whose untimely death in a car accident in South Africa we mourn, and with whom I had the rare privilege of working closely at the WCC World Mission Conference at San Antonio, Texas. "What he had set out to do in his book," I claimed, "was to give a comprehensive survey of the terrain and the shifts that had and were taking place, rather than to propose a new paradigm for mission." She was only partly satisfied.

But her concern was revealing. Not only in Bosch, but also in most writings on Christian mission, often there is clear analysis and recognition of the deep theological issues and the profound challenges we face in mission today. They are accompanied, however, by a characteristic reluctance to draw the necessary consequences of it to our understanding and practice of mission. What do I mean by this?

IS THERE A PROTESTANT 'PARTY LINE' WHEN IT COMES TO MISSION DISCUSSIONS?

In my book published by the WCC, *Not Without My Neighbour: Issues in Interfaith Relations,* I have argued that from my observation of mission discussions at three WCC Assemblies, two World Mission Conferences and several church meetings, I have concluded that Protestant discussions on mission appear to have a 'party line', with some 'required affirmations' and several 'no-go areas'. Mission discussions are like a minefield, where one walks carefully, avoiding the red flags that mark 'syncretism', 'relativism', and 'universalism'. These discussions also have to live with what I have elsewhere described as the 'three classical fears' of the missionary movement: the fears of compromising the uniqueness of Christ, of losing the urgency of world mission, and of acknowledging the salvific significance in the religious life of our neighbors.

Then, there always needs to be the three positive affirmations: Of the mandate given in Matthew 28 to go out into all the world to preach the Gospel; the John 14:6 affirmation that Jesus is the way, the truth, and the life and that no one can come to the Father except through him; that Christ is the 'only way' to salvation, and that eventually 'every knee would bow and every tongue confess that Jesus Christ is Lord.'

There have of course been very courageous statements, understandings, and practices of mission in concrete situations that go well beyond the caricature that I have drawn above, and several forward-looking and even daring explorations of the meaning of mission in the context of socio-economic oppression, religio-cultural diversity, and in the context of the impact of the secular-consumerist culture. And yet, official church discussions and statements on mission appears to me to be bound by the 'party line' that respects the fears of the missionary movement, and are compelled to make the affirmations that have always been made. I hope that I am wrong in this assessment. In fact, I would like to be wrong. But my fear, especially based on my experience with mission discussions in the churches in Asia, is that I may well be right.

Whether these 'fears' and 'affirmations' are right or wrong, biblical or not, are in themselves legitimate questions for exploration, but lie beyond the scope of this presentation. What interest me about these classical 'fears' and 'affirmations' are some of the open and hidden theological assumptions about God, the world, and the peoples of other religious traditions on the one hand, and of the meaning, purpose and goal of mission on the other. Since these assumptions have become sacrosanct, it has become difficult to do bold theological explorations on mission within the missionary movement. And yet, I believe that the future of Christian mission in our world today, especially as we look to the future generations, depend on our willingness to move beyond these self-imposed limits. Otherwise creative and relevant mission theology and practice would continue to happen only at the margins of the church.

For my part, I believe that there need to be four 'shifts' in our mission thinking in order to arrive at an understanding of mission for our day. None of them, I must admit, are original, in the sense that these have already been part of one or another of the explorations of the meaning of mission or the challenges it faces in our day. What I hope to argue for, however, is that these four 'shifts' *together* should constitute a basis for a new missiology *within the church*, and that only such a missiology would form a more adequate basis for mission, especially as we think about youth, the children and the generations to come.

GROWING DISQUIET OVER THE CURRENT STATE OF MISSION DISCUSSIONS

In his review of developments in mission theology from 1948 to 1975, Rodger C. Bassham says that "the question of God's activity in the world raises one of the most acute points of tension in the contemporary discussion of mission." He points out that there is of course general agreement that God is at work in the world. But "it is far more difficult to answer how and where God is acting, and what the relationship is between his work of salvation in Jesus Christ and his presence and activity in the whole world, including other religions." "This question," in Bassham's view, "which has such broad ramifications for mission theology, remains the key issue in the current debate."[1]

Bassham is right in his assessment that the debate has become more intense, divisive, and urgent with the rise of the new theological awareness of religious plurality. The issue itself, however, has been with the missionary movement from the very beginning.

Are we in mission because God is absent in the world, or because God is present in it? If God is already present and active in the world, where and how does God act in it and what is our own role within it? If God is active and present in the world to bring it unto Godself, does God use agents other than us in the healing of the world? And if God is active in the world, which of course also means in the life of human beings, what do we make of the responses people have made to the presence and activity of God in their religious lives?

Those who are familiar with mission history would be aware of the developments that have taken place in the understanding of mission in relation to this issue. When the first World Missionary Conference was called in Edinburgh in 1910, mission was seen primarily as that of Christians, who were mostly lay men and women, who had formed Missionary Societies to make their task more effective. Their

---

1. Rodger C. Bassham, "Mission Theology: 1948–1975," *International Bulletin of Missionary Research* IV, no. 2 (April 1980): 57.

own personal experience of Christ and the urge to share it with others was the basic rationale for missions.

But by the third World Mission Conference in Tambaram, 1938, (which was called by the International Missionary Council, which had since come into being), the emphasis changed. Tambaram meeting is remembered mostly for the debate on the theology of religions, provoked by Hendrik Kraemer's epoch making preparatory volume, *The Christian Message in a Non-Christian World*. But one of the major contributions of Tambaram was its advocacy of the *church* as the primary agent of mission. Concepts such as "The missionary nature of the church," "Churches in mission," "Missionary structure of the congregation," etc. were to emerge out of this conviction, and soon mission was seen as the basic rationale of the church.

With the integration of the missionary movement into the WCC (as the Commission on World Mission and Evangelism) and its consequent exposure to the social concerns led by the Life and Work movement, the emphasis changed again. By the first meeting of the Commission on World Mission and Evangelism (Mexico City, 1963) the concept of the *missio Dei*, the mission of God, first put forward at the World Missionary Conference at Willingen, Germany (1952), emerged as a primary paradigm of mission.

THE NEW OPENINGS OFFERED BY THE CONCEPT OF THE 'MISSION OF GOD'

Bosch rightly identifies this shift from the 'mission of the church' to the 'mission of God' as a significant leap forward in our understanding of mission. It helped to put many things in perspective. First, it clearly establishes the link between God and the world and sets forth the primary motive of mission as the love of God toward all of God's creation. Thus mission originates in and flows from the heart of God. It is rooted in the Trinitarian life of God.

Second, it understands the church as an instrument in the hand of God, participating in God's mission for God's own purposes. The church does not justify the existence of mission; rather, the mission of God justifies the existence of the church, which is called to participate in the movement of God's love toward people.

Third, the concept of the 'mission of God' in the world enables us to make sense of all the creative and healing activities that happen in the world, which does not come under the umbrella of the church. It enables us to join hands with all that are committed to the cause of justice for the poor. It helps us to affirm the fruit of the Spirit evident in the lives of women and men who do not bear the name we bear.

It is also significant that the concept of the 'mission of God', in one form or other, has become acceptable to all branches of the church and to those with different emphases on mission and evangelism within them. "The recognition that mission is God's mission," says Bosch, "represents a crucial breakthrough in respect of the preceding centuries. It is inconceivable that we could again revert to a narrow, ecclesio-centric view of mission."[2]

THE ECUMENICAL AND EVANGELICAL DIVIDE

And yet, as Bassham has pointed out, soon deep divisions were to appear within mission discussions on the relationship between God, the church, and the world. This is a fascinating story and is still at the heart of the so-called 'ecumenical' and 'evangelical' divide on our understanding of mission. The story also has many interpretations depending on who tells it. To make a long story short, too short for my liking, (and of course to give my own reading of it), it is believed by some groups that within the Ecumenical Movement, especially in its expression in the World Council of Churches, a tendency arose (especially in the sixties and seventies) to equate mission almost exclusively to God's activity in the world. It is believed that this tendency led, on the one hand, to an uncritical affirmation and solidarity with what was going on in the world, and on the other, to the neglect of the church and its missionary mandate.

Charles Van Engen, in his sensitive study of this period, holds that this development led to the two-pronged loss of both church and mission.' Of even greater concern to him is that the concept of the 'mission of God' was developed in such a way as to confirm Stephen Neill's fear of confusing everything with the mission of God: "Stephen Neill's axiom has proven to be true. Never was there a time when one could say so confidently that everything is mission. But by the same token, never has there been a time of such massive confusion about mission. Unfortunately, Neill was right: 'When every

2. David J. Bosch, *Transforming Mission: Paradigm Shifts in Theology of Mission* (Maryknoll, NY: Orbis, 1994), 389–93.

thing is mission, nothing is mission'. In such a situation both church and mission can get lost."[3] Engen, however, sees signs of recovery of the church and its mission in more recent ecumenical discussions.

As I mentioned earlier, and as Engen also points out, there are other readings of the story. Some continue to insist that the 'ecumenical paradigm' of mission was not only a necessary corrective to an overly church-centered understanding of mission, but to our very understanding of mission itself and of its scope and purpose.

THE EMERGENCE OF INTEREST
IN RELIGIOUS PLURALISM

But what is of interest is that the issue has re-emerged in a new way with our increasing awareness of religious plurality and our attempts to struggle again with the question of God's presence and activity in the religious life of our neighbors. During the last two decades hundreds of volumes have appeared on pluralism, dialogue, theology of religions, and on an appropriate Christology in the context of plurality.

This is accompanied by the increasing realization that we would indeed live in a religiously plural world in the foreseeable future. There are also some doubts as to whether the task of 'winning the world for Christ' constitutes replacing the world religions with the church. Such a vision, which was one of the initial prime motives of 'world evangelization', has been frustrated, for example, in Asia. Moreover, the gradual erosion of the church in the fully 'Christianized West' has brought in greater awareness that mission has to do with something much deeper than making Christians out of the peoples of the world. Barth's criticism of all religion (including Christianity) as unbelief, and Bonheoffer's advocacy for a 'religionless Christianity' stems from their utter disillusionment with the 'missionized' and 'Christianized' Europe. In recent years, Rwanda left a permanent scare in human consciousness on the levels to which human brutality to one another could descend. And yet, it was also the most 'Christianized' nation in Africa.

My intention here is not to engage in an anti-world-mission rhetoric. I am aware that everyone who advocates world mission

3. Charles Van Engen, *Mission on the Way: Issues in Mission Theology* (Grand Rapids, MI: Baker Books, 1996), 153.

would argue that their purpose is not to produce nominal Christians but 'true disciples' of Christ, by presenting the challenge of the gospel and the demands it makes on people's lives. One also readily recognizes the enormous humanization and liberation that the message of the gospel brought into the human community. And yet, the failure of Mott's vision of 'evangelization of the world in this (his) generation'; the erosion of faith and of the influence of the church in the Western world, especially on its public life and values; the resurgence of awareness of world religions; Christian interest in a new relationship to them; new developments in science and technology, which has created a whole new culture among the youth; all these and more have contributed to searching questions about the future of Christian mission.

END OF ONE OF THE PARADIGMS OF MISSION

To me it appears that these complex contemporary developments, both in the East and the West, and the virtual missionary paralysis that has befallen the mainline churches, points to the end of the kind of mission envisaged in the eighteenth and nineteenth centuries. This paradigm of mission, however, has also been and continues to be the dominant paradigm of mission in most of our churches to this day. It is an understanding of mission that divides the peoples of the world into the 'saved' and the 'unsaved', which puts its emphasis on the numerical increase of the church, and which does not make common cause with all those peoples and forces that are striving for the kingdom and its righteousness. This mission appears to me to be at its end.

IN SEARCH OF A NEW PARADIGM

As part of the search for new paradigm on mission I have ventured to suggest four important 'shifts' that should take place within mainline missiology:

- From exclusive to inclusive;
- From conversion to healing;
- From majority to minority, and
- From doctrinal to spiritual.

A genuine breakthrough in missiology would happen only when such 'shifts' become part of the missionary perceptions in our churches. No doubt, others coming from other experiences would see other 'shifts' that would make for a relevant understanding for mission for our day.

If Christian mission is about participation in the mission of God, and to be where God is, we need greater discernment and greater willingness to change; we should also be willing to be led into new ways of thinking. It is precisely at the time of the restoration of Israel, after the painful experience of exile, that God tells them not to think as they have always thought or to expect things to be as they have always been:

> Do not remember the former things,
> or consider the things of old.
> I am about to do a new thing;
> Now it springs forth,
> do you not perceive it?" (Isa 43:18–19)

The evaluative report of the last WCC World Mission Conference in Salvador, Brazil, has an attractive title, which reads, 'The Sign Posts of the New in Mission at Salvador'. What we appear to need in our day are also sign posts for a 'new mission', which would still be a mission about Jesus Christ and what God has done among us in him. I hope that the proposed call for four shifts in mission thinking is among the sign posts that point to the 'new in mission'.

I. FROM AN EXCLUSIVE TO AN INCLUSIVE
UNDERSTANDING OF MISSION

It is important to re-conceive an inclusive mission based on a new discussion of the concept of the *missio Dei* or the mission of God, which would, hopefully, avoid some of the pitfalls that created the 'ecumenical' and 'evangelical' polarization. Neill is right in saying that when everything is mission, nothing is mission. But, at the same time, it is also true that mission is about everything and everything that we do has a missionary implication. It is also true that nothing is outside the scope of God's mission and that there is nothing that God cannot use in the fulfillment of God's mission.

My Sri Lankan Experience

Let me illustrate the concern from my own personal situation. In Sri Lanka, 65 percent of the population are Buddhists and 18 percent are Hindus. Only 6.8 percent constitute the Christian minority that is also divided into all possible confessions, denominations, and para-church groups. Among the many problems facing the nation, the major one is the armed conflict between the two ethnic groups that constitute the island, which has already claimed the lives of many thousands of people.

If one were to conduct a survey among the churches with the question, 'What constitutes the mission of the church in Sri Lanka today?' a majority would no doubt answer: 'The church's mission is to preach the Gospel and to bring the Buddhists, Hindus, and Muslims to Christ.' What is important is to note that most of them are well aware that in the context of the resurgence of Buddhism, Hinduism, and Islam, only a small fraction of the people would be receptive of the Christian message to the point of 'accepting Christ' and make an open display of it by 'becoming a part of the church'. As someone who has ministered to congregations there, I am also aware that most of them, despite what they say about mission, have no real intention to preach Christ to their neighbors, despite the repeated reminders from the pulpit of their 'missionary obligation' and the revival meetings held regularly to enhance their missionary zeal.

And yet, at the theological level, we have to affirm that God, whom we know in Jesus Christ as the creator and sustainer, and as one who seeks to redeem all of life from the forces of death, is also in Sri Lanka; that God participates in the sufferings of the people; that God loves, reconciles, and heals them and is using all those people and forces (which are not necessarily part of the church) to bring about just peace and reconciliation.

Most Christians in Sri Lanka, however, would not too readily discern or acknowledge God's saving presence and activity unless it is an activity in which Christians are engaged, or it is one that is aimed at making Christians of people from other religious traditions. This does not mean that Christians are not engaged in the attempts to bring about peace and reconciliation along with neighbors of other faiths. But they would see this as part of their exercise of 'discipleship', rather than participation in the mission of God. The suggestion that

God may be calling them for the *mission* of healing and reconciling the nation, and that for this purpose they must work with Buddhists and Hindus, is not always acceptable to them. In the context of an understanding of mission as converting others into the Christian fold, it would be put down as 'lack of evangelistic zeal' and 'betrayal of the true mission of the church'.

II. FROM CONVERSION TO HEALING

Several years ago I was responsible for the organization of a Hindu–Christian dialogue at Rajpur in India. During one of the breaks, one of the Hindu participants got into a conversation with me. He told me that Hindus admired Jesus for his teachings, life, and spirituality, and also admired the church for the "lot of good things" it does for the people. Our real problem with the church is about conversion. "We have the same problem with Islam," he continued, "why do you insist on converting people out of their communities?"

I knew that this was going to be a difficult dialogue because we would be approaching the question from two very different perspectives. But I had to respond to the question. "Conversion, in the sense of dragging a person from one community to another, is not the aim of Christian mission," I explained, "Conversion is what happens when we preach the message of God's love and forgiveness. In fact, most Christians believe that conversion is what God or the Spirit of God does in the lives of people. Conversion is not what the preacher does but how the hearer responds."

"Of course there are many who live unspiritual lives; they must be brought closer to God. But why is it that one must become a Christian, or become part of the church, in order to get closer to God?" he asked.

I decided to give a more direct answer, one that many Christians in Sri Lanka would give if they were asked this question.

"Christians believe that God's love and forgiveness is offered to all people in the life, death, and resurrection of Jesus Christ, and that by believing in him and becoming part of the community, those who accept Christ would participate in this love, forgiveness, and new life that God offers." I said.

There was silence. A rather long silence, during which which my

Hindu friend was attempting to understand and figure out the implications of what I had said.

"I don't understand this," he finally told me, "For one thing, love and forgiveness of God are also in Hinduism. In any case, why should one move from one community to the other to receive God's forgiveness when God is everywhere and in every one's life?"

I have used the incident above on other occasions to illustrate that dialogue often offers opportunities for Christian witness and that in some sense it is more demanding and challenging to witness in the dialogue context than in an evangelistic convention where a safe distance separates the preacher from the hearers.

Whether my witness was adequate is another issue. But I recall the incident here to indicate the second 'shift' I believe that needs to take place in a new paradigm on mission as we look to the future, namely, a move away from 'conversion' language to that of 'healing'.

I am aware of the positive theological content that one can give to the word 'conversion', especially as the transforming activity of the Spirit in the lives of individuals and communities. But it has come to mean, especially in the context of plurality of faiths, an activity aimed at dragging persons from one community to another. In fact, my Hindu friend is right in assuming that Christians commonly believe that conversion is complete only when someone had moved into their own community. We do still think of the 'success' of mission in terms of how many converts have been made.

It is of interest that the call to repentance (to a life oriented toward God and one's neighbor), healing, teaching, and casting out of evil spirits constituted the mission and ministry of Christ. No doubt, the idea of 'conversion' as becoming a part of a new faith community is present in the Acts of the Apostles. Rightly understood, the word can have rich meaning. But still, it is a much-misunderstood word among peoples of other faiths, also because there had been missions (which continue to this day) that place the primary emphasis on harvesting 'converts'.

But as we look at the world we live in, the words that can truly capture the mission that the church needs to engage in along with God are 'healing', 'reconciliation', 'wholeness', etc. The urgency of these would be readily understood both by Christians and others. The word 'conversion', and phrases like 'winning the world for Christ' look almost out of place in a world in turmoil.

Returning to my Hindu friend, I am certain that he would have had no difficulty in understanding the need for healing—physical, spiritual, and social—in the world and within the Hindu community. He would not have had any difficulty in receiving our witness of the experience of healing, and that we are in a ministry of healing lives in the name of Christ. He would also have been open to explore, lift up, and employ the resources for healing and reconciliation that are present within Hinduism, despite the fact that there are other dimensions of Hinduism that have been used to perpetuate unjust social structures.

I have used the word 'healing' because it has for me a rich connotation that goes beyond physical well-being to spiritual, social, and ecological dimensions. Other more suitable words may be available that connote the picture of shalom, where the intention is to bring all of life to what God intends it to be.

Some would argue that the emphasis on healing moves away from an important word in mission: salvation. The Christian mission, it would be said, is about the salvation of the world. Jesus has to be preached because he is the savior of the world. Conversion is necessary because one participates in salvation by believing in him.

This question merits a discussion all of its own, and is familiar to all that have followed the controversies within the church on the person and work of Christ, both classical and modern. All that can be said is that we are aware that there has already been a plurality of understanding of what God has done in Christ and what significance it has for the life of the world both within the New Testament and within the early church.

What is significant in more recent mission discussions is that there is less insistence on the unqualified affirmation that there is no salvation outside that act of persons naming the name and becoming part of the Christian community. However, I am aware that quite a number of Christians and theological streams would still make the call to explicit acceptance of Christ as the basis of salvation and therefore as the primary purpose of mission.

Advances Made at San Antonio Mission Conference

The report of the WCC World Mission Conference at San Antonio, Texas, which did include many streams of mission

142 STRANGERS OR CO-PILGRIMS?

thinking, however, shows signs of a new willingness on the part of the Christians to do fresh thinking on this issue. While affirming the belief that salvation is offered to all through Christ, and that our mission to witness to Christ can never be given up, San Antonio confessed that there is a tension between our call to such witness and our affirmation about 'God being present and at work in people of other faiths'. In view of the unresolved theological issues in making these affirmations San Antonio could only conclude, "We appreciate this tension, and do not attempt to resolve it."[4]

The 'nervousness' about resolving this tension is understandable because it can never be resolved within the parameters, fears and self-imposed limits that operate within the church discussions on mission. If there is to be a genuine 'shift' in the missionary paradigm for a new period ahead, it has to do with our honest attempt to resolve this tension. The call to move from 'conversion' to 'healing' is part of that effort.

III. FROM MAJORITY TO MINORITY

One of the divisive issues in mission discussions has to do with the intention of mission in terms of its ultimate goal. To some, the goal of mission is to make everyone accept Jesus Christ as their Lord and savior, because otherwise they would be 'lost'. The 'perishing millions' provide the urgency and the obligation for mission. Even other missiological thinking that does not go in the direction of 'the millions that are perishing for having not heard the Gospel', when analyzed, would reveal that they too are based on the assumption that mission constitute the conversion of the world to Christ. It is natural that this thinking persists, if only in the background, because much of the Protestant missiology took shape before the concept of the 'mission of God' became a key concept in mission. It also took shape within a Theology of Religions that saw no possibility of a life in God through other faith traditions.

The intention to be the majority also comes from the imperial and colonial history of the church, where political power held out

4. Frederick R. Wilson, *The San Antonio Report: Your Will be Done: Mission in Chris's Way* (Geneva: WCC, 1990), 33. It is of interest that one of the main drafters of this section was David Bosch.

the possibility of Christianity, the religion of the colonizing powers, becoming the religion of all people in one way or another.

Understandings of Mission in the Scriptures

It is interesting that in the Old Testament there is no anxiety that the status of the 'people of God' should be extended to include all nations. On the contrary, it would appear that there is greater interest that the small nation of Israel and, at times, even a remnant minority from within it, should remain faithful to Yahweh. But Yahweh remains the Lord of all nations. Israel, despite the fact that it is small, weak, and often overcome and scattered, is called to be a 'light to the nations' and to 'live out the righteousness of God among the nations'.

We are aware of the plurality of perspectives on mission that can be drawn from the New Testament. It is not surprising that the Matthew 28 passage on going out into the world and making disciples of nations play a crucial role in mission discussion, for it confirms what mission eventually became after the earthly life of Jesus. In his own mission, however, Jesus appears not only to shun any attempts to form a community rival to his own Jewish community, but insists that only a few would find and walk in the narrow path that leads to life.

There is also a rich diversity of perspective among New Testament scholars on the Pauline understanding and practice of mission, carried under the belief of the impending eschatological summing up of all things. What is most interesting is that while Paul went about establishing Christian communities in the known world, and insisted that the life of the communities have to be lived in witness to the truth of the gospel, in none of his letters does he call upon the churches he had established to launch out a mission campaign to convert the rest of the community. For all his zeal to prove that Jesus was the long expected Messiah, he spends no energy in whipping up the enthusiasm of his congregations to engage in world mission. He was, however, ruthless in demanding of them a life in Christ, which would serve as a visible witness to those around them.

Pauline Understanding of Mission

There are different interpretations of Paul's silence on the missionary imperative of his congregations. Some hold that Paul just assumes the missionary vocation of his congregations and was aware that there were evangelists in each of his congregations that were engaged in the proclamation of the word among the non-believers. While this may well be true, it is still note worthy that Paul, a man fired with the zeal for the preaching of the gospel to the point of willing to lay down his life for it, would not make that the primary vocation of the congregations he had formed.

A more convincing explanation is to be sought in Paul's apocalyptic understanding of the context of his mission. Paul was convinced that in Jesus, not only has the new age been inaugurated, but that it would also soon be brought to its consummation. In fact, Paul believed in God's imminent intervention in human history. Christians are people upon whom "the end of the age has come" (1 Cor 10:11). It was time for the believers to be fully awake and to be ready "for salvation is nearer to us now than when we first believed; the night is far gone, the day is at hand" (Rom 13:11).

This salvation for Paul is also of cosmic proportions for it is not only we who groan inwardly but also the whole created order that has been groaning in travail, as it were in childbirth, is to be set free from its bondage to decay to share in the glory of the children of God (Romans 8). God's gathering in of the Gentiles, and their response to the gospel is the essential elements of God's eschatological ingathering of all of creation. But, the Gentiles can never discern the truth of the gospel if those who claim to have already had the foretaste of this new life and glory live in ways that manifest their old selves. Paul's emphasis for his congregations was to 'witness' rather than to the 'evangelization of the world.'

It is not my intention to go into the complex and controversial issue of sorting out Paul's missionary intentions. But it is important to note that Paul, a Jewish rabbi, combines his missionary zeal of announcing what God has done in Christ with the time-honored understanding of mission within his tradition, namely to be a community that is a 'sign', the 'symbol' of God's presence in the world. It is a community that lives out a life that gives 'witnesses' to what God requires of all human kind, and lives as a 'promise' to what God intends to do with all of creation. Jesus also owned this Jewish under-standing of mission when he spoke of the community that has come under the Reign of God as the 'lamp' that is put on the lamp stand or a 'city' that is set on a hill.

Willingness to be a Minority

The essence of such a missionary self-understanding of a community is its willingness to be a minority. The missionary vocation of such a community includes its willingness to live a vicarious life on behalf of others. The faith of such a community lies not on what they see or what they can accomplish by their efforts, but in the living hope of what God would bring to pass with, without and even in spite of them. To be a missionary community is to own what God has done, and to have confidence in what God would do.

It is fascinating that in the Orthodox tradition of the church the Eucharist is the primary missionary event. It is 'missionary' in so far as it is a celebration in which the past and the future are held together. The Eucharist, in this understanding, is not only a commemoration by the church of the mystery of the Christ event, but also, in fact more so, an uplifting of the whole created order before its creator. It is *theosis* in anticipation, a pre-living of the glorification of all things in God.[5]

It is in this context of the confidence and hope that the Protestant anxiety about the souls that are being lost, its activism in wanting to convert the world to Christ, its self-flagellation about the lack of interest in evangelism in its churches, its sense of defeatism when other religions increase in their numbers, and its triumphalism about the little advances it is making in Africa and Asia in adding more members for the church, let me be honest here, is quite troubling.

The 'Troubling' Dimension of Mission

The 'troubling' is not about the preaching of the gospel or about the fact that in the parts of the world the church has grown in numbers. It has more to do with the assumption that the advance of the mission has to do with numbers, and that the success or failure of mission, like

---

5. Cf. Petros Vassiliadis, *Eucharist and Witness: Orthodox Perspectives on the Unity and Mission of the Church* (Geneva: WCC, 1998), 49–66.

that of a commercial corporation, can be quantified. It is troubling because of the enormous emphasis it puts on individual conversions and its incapacity to understand the rich biblical concept of vicarious representation. It is troubling because most Christians, at least in my part of the world, live and die with a sense of guilt for not having made Christians of their immediate neighbors, which the church has repeatedly told them is their primary Christian vocation. It is troubling because it discounts the many other ways and means by which God can and does draw the world unto Godself.

It is this understanding of mission that is in crisis and is perhaps at the beginning of its end. We need to rediscover, re-own and learn to be at home as a minority mission community whose life is rooted in God and whose life is lived in, for and on behalf of the world.

The Ambiguity of some of the Contemporary Missions

Therefore, I also have some reservation about too quickly identifying the future of the church or of Christianity with Africa, Latin America, Asia, and Oceania, simply because it is there that the churches are growing faster. The loss of nerve about mission in Europe and channeling of more and more mission funds to the 'third world' by the European churches in order to "advance the growth of the church in the 'third world'" is, in my opinion, quite misplaced.

In Jesus's teaching, that which stands against the kingdom is not other religions, but Mammon. He was unequivocal in his insistence that no one can serve both God and Mammon. It is of interest that the temptations that were intended to block and destroy Jesus's own mission were from the world of Mammon: to go for the bread (instead of the word by which one lives), to display power (rather than to put one's confidence in God) and to abandon God (the only one whom Christians are called to serve) in exchange for all the material wealth that the Tempter was willing to promise.

The 'majoritarian mentality' goes with the values of Mammon. The minority status to which the church has been reduced in Europe has opened their eyes to a new sense of mission, to a greater awareness and sense of solidarity with the poor and the oppressed, a fuller awareness of the economic and political injustices perpetuated by their nations on other nations through unjust economic, monitory and trading structures, to the awareness of the contribution their nations make to wars and conflicts all over the world through the production and sales of arms etc.

Jesus's teaching that it is easier for a camel to enter the eye of a needle than for a rich person to enter the kingdom is neither an anti-rich rhetoric nor unsympathetic attitude toward the rich. The rich young ruler who comes to Jesus with an interest in eternal life himself proves the point that Jesus was making: The hold of Mammon is not easy to break out of. And therefore, the gospel is the anti-thesis of the culture of Mammon. On this issue Jesus is clear: "No one can serve two masters; for a slave will either hate the one and serve the other, or be devoted to the one and despise the other. You cannot serve God and wealth [Mammon]" (Matt 6:24).

On this issue a whole new beginning in our understanding of mission is called for both in the East and the West. Without it, there can even be, despite all good intentions, an evangelization of the cause of Mammon.

IV. FROM A DOCTRINAL TO A SPIRITUAL UNDERSTANDING OF MISSION

Some years ago I wrote a letter to my Hindu friend and dialogue partner, Dr. Anantanand Rambachan, asking him to write a few pages on "Who he says Jesus is." Soon I received a four-page reply, which was quite rich and fascinating. "From the perspective and background of my own Hindu tradition," wrote Rambachan, "I did not find it difficult to identify with the figure of Jesus. In fact I found him positively attractive."

Why would a Hindu Brahmin young man be so attracted by the figure of Jesus? Rambachan also provided the answer:

Deeply attracted as I was, at that time, by the ideal of the Hindu *sannyasin* (monk), I was able to immediately see in Jesus many of the qualities of this ideal. Here also was a wandering spiritual teacher without home or possessions, fired by the true spirit of renunciation (*vairagya*). Here also was one who spoke with authority about the limitations and futility of the life, which was spent solely in the selfish accumulation of wealth (*artha*) and transitory sense enjoyment (*kama*)"
    [...]
What, therefore, initially attracted me in the personality of Jesus is the embodiment in him of what I consider to be, from my Hindu view

point, the ideals and values of the authentic spiritual life. This dimension of Jesus has always continued to have meaning and appeal for me.[6]

I must confess that his letter moved me. Rambachan, however, is not the first Hindu to be fascinated by Jesus and his spirituality, but stands in a long line of Hindus who found inspiration in Jesus's life and teachings.

What also interested me in Rambachan's letter was his gentle, and yet profoundly penetrating "complaint" about what we Christians have done with Jesus, and why. Let me allow him to speak for himself:

> From my own limited perspective of Christianity, I think that this primary aspect of the personality of Christ is not always sufficiently emphasized in presenting him. I imagine that it will always be difficult to represent one who cared so little for the comforts and possessions, which is usually the focus of our energies and aspirations, and whose life was so totally a reflection of its center in a higher reality.
>
> As human beings, we have mastered the art of subtly and nakedly using our respective spiritual traditions and ideas to mask and serve our own insatiable ego-centered ambitions. It seems hopeless when that which is meant to free us from the constraints of the ego becomes the servant of its narrow interests.
>
> Perhaps in its concern to stress the uniqueness and originality (decisiveness) of Jesus, Christianity has ignored some of the identities in the definition of the spiritual life, which Jesus shares with the tradition of Hinduism."[7]

Rambachan puts his finger on the most crucial problem we face in our mission with the youth and children of our day, and to a generation that is said to be entering a post-modern world. Our understanding of the human predicament, what we need for our life to become more meaningful, and our witness to who Jesus is, and what significance he has for us, are wrapped up in doctrinal formulations that make little sense to our youth, and especially to those outside our fold.

6. The full text is published in Rambachan's *A Hindu Vision of Life* (paragraph subdivisions mine).

7. Anantanand Rambachan, "A Hindu Response to Jesus," in *My Neighbors Faith – and Mine: Theological Discoveries through Interfaith Dialogue, A Study Guide* (Geneva: WCC, 1987), 18–19. The full text is published also in Rambachan's *A Hindu Vision of Life* (paragraph subdivisions mine).

Our discussions on whether Christ is 'unique', 'final', 'the only way', or 'of one substance with the Father' is irrelevant to our mission, if our youth, while attending Sunday services to maintain their religious identity, need to go on Wednesday evenings to the Buddhist meditation halls to center their lives, or to Hindu gurus to learn about authentic spirituality. Our witness to Christ among peoples of other faiths would continue to have little meaning if the intention is to isolate them from their religious community than to give them new dimensions of the challenge of living with God and ones neighbour that we have found in Christ.

Mission based on doctrinaire Christology, on the claim to uniqueness or superiority or for the purpose of building a rival religious community appears to me to have no future. And yet the need for a relevant mission has never been more urgent. We live in a period of history in which there is an intense search for meaning and for authentic spiritual life. We hear the cry for economic justice and for just dealings in international relations as never before. In a civilization which is being built on the confidence on wealth and power, and which is so rife with violence, there is a quest for the forces of reconciliation at all levels and areas of life.

Let me not suggest that Christians and churches are not alive to these issues or are not responding to them, at times at considerable cost. Nor do I suggest that some of these concerns have not been part of our own understandings of and thinking on mission. And yet, these are all at the margins while we continue to protect, sometimes at the cost of much division and rivalry, an understanding of mission, which needs to die. And the new thinking on mission can never emerge and become part of the Church's mainline thinking and action if we continued to nurse the old fears or seek to fit the new perspectives into the theological and doctrinal presuppositions of the eighteenth and nineteenth centuries. New wine needs new wine skins.

PART V

Dialogue and Religions

9.

Jewish-Christian Dialogue: Toward a Fourth Phase in Jewish-Christian Relations: An Asian Perspective

WHERE DO I COME FROM TO THIS DISCUSSION?

I must begin with the admission that even though I have worked in the field of interfaith relations for some three decades, I am not an expert in Jewish-Christian relations. My own field has been Christian-Hindu, Christian-Buddhist relationships. In 1981, I was invited to work in the Interfaith Dialogue program of the World Council of Churches, and served as the Director of the program for ten years.

All through those years an immediate colleague was responsible for Jewish-Christian Relations. However, as the Director of the overall dialogue program, I had been part of the joys and frustrations of my colleague responsible for Jewish-Christian relations, and had to relate at different levels with our Jewish partners. Much has been achieved through the WCC program to establish and sustain Jewish-Christian relations. We should also acknowledge the contribution of many Christian and Jewish theologians that have devoted their life to rebuilding this relationship ravaged by the vicissitudes of history.

I had also been part of the struggle to produce the 'Ecumenical

Considerations on Jewish Christian Dialogue', drawn up by the WCC Dialogue Program along with the Consultation on the Church and the Jewish People (CCJP) and the International Jewish Committee on Interreligious Consultations (IJCIRC). It has also been my role to be at difficult meetings between the WCC and the World Jewish Congress on attempts to resolve difficult problems in our relationships. I have also tried to keep abreast with the thinking that has been going on in Jewish-Christian dialogue.

I say all this to indicate that I am both an 'outsider' and an 'insider' to this relationship. I come from a country (Sri Lanka) where there is no resident Jewish community, but with a work history that has helped me to watch this relationship from close quarters. This may well be the reason why I, as an Asian, have been invited to give some reflections on this relationship and on my sense of the directions in which Jewish-Christian dialogue might move as we look to the future.

DISQUIET OVER JEWISH-CHRISTIAN DIALOGUE

My own sense during these years has been that, despite the advances made and the relationships that have been built, for one reason or another, the Jewish-Christian dialogue lacked promise and vitality. For all the closeness claimed for the two traditions, this particular dialogue, especially at the global level, lacked spontaneity and appeared to lag behind in comparison to other relationships. In this relationship there were 'no-go' areas, boundaries that had to be observed, language that had to be watched, sensitivities that had to be respected, and politics that had to be mediated. These realities were, of course, present in other relationships as well, but in this dialogue, at least at the moment, the problems appear to stand out more than the promises.

The reasons for the difficulties that trouble Jewish-Christian relations are of course well-known: the polemics that attended the growth of Christianity from within Judaism, the troubled history of European Christianity and the Jewish people, the horror of the Holocaust, the political realities in the Middle East, pronounced internal diversity within both Judaism and Christianity on the appropriate approach to one another's religion etc., loom large, none of which needs elaboration here.

Much pain had marked this relationship and much healing needed to take place. But as we look to the future, are we going in the right direction to bring about a new, lasting, and creative relationship between Christians and the Jewish people? What lessons have we learnt from our nearly sixty years of relationship and dialogue? What light do the emerging new relationships between religious traditions in general throw on this particular relationship? What do I, as a Christian from the 'third world' and from churches that have not had immediate relationship with Jewish communities, make of the current trends in Jewish-Christian dialogue?

It is these questions that lead me to indulge in these tentative reflections on what I have called the need for a 'fourth phase' in Jewish-Christian relations.

CHRISTIANITY IN JEWISH CONTEXT

Much has been written and said about the first two phases. In the first phase, Christianity, which originated as one of many movements within the Judaism at that time, had to cope with the vicissitudes faced by all reform movements in the hands of those who seek to maintain the status quo. There is every reason to believe that, under different set of circumstances, Jesus Movement may well have ended up as one of the streams within Judaism. But three reasons appear to have led progressively to the alienation of the Jesus movement within the Jewish milieu.

First has to do with Jesus himself. We are of course in much difficulty here, because scholars of the Christian scriptures are not agreed on how much we do in fact know about the historical Jesus. Most scholars agree that the Gospel narratives are interpretations of the 'Christ of Faith', and to that extent compromise history. They are undoubtedly affected by the interests of the writers and the circumstances and the audience to which they wrote them. Yet, I am convinced that despite reasonable doubts about the authenticity of many sayings attributed to Jesus and interpretation of events related to his life, we have a reasonable picture of the man, his life, and the direction of his overall teachings.

Jesus that emerges from the narratives, in my own assessment, is not just another teacher, prophet, or reformer, but someone who called for a radical reorientation of the prevalent understandings of

God, attitude to one's neighbor, one's religious practices, and the place and role of the Temple. There is also no doubt that Jesus looked upon his ministry as an internal struggle within the Jewish community, to which he belonged, in order to challenge the community to move toward what he considered a more authentic practice of the intentions of the Torah.

It also appears to me that his teachings and ministry took him to the margins of Judaism. One of the central issues in this regard had to do with Jesus's understanding of universalism, which was in conflict with the eschatological universalism of the Jewish tradition. This is of course a much-debated issue and we need to return to this at a later stage.

The second is the conviction among Jesus's Jewish followers that he had been raised from the dead, that he was indeed the long expected Messiah, and that in his person the coming of the Messianic Age had already been inaugurated. There is disagreement on the extent to which this claim led to the eventual separation between the Jewish community and the Christian community that was evolving within Judaism. Some would place greater emphasis on the Hellenization of the Christian community, although it clear that Judaism of the first century was also undergoing considerable Hellenization before Christianity became incompatible with Judaism.[1]

The third, which was to be the decisive role, was the actual incorporation of Gentiles into the church, which had until then been a Jewish sect, without the requirement that they come under the Torah and be circumcised as a mark of belonging to the Covenant community. This first period was the painful period for the church, facing opposition from the Jewish community on the one hand and from the Roman emperors on the other.

There were many Jewish followers and others with Jewish leanings that attempted to hold Judaism and Christianity together. Paul, in his Letter to the Romans, and some of the early church 'Fathers', made Herculean efforts to give new interpretations to both Christianity and Judaism in their attempt see them as part of a single tradition, eventually to no avail. Gradually the new church became Gentile, and

---

1. Jacob Neusner, in his *Jews and Christians: The Myth of a Common Tradition* (Philadelphia: Trinity Press, 1991) and other scholars on this period argue that Judaism of the first Century, itself subjected to Hellenization, was a very diverse reality represented by the Priests, Scribes, Pharisees, Zealots, Sages, Prophets, and Messianic cults with apocalyptic hopes. Jesus Movement, therefore, was one of many movements. The Christian teaching that Jesus Movement somehow displaced Judaism is farfetched and devoid of any historical veracity.

with it the Hellenization of its theology and especially its social life, it had moved far away from the religious tradition from which it had emerged.[2]

One of the divisive debates within the church was whether it should completely divest itself of its Jewish roots and become a religion in its own right. Marcion, for instance, fought a losing battle on removing the Hebrew scriptures as part of the scriptures of the church. However, since all the early followers and the leaders of the emerging church had been from the Jewish tradition, and since much of the early interpretation of the significance of the life, death, and resurrection of Jesus had been made by Jews who had become Christian, and since much of the interpretations of Jesus were based on Jewish symbol system, it was too difficult for the church to admit the reality that it had become Gentile, and that by continuing to interpret Christianity within Judaism it was increasingly doing violence to the Jewish tradition itself and its own self-understanding.[3]

The Christian ambivalence over this issue continues to plague Christianity to our day.

JUDAISM IN THE CHRISTIAN CONTEXT

The fortune of the church changed with the conversion of Emperor Constantine. In this second phase of Jewish-Christian relations, Christianity as the powerful imperial religion began to deal harshly with Judaism—theologically, psychologically, and even physically. The supersessionist understanding became part of Christian theology, leading to anti-Jewish polemics, anti-Judaism, anti-Semitism, and eventual 'hatred' of Jews within sections of European Christianity, leading to massive injustices to the community, paving the way that made such a horrendous event as the Holocaust possible.

2. Here I follow Alan Segal's argument that claims to Messiahship was something that Jewish community could handle but that it was the increasing social incompatibility that led to the eventual separation of the two traditions. See his *Rebecca's Children – Judaism and Christianity in the Roman World* (Cambridge: Harvard University Press, 1986), 160f.

3. There is much debate among scholars on when and why the separation between Judaism and Christianity became a reality. We are, however, certain that the break did not occur with the destruction of the Temple in 70 CE. The rise of Rabbinic Judaism as a major force in the second century was certainly one of the factors that facilitated the separation. But it is reasonable to assume that the process was gradual, at different stages at different parts of the Empire, and that a more decisive separation took place in the fourth century. Even in the fourth century Jerome could make a comment about some of the Nazarenes who were trying to be both Jews and Christians, and that in his opinion they were neither.

Again, the complicated social, political, economic, psychological, and theological circumstances that led to this deepest wound in Jewish-Christian relations has been studied and written on and needs no repetition here. Suffice to say that the holocaust, and the circumstances that made it possible, left the conscience of the European and North American churches deeply shaken. After the Second World War, the founding assembly of the World Council of Churches, meeting in 1948 in Amsterdam, which was at that time composed mainly of the churches of the European and North American parts of the world, confessed that "We have failed to fight with all our strength the age-old disorder of man which anti-Semitism represents" and called upon the churches "To denounce anti-Semitism as absolutely irreconcilable with the Christian faith. Anti-Semitism is sin against God and man."

Out of this conviction arose the agenda of 'theological reparation': the attempt to clear Christian theology and liturgy of its anti-Semitic elements, the attempts to re-understand both Judaism and Christianity in ways that do not exclude each other, and the building up Jewish-Christian relations on new foundations. The third phase of relationship had been put in place.

JEWS AND CHRISTIANS DEFINING THEMSELVES

This third phase of relationship was very important. Here the Jewish community called the churches to account, and churches have responded with repentance and theological reparation. I am not unaware that there are different levels of satisfaction within the Jewish community about the degree and extent to which Christian repentance has been openly manifested. However, much must be said in praise of those Christian scholars and leaders that have done the patient and difficult task of attempting to rebuild Christian-Jewish relations and to interpret the Bible and the Christian faith in ways that moves away from anti-Judaism and anti-Semitism. We should also acknowledge the courage and fortitude of our Jewish partners who, despite doubts and reservations on the part of some within their own community, have worked alongside Christians toward building a new relationship. A number of churches and interfaith groups have made important Statements and much theological work has been done.

Despite the admiration I have for these efforts, as someone coming from the churches in the 'third world' and as one who has given much thought to the theory and practice of interfaith dialogue and the Theology of Religions, I have begun to feel that this third phase was a necessary and important, but must eventually give way to a fourth phase of relationship. The third phase, despite the contributions it had made, has also become the reason for the stagnation of Jewish-Christian dialogue, with little hope of moving this relationship to higher levels of interaction.

THE LIMITATIONS OF THE THIRD PHASE

There are four reasons why I believe we need to move beyond the third phase. First, much of the Jewish-Christian relations and dialogue in this phase is overshadowed by the unfortunate history of the relationship between the European churches and the European Jewish communities. It is, of course, natural and normal that such a devastating event like the holocaust, and the history of Christian attitude to Jews in European history that contributed to it, has shaped, colored and set the parameters of much of the conversations since then. Addressing Jewish-Christian relations from that perspective was necessary to bring the needed correctives to the interpretations of Christian faith and practice in relation to the Jewish community.

It must be remembered, however, that Christianity is a world religion, and that the center of gravity of the Christian religious tradition has long since moved out of Europe. Much of the church in our day does not share the common history and memory that drives the European–Euro-North American relationship with the Jewish people. I am of course aware of the argument that what happened in Europe cannot be isolated and that there is a sense in which the Church as a whole needs to bear the responsibility for what had happened. This argument is further reinforced by pointing out that the whole church shares supersessionist ideas in the Bible and Christian theology. I do believe that history should neither be denied nor swept under the carpet. There is also truth in the call for corporate responsibility, but as a Christian from the 'third world', I find it difficult to accept that our current relationship with the Jewish people has to be shaped primarily in terms of this history.

The Christian history that emanates from Europe, to say the least, is enormously ambiguous. When looked at it from the 'third world' perspective, we are left with a so-called 'Christian' history that perpetrated genocide on the native peoples of North and South America, totally eliminating some of the 'nations' as a whole. It is part of the 'Christian' history that brought about the decimation of the aboriginal peoples of Australia and many other indigenous peoples in the Asian region. Africa has suffered the history of the brutal slave trade in which hundreds of thousands of slaves died on the way to the slave ships, in the ships, and in slave labor. In Asia, some of the highly developed and spiritually profound religious traditions were treated with indignity and rejected as 'pagan' with the claim that their people have to convert to Christianity to have any knowledge of God.

It is of course true that one atrocity does not minimize the horrendous nature of another; and each people's experience has to be looked at in its own specificity. I want to make a different point here. Christians from the 'third world' do recognize these as part of the history of the church, but they see no reason either to 'own' it as 'their history' or feel guilty about it. Since so much of what happened has so little to do with the foundations of Christian faith and is so closely tied up with the social, cultural, economic, political, and theological realities that belong to people of one part of the world, there are limits to how much we want to own as our common Christian history. We reject it, and learn lessons from it, but do not own it.

Applying the principle to our own day, I for one, for instance, do not expect the Muslims as a people to own the responsibility for what happened on 9/11, the Jewish people for the actions of the current Israeli government, or the people of the United States for the actions of the current administration in Iraq. Too many things are being done in our name and there are limits to what we want to own. During the Iraqi war many of the intellectuals of this country had to begin a movement that had to say, "Not in our name." We need not only to own, but also disown history that is made by others in our name. The feeling among the 'third world' Christians is that the Jewish-Christian relationship has not only become prisoner to the European history, but is also reluctant to break out of that box.

The second reason has to do with the way the third phase is bringing deep divisions within both the Christian and Jewish communities over the State of Israel. Speaking for the situation within the Christian community, I have not known any other issue over which Christians from the 'third world' are so deeply alienated from the Christians of the Western world. It is not my intension to go here into the complex issues of the state of Israel and the plight of the Palestinian people. The question of the need of a permanent and secure homeland for the Jewish people, the rights of Palestinians, accountability on the part of the state of Israel as a modern state, international law, terrorism, militarism, state terrorism etc. are complex issues relevant to this discussion and are not easily resolved. And yet, the resolution of the issue is key to the well being of both Jews and the Palestinians and the future of Jewish-Christian dialogue.

It is no secret that Christians in Jewish-Christian dialogue, most of whom are deeply committed to both the Jewish people and to justice issues, have to walk on eggs when it comes to the question of the Middle East. On the one hand, Christians in Jewish-Christian dialogue are the most informed of the Jewish sentiments and are committed to the well-being of the future of the Jewish community. At the same time, they appear to be the least able to speak their mind, to stand up for justice for all concerned, and to play the kind of role that can bring about a just peace in the Middle East.

The unspoken ground rules, in the third phase of our relationship, appear to me to prevent the Christian partners from engaging the Jewish partners publicly in a serious dialogue on the Middle East issue. Some from within the Jewish community itself accuse the Christians in dialogue of having made an 'ecumenical pact' with their Jewish partners or of maintaining a 'conspiracy of silence' when it comes to justice issues in the Middle East. Christians from other parts of the world increasingly look upon those Christians in Jewish-Christian dialogue as those who have 'crossed over to the other side' and are no longer able to play any meaningful role in the struggle for justice and peace for all communities.

The third issue has to do with Christian affirmations within this dialogue about Judaism that, from the perspective of the Theology of Religions, goes beyond what a religious tradition would say or not say about another religious tradition. Interfaith relations are built on the basis that we need to 'respect', but not necessarily 'accept' the religious self-understanding and faith-claims of other religious traditions. Thus the Christian claim that Jesus was 'Divine' or is the 'Son of God' or is the 'Savior of the World' may be important to Christians, but one does not expect the other communities to either accept or affirm such claims. Truth or otherwise of 'faith claims' made by one community is not the province of another to confirm or deny.

A statement by a Christian Scholars Group on Jewish Christian Relations, dated September 1, 2002, speaks of 'A Sacred Obligation' on the part of the Christians to rethink Christian Faith in relation to Judaism and Jewish People. There are a number among the ten affirmations made by this group that are important reminders to Christians about the way they should think about Judaism and the Jewish people. Two of the affirmations, however, alerted my 'Theology of Religions' mind-set. The first, "God's covenant with the Jewish people endures forever," and then, "We affirm the importance of the land of Israel for the life of the Jewish People."[4]

I do understand the spirit in which Churches and Jewish-Christian groups in the Western Hemisphere make these and many other statements on Jewish Christian Relations. However, seen from an Asian religious perspective, whether God chooses or makes a covenant with any people, be they Jews or Christians, is an open question. Similarly, whether God promises a particular geographical piece of land to a specific people, or has commanded a people to "Go out and make disciples of all nations" is also an open question. These may well be understood as the 'self-understandings' and 'faith claims' of particular religious groups. Many Christians from other parts of the world would see no need for Christians to have to affirm the Jewish self-understandings or for the Jews to affirm the Christian claims and self-understandings.

In the year 2000, a group of Christian and Jewish scholars published a volume entitled *Christianity in Jewish Terms*. There is also increasing insistence on the 'Jewishness' of Jesus, and claims that Christianity cannot be fully understood outside its Jewish milieu. In this volume, and in other recent writings, there are also indications of tentative Jewish theological moves toward responding to Christian claims. Some of the Christians see the re-emphasis of the Jewishness of Jesus, and the attempts to understand Christianity in Jewish terms, as an attempt to correct the over-Hellenization of the Christian faith, its theology and Christology so that Christianity might be brought back to the theological milieu where it actually belongs. This to me is

---

4. *A Sacred Obligation: Rethinking Christian Faith in Relation to Judaism and the Jewish People*, http://jcrelations.net/en/displayItem.php?id=986.

a futile attempt. The horse has bolted the stable quite some while ago; Christianity, whether we like it or not, is now a Gentile religion.

Again I would like to reiterate that I understand the spirit in which these dialogues and theological reflections are taking place. But over a period of time I have begun to wonder whether this theological work takes full account of the revolutionary changes that have taken place within Christian theology on our understanding of God, of the place and authority of scripture, and especially of the meaning and significance of Christ. While supersessionism, concepts of 'old' and 'new' covenants, chosenness, etc., linger in Christian theology, much of the theological reflections today have little resemblance to the European theology that was so beholden to interpret itself in relation to or against the Jewish tradition.

There is of course no uniformity in Christian theology, and there would always be the strand of theology that is supersessionist, as there would be streams within Jewish traditions that would refuse to accept any of the claims of Christianity. Christians should not stop challenging theological traditions within Christianity that are negative to Jewish or any other religious tradition in a supersessionist or superior-to-others mentality.

The problem in the third phase of Jewish-Christian dialogue is that it appears not to be informed by some of the radical changes that have taken place within Christian theology and Christology that would make the whole supersessionist theology totally irrelevant. Are we wasting our time repairing an outdated theology, which is beyond repair, to form the basis for a contemporary relationship?

This discussion brings me my fourth reason, which for me is the most important argument for moving to a fourth phase. As said earlier, Christianity is a world religion, and the bulk of Christianity today is outside the European context. This means that a majority of the Christians of our day have had no direct relationship to the troubled history of Jewish-Christian relations in Europe and would not own it as part of their history. Asian, Latin American, and African theologies have entirely different starting points and are geared to the issues and problems faced in their own contexts. They are more concerned about what the missionary movement has done to their own cultures and religious traditions.

While Israel as a modern state especially in its encounter with the Palestinian people is very much in their focus, they look upon

Judaism as yet another religious tradition like others. There is no anxiety whatsoever about the Jewishness or otherwise of Jesus, whose significance is interpreted in terms of their own history.

In fact, some years back the WCC, as part of its Jewish-Christian dialogue program, organized dialogue events between Jews and African Christians, and between Jews and Asian Christians. This was an eye-opener to the Jewish partners because they were for the first time in a dialogue with Christians that was not weighed down by history or by the classical controversies in Jewish-Christian dialogue.

In other words, the third phase keeps the Jewish-Christian dialogue prisoner to the past and in a dialogue that is overly circumscribed. This relationship, more than any other, needs some fresh initiatives and a new agenda.

MOVING TOWARD A FOURTH PHASE

A religious movement growing out of an existing religion, borrowing much from its parent religion, and still establishing itself as a new religion is not a new phenomenon. In India, long before the Common Era, Buddhism and Jainism grew out of Hinduism and have established themselves as new religious traditions. Not all religious movements within a religious tradition become separate religious traditions. Some fizzle out after a time; others are not too far from the original tradition and therefore become a sect, denomination, or stream within the main tradition. Still, some move so far away from the fundamental affirmations of the religion from which they emerge that they become a new religious tradition.

The Buddha was a Hindu prince who was dissatisfied with what his own religious tradition was offering him to grasp the meaning of existence. His intense search resulted in an experience of enlightenment that convinced him that he had a message to his people and to all peoples on the true nature of human existence. Even though he retained the central concept of a series of births (*karma samsara*) that was part and parcel of Hinduism, his overall teachings and his own interpretation of *karma samsara* took him far away from Hinduism. He and his followers moved so far from many of the religious practices, and especially the social organization that defined Hinduism, that soon Buddhism had become a distinct religious tradition.

The Buddhist-Hindu relation in the beginnings was a difficult one (as one might expect) and included brief periods of persecution of the one by the other. But today Buddhism and Hinduism respect each other as distinct religious traditions. Anyone who really wants to delve into the historical circumstances and the religious milieu in which Buddhism arose, of course, needs to know the Buddha's Hindu origins and of the Hinduism of that time. But there is no insistence that Buddhism cannot be understood without Hinduism, or that we must emphasize the 'Hinduness' of the Buddha to be able to understand him and his teachings. Once a religious movement renounces some of the central beliefs and practices of the religion from which it emerges, it becomes a distinct tradition and must be understood in its own terms.

It is often argued that since the Christians worship the 'Jewish God', follow Jesus (who was a Jew to the very end of his life), retained the Hebrew Scriptures as part of their own scriptures, and inherited the prophetic passion for justice, etc., their religion can only be understood in Jewish terms. But Christianity also abandoned much of what is central to Judaism- the place of the Torah in religious life, the oral Torah, acceptance of circumcision as mark of the covenant community, keeping of the Sabbath, and other feasts and festivals. In fact, few Christians are aware that Judaism of Jesus's own time was not the Judaism they know from reading the Hebrew Scriptures in their Bible. Few have any knowledge or contact with Rabbinic Judaism.

In any case, in spite of adopting the Hebrew Scriptures and borrowing many of the Jewish beliefs and distorting them, the Christian Church today is a Gentile church and has little or no relationship to Judaism of our day. There is no doubt in my mind that Christianity moved away from Judaism as far as Buddhism moved away from Hinduism. Attempts to cast Christianity in Jewish terms appear to me to be as difficult as any attempt to spell out Buddhism in Hindu terms.

While the intensions may be noble and genuine, the effect will be to deny the enormously diverse ways in which the Christian tradition has developed as it moved from culture to culture. And most attempts to understand Christianity within Judaism would end up doing less than justice to Judaism. Polemics and supersessionist attitudes are part of all religious traditions that grow out and separate from another. They are often unavoidable. The trick is to outgrow this stage and for the new religious tradition to establish foundations of its own. The church of the early centuries obviously made a mess of this process.

In other words, the fourth phase for me is a relationship in which Christians and Jews encounter each other as two distinct religious traditions. In fact, despite the knowledge I have of Christian origins and the fact that, for historical reasons, the Hebrew Scripture has become part of my own heritage too, I have always looked at Judaism as I would look at Islam, Hinduism, or Buddhism. Knowing the theological diversity within the Christian tradition, and the extent to which contemporary Christianity has moved away from what is known as 'classical Christianity', today I find closer resemblance between Judaism and Islam than between Judaism and Christianity.

I have come to believe that to look at Christianity as a distinct religious tradition from Judaism is to afford the respect and particularity that is due to both religious traditions. Attempts to interpret Christianity in 'Jewish terms', or to seek to elicit a place for Jesus and the Christian tradition within the Jewish theological framework are likely to produce even more theological complications than what we already have to live with.

For this reason, I have also had difficulties in relating to the concepts of 'Abrahamic religions' and to the identification of Judaism, Christianity and Islam as the 'the three great monotheistic traditions.' Despite the common roots, when examined closely, the conceptions of God differ very much: Abraham is not regarded in the same way, and it is not true that these three are the only solid monotheistic traditions of the world. Monotheism is one of the strongest themes within the Indian tradition. Further, the understandings of the Ultimate Reality as 'monotheistic' and 'transcendental' have come under much pressure in some of the Christian discussions today.

As a Christian coming from Asia I feel closer affinity to Hinduism and Buddhism than to Judaism and Islam, as they have not been part of my own historical experience. Christopher Duraisingh speaks of Christians of India as 'double-scripted' people. They inherit not only part of the Jewish tradition through the Hebrew Scriptures, but also the Hindu tradition, which provided the scriptures of their forefathers and mothers.

THE IMPLICATIONS OF MOVING
TO THE FOURTH PHASE

The call for the fourth phase does not mean that we abandon repairing the troubled relationship between Christianity and Judaism. Nor does it deny that there are still streams of interpretations of Christianity that continue to undermine the reality of continuing Judaism, and of the need to challenge and correct them. But it does call us to free ourselves from the shackles of history and of the need to have to always interpret each in terms of the other.

Over the past one thousand years Judaism has grown into a rich and diverse tradition; and so has the Christian faith. Neither Judaism nor Christianity is where they were at the time of the Jesus movement or at the period of the Second World War. Today they are two mature, self-assured, and distinct religious traditions that need to be in dialogue as any other two religious traditions do, based on mutual respect. And both sides need to reflect the rich diversity of their tradition.

In all my travels in the 'third world' countries I have heard many anti-Israeli sentiments that are basically political, but never those of anti-Semitism, or anti-Judaism, thus pointing to the urgency to find a just solution to the Middle-East crisis. Jewish-Christian dialogue can ill-afford to keep setting this pressing problem aside. As partners in dialogue we are equipped to be honest with each other, to hear out each other with patience and understanding, and seek to work together toward peace with justice to all, not only in the Middle East but in all parts of our broken world.

In other words, the future of Jewish-Christian dialogue may well depend on our capacity to look well beyond our own historical problems to the wider issue of mending God's creation that is so fractured in our day. To that end we do have a common mandate from both our respective religious traditions.

10.

Muslim-Christian Dialogue: "What is it Between Christians and Muslims?"

I was invited in September 1997 to take up the position of Professor of Ecumenical Theology at the Drew University School of Theology here in Madison, New Jersey. In looking through the course offerings of the School of Theology at that time, I found that there were no courses on any religion other than Christianity, and that there was not even an introductory course on world religions. Once I settled down at the school, I decided to raise the issue at one of the faculty meetings. "The United States today is one of the most religiously diverse countries in the world, and all the students we are training for ministry would be serving in multi-faith contexts" I said, "Why is it that we don't have a course on world religions? I think it should be required in our curriculum."

It turned out that the faculty was well-aware of the problem, but did not have someone in the team who felt able to offer such a course. "We cannot add any more required courses," the Dean said, "but now that we have you here, feel free to give an elective on World Religions." I was not happy that the course would not be a required course, but decided to give an elective called "Challenge of World Religions to Christian Faith and Practice." The idea was not only to help students learn the beliefs, practices, and histories of other religions, but also to relate them to their own Christian faith and practices. When the lecture course was announced, there were about forty applicants for the course intended for only twenty-five or thirty students. I knew that it had nothing to do with me; I was new, and students had no idea how good or bad a professor I would be. It simply showed that the student body was beginning to be aware of the changing landscape of their country and the challenge of ministering to multi-faith communities.

Then 9/11 happened in 2001. New Jersey, just across the Hudson River, provided many of the suburbs for residence of those who worked in New York City. Many persons killed in the 9/11 attack had lived across the river in New Jersey, including Madison. The theological school organized a number of counseling sessions to help the students who were deeply affected by the tragedy. The questions that were raised included: "Why us?", "Why would 19 young men give up their own lives to kill so many people who had done nothing against them?", and "What is it between Christianity and Islam that motivated them to perpetrate such an atrocity on innocent civilians?"

The question that intrigued me most was: "What is it between Christianity and Islam?" What *is* the problem? It turned out that most students had no idea what Muslims believed, what the Islamic religious practices were, and what the history between Christianity and Islam had been from the Islam emerged in the Middle East as a possible alternative to Judaism and Christianity. At the same time, most of them thought that they had some knowledge of Islam, mostly fed by the media, in which words like 'Arab', 'Middle East', 'Jihad', 'Islamic terrorism', 'fundamentalism', etc were dominant. The level of ignorance about a religion with which Christianity has co-existed for so many centuries really shocked the faculty. Soon the course on world religions, which included visits to places of worship, conversation with people of other religions, and assignments to explore the teachings and practices of other religions, was made a required course.

I have given this introduction in order to highlight four issues in Muslim-Christian relations that would throw some light on exploring the question, "What is it between Christians and Muslims" that makes this relationship a difficult one? Why is there some form of unacknowledged (but discernible) alienation, even fear, leading to what is loosely described as "Islamophobia" within sections of the Christian community in many of the Western countries?

A RELATIONSHIP MARKED BY IGNORANCE
OF EACH OTHER

The first has to do with mutual ignorance and the prejudices that play a significant role in shaping the perceptions of each other. For instance, there was very little knowledge among the students on the place Islam occupies in the world as a religious tradition. The Pew Research Center estimates that there are some 1.6 billion Muslims in the world, constituting about 23% of the world's population, which makes it the second largest religion of the world. The students' impression that it is the religion of the Arabs in the Middle East is right only in relation to its origins and the use of Arabic as the sole language of its scripture. In reality, the largest Islamic country in the world is Indonesia, there are more than 990 million Muslims in the Asian-Pacific region, and nearly 250 million in Sub-Saharan Africa, over against the 318 million in the Middle East and North Africa combined. Nearly 3.5 million Muslims live in the United States.

There was also little knowledge among most of the students that Islam is as widespread and culturally diverse as Christianity is, and that today millions of Muslims, Christians, Buddhists, Hindus, and others live together peacefully in many multi-faith societies around the world. In addition, there was very little knowledge of Islam as a religious tradition that nourishes the spiritual and ethical lives of millions of its followers. Equal level of ignorance about the Christian tradition also bedevils the Islamic world. In the absence of informed understanding of one other, the Muslim-Christian relationship, more than most of the other interfaith relationships, is marked by unexamined prejudices and caricatures.

THEOLOGICAL ISSUES

The second relates to theological issues. The birth of Islam raised a number of problems to Christian identity and self-understanding, in that it presented a radical theological challenge to some of the cherished Christian beliefs. The prevalent Christian position was that God, who had been revealing Godself though the ages, had made the final and decisive revelation in Jesus Christ, and had acted in the life, death, and resurrection of Christ for the salvation of all humankind. Christianity, therefore, had problems with accepting the

Islamic claim that God had made the final and decisive revelation in the Qur'an through the prophet Muhammad.

Christian qualms on the status of the Muhammad as the receiver of a new revelation and of the Qur'an as God's final word continued through the centuries. From the perspective of Islam, in order to justify the need for a new revelation, Islam claimed that God had to give this new and final revelation because Jews and Christians had corrupted the earlier revelations given through a series of prophets, including Moses and Jesus. In so doing, Islam was seen to undermine both the Hebrew and Christian scriptures. Some of the early Christian writings attempted to present Prophet Muhammad as an imposter who borrowed from Jewish and Christian scriptures to create a new movement based on a fictitious claim to have received new revelations from God.

Yet it is of interest that the Qur'an has significant teachings about Jesus (*Isa*). It affirms that he had a miraculous birth through the Virgin Mary (Qur'an 19:19–21). In fact, there are more references to Mary (*Miriam*) in the Qur'an than in the New Testament. It holds that Jesus was a humble servant of God, strengthened by the Holy Spirit (2:87), and a righteous prophet through whom God announced his gospel. For the Muslims, the proof that he was a true prophet from God is shown by the power he had to perform many miracles and healings as a sign of God's approval (19:30–35).

In spite of these positive affirmations of Jesus and his ministry, the Qur'an has other teachings about Jesus that disturbed the Christians and challenged some of their basic beliefs. It held that the Christian claim that he was the 'Son of God' was blasphemous: "It is not befitting to (the majesty of) Allah that He should beget a son" (19:35). The denial of this claim is rather dramatically put in Sura 5:116, where Jesus is presented as giving an account on this matter to Allah: "And behold! Allah will say: 'O Jesus the son of Mary! Did you say unto men, worship me and my mother as gods in derogation of Allah'? He will say: 'Glory to Thee! Never could I say what I have no right (to say). Had I said such a thing, thou wouldst indeed know it.'" . . .

The problem was even more troubling to the Christians when the Islamic tradition denied that Jesus was crucified: " . . . they said (in boast), 'we killed Christ Jesus the son of Mary, the messenger of Allah'; but they killed him not, nor crucified him, but so it was made appear to them . . . ' (4:157). Instead, Muslims believe that Jesus, one of the most righteous among prophets, was taken bodily to heaven: "Behold! Allah says: 'O Jesus! I will take thee and raise thee to Myself and clear thee (of the falsehood) of those who blaspheme . . . '" (3:55).

The difficulties these teachings raised for the Christians are obvious. The Qur'an teachings denied two of the doctrinal pillars of Christian theology: Trinity, and the significance of Jesus's passion and death on the cross for human salvation. The Christian-Muslim divide over the significance of Jesus persists to this day. The respective positions they held on this question were irreconcilable and yet central to each of the faith traditions.

POLITICAL ISSUES

The third difficulty is political. If Islam had remained a religion in the area where it originated, the polemical relations between Islam and Christianity would have remained at the theological level. But already during the Prophet's time Islam began to spread into the Arabian Peninsula. Soon after, it began to extend its reach much further, conquering first the territories of what had been the Persian Empire and then many parts of the Roman Byzantine Empire. In the wake of political and economic weaknesses caused by constant warfare and internal divisions that plagued the Roman rule, Islam was able to conquer and establish itself in large parts of what had traditionally been 'Christian lands'. Soon Islamic rule stretched from the boarders of China and India, across Central Asia, the Middle East, North Africa, Sicily, and the Iberian Peninsula.

The Islamic expansion, however, was not all military conquests. Under a number of enlightened rulers, an Islamic civilization grew with many centers of culture and science and produced notable astronomers, mathematicians, doctors and philosophers during what was considered the Golden Age of Islam. Investments were made in economic infrastructure, such as irrigation systems and canals. Further the emphasis on reading and reciting the Qur'an produced a comparatively high level of literacy in the general populace.

However, from the Christian perspective, what had been some of the most important and celebrated centers of Christian teaching and thought were now under Muslim rule. What is more, the Holy Land, which had so much meaning to Jews and housed the pilgrimage sites for Christians, had been taken over in the Islamic conquest. The

attempts led by the Roman Catholic Church, and what remained of
the Roman Empire, to free Jerusalem, and where possible to liberate
the former Christian territories, led to a series of partly religion-moti-
vated brutal and bloody wars between Muslims and Christians, generally called the crusades.

What I have described here is an overly simplified expression of a
very complex history, over which there is considerable dispute and
disagreements among historians and scholars of religious studies. The
purpose, however, is not to give an accurate account of the history
but to say how Christian-Muslim relations were vitiated by both religions' embroilment with empires that rarely had any respect for religion but only to expand their power by conquering more and more
territories.

An important point for our reflection is that no other religion has
posed a threat to Christian political power and was able to take control of and radically change the Christian territories as Islam was able
to do. The loss to Islam of the ancient Christian centers of teaching
and the areas that had the holy sites of Christianity left an indelible
mark on Christian consciousness. This historical memory, conscious
and unconscious, has led many Christians to associate conquest, militarism, etc., with Islam, creating in them a generalized suspicion and
fear, and an adversarial image of Islam.

This unfortunate history did not end there. Eventually, the historical fortunes changed again. With the fall of the Ottoman Empire,
many of the Islamic countries in the Middle East came under the control of Western powers. Originally they were intended to be 'pro-
tectorates' under the British and French colonial rule. The colonizers,
however, were less interested in the welfare of the people and supported rulers that served their own economic interests. Soon Muslims
began to look at the colonizers as Christians who have done enormous injustices to them by supporting and protecting their oppressive leaders. Therefore, the recent struggles of the Muslim masses
against their despotic leaders also became a struggle against the Christian West.

Thus, Christian-Muslim relations were marred not only by the
theological difficulties but also by centuries of political rivalry,
enmity, and wars. Not everyone on either side knows exactly what
the history was, but they act out of a collective memory that has
been passed down through generations. The nineteen terrorists that

brought down the twin towers on 9/11 had nothing against anyone who was working in the towers; they were not guilty personally, but are guilty by association—by belonging to a group that is collectively looked upon as the enemy.

SOCIAL ISSUES

The fourth concerns the wide gap between Christianity and Islam on social questions. It is unfortunate that the political rivalries and conflicts that marked the beginning of their relationship resulted in the two traditions moving in separate directions regarding the way they spelt out social and political norms for their respective societies. The two religions were subjected to and impacted by different movements of history, resulting in different types of internal religious developments. This is a large and complex subject, but one can take three examples to show where Christians and Muslims appear to have differences that create false images of each other.

The first relates to their respective scriptures and the consequences of the approach taken to them. Broadly speaking, both Christianity and Islam consider their scriptures as the word of God. Over a period of time Christians have had considerable struggles on what it means to call the Bible the word of God, resulting in a variety of positions that are generally tolerated within the Christian reality. While the Bible still has a kind of authority, it does not play the central role, as it once did, in shaping Christian life, social practices, and norms.

Islam, for its part, considers the Qur'an not only as the word of God, but the very *words* of God, directly delivered by God to Prophet Muhammad through the agency of the angel Gabriel. Even the Arabic language in which it was delivered is believed to be intrinsic to the Qur'an. Further, many Muslims believe that Qur'an gives a comprehensive guide to personal, family, social, economic, and political life in society. One must note here that Islam also has number of other authorities, like the *hadith*, which is a collection of the teachings, actions, and habits of Prophet Muhammad, to give guidance on matters not directly dealt with in the Qur'an. Further, there are extensive scholarly commentaries on the Qur'an and well-developed schools of Jurisprudence spelling out the significance of the teachings in the Qur'an for life in society.

However, since all the words in the Qur'an are said to have been directly given by God, extremists could quote an isolated verse of the Qur'an, often out of its context, and use it as a command of God, not recognizing that it may be against the overall teaching of the Qur'an, or even opposed to other verses in the Qur'an. Further, while *sharia* can mean Islamic law in a broad sense, the extremist can give it a very narrow interpretation, insisting that what had been the practice centuries back must guide us also in the present.

The fundamentalist groups' interpretations of the place and role of women, the place and rights of minorities in Islamic societies, abuse of blasphemy laws, the nature of punishments applied for wrong doers, etc., are some examples of issues on which Christians have reservations. From the side of Islam, there is persistent criticism of Christians and Christianity for building societies that are increasingly secularized, where religious beliefs and convictions play little role in shaping individual and social values and norms. This, Muslims claim, is the result of moving away from life that is centered on God's will and revelation.

My purpose is not to say that one approach to the scripture is better than the other, or to deny that extremists and fundamentalists are found within both religions, but to say that the approach to the scripture within these two religions is one that leads to mutual misunderstanding. There is, of course, internal diversity of approaches within both religions to their scriptures, but the place and role of scripture is certainly one of the issues that stand out.

The second example would be on the relationship between religion and state. Islam sees family, social, economic, political, and cultural life in a continuum, and draws its primary inspiration for them from the teachings of the Qur'an. This, in general, can mean that religion and state cannot be separated, although a survey of Islam-majority countries would show that this belief is applied in different ways in concrete cases. Religion and state relationships are not the same in Saudi Arabia, Jordan, Morocco, and Indonesia. However, Christians have been made to believe, wrongly, that Islam believes only in theocracy. We should note that Christians have also had state-sponsored churches for a good part of their history and the separation of church and state is a comparatively new phenomenon. But misunderstandings over religion and state continue to persist.

The third relates to a number of cultural issues, like status of women in family and society, where Christians and Muslims approach the questions from different perspectives. On such questions there is internal diversity within both religions. Some place the rights of individuals over the rights of the community. Others place religious rights and human rights in competition to one another. Still others hold different positions on the rights of majorities and minorities within a nation. In brief, there are considerable cultural differences between Christians and Muslims that play out in different ways.

We began with the question, "What is it between Christians and Muslims?" The discussion above is a general survey of matters that play some role in shaping the Christian-Muslim relations. It is important, however, to also note some of the contemporary developments that have begun to adversely affect this relationship.

THE IMPACT OF TERRORISM

The communications revolution and the many forms of globalization of human life have had considerable impact in the internal life of all nations, including nations where Muslims are a majority. One of the consequences of this development is that masses in a number of Islamic countries, especially in the Middle East and North Africa, have begun to challenge the dictatorial regimes that have kept them in poverty and depravation for much of their history. Even when democracy is said to be the governing ideal in some of these Muslim-majority nations, people increasingly realize that the election process is often rigged to support those already in power. This political awakening and wide-spread unemployment among the youth has eventually resulted in organized mass-revolts in a number of Islamic countries.

It is not my intention here to explore this question in detail, because one needs deeper study and analysis of the multi-faceted forces at work and the degrees to which they have succeeded or failed in changing the political realities in these countries. However, three dimensions of the contemporary situation are relevant to our discussion.

First, the upheavals against the prevalent regimes have taken two forms. One is 'popular uprising' that is essentially non-violent, calling for the establishment of genuinely democratic forms of government. The other is resorting to militancy and terrorism, often accompanied by the abuse of the Qur'an and Islamic teachings. The indiscriminate violent acts are intended to register the protest, and where possible, to make the nation ungovernable as a way to bring about the desired change.

The second is the reality that these struggles have re-energized the divide of the Islamic community into Sunnis and Shiites, which began with the controversy on who should be the legitimate successor of the prophet when he passed away. To briefly state a complex history, the prophet passed away without designating a successor, and he did not have a son who might have become his immediate successor. The leadership fell on his closest associate, Abu Bakr. But soon others insisted that it is the prophet's son-in-law, Ali, that should be his successor. The succession struggle, accompanied by different theological emphases, led to enmity between the two groups. The latent animosities have received new prominence in our day, pitching Muslims against Muslims.

The third, more relevant to our discussion, is that many that are revolting against dictatorial regimes, especially the militant and terrorist groups, accuse the Western 'Christian' powers, first for having colonized their lands, and then for supporting and protecting the oppressive leaders in the Middle East and North Africa for their own economic interests. They also see the global media culture, also identified as 'Christian', as an organized attempt to undermine the Islamic culture and way of life. On this basis, they see targeting Western Christian groups and institutions as part of their protest. Further, Western powers, especially the United States, got embroiled in the internal struggle within Islam, partly for their own economic interests, partly to preserve their military and economic alliances in the Middle East, and in the hope of shaping the political future of the Middle East to serve their best interests.

The groups that direct terrorist attacks against the Western and Christian people and institutions are at the margins of the Islamic world. But they are experienced, also because of the nature of the coverage given by the media, by many Christians as the contemporary face of Islam as a whole. This is accentuated by the latent fears fed by the historical rivalries between Christianity and Islam and the prevalent ignorance about Islam as a religious tradition in most Christian communities.

Much more needs to be said, but the forgoing discussion shows that there are many issues to be resolved and bridges to be built in order to foster a positive and creative relationship between Christians and Muslims.

THE OTHER SIDE OF THE RELATIONSHIP

Fortunately, this is not the whole story. In what follows I would like to point to significant advances that have been made in attempts to overcome some of the hurdles that stand in the way of Christian-Muslim relations. This discussion, however, should begin with the recognition that there had been a number of periods in history where Islam and Christianity have co-existed and had been in a dialogical relationship, and that today, in many countries, including those in the Middle East, there is an ongoing dialogue of life, where groups of Christian and Muslims live in peace and harmony.

Equally important, however, are specialized attempts that have been initiated and are in progress that seek to move beyond the traditional animosities and help Christians and Muslims to foster good relationships that would defy the extremists' attempts from both sides to pitch one community against the other. This was facilitated by some of the rethinking that began to take place in the 1950s, both within the Roman Catholic and Protestant churches, on their attitude and approach to other religions, including Islam. The most significant result of the new mood within the Roman Catholic Church was the creation of the 'Vatican Secretariat for Non-Christians' by Pope Paul VI (May 1964), renamed in June 1988 by Pope John Paul II as the 'Pontifical Council for Interreligious Dialogue' (PCID). A special commission, 'Pontifical Commission for Religious Relations with Muslims', which is affiliated with the PCID, pointed to the special emphasis the Roman Catholic Church was giving to relations with the Muslims. One of the significant documents promulgated at the Second Vatican Council on interreligious relations, *Nostra Aetate,* had this to say about the Muslims in its third paragraph:

> The Church regards with esteem also the Moslems. They adore the one God, living and subsisting in Himself; merciful and all-powerful, the Creator of heaven and earth, (5) who has spoken to men; they take pains to submit wholeheartedly to even His inscrutable decrees, just as Abraham, with whom the faith of Islam takes pleasure in linking itself, submitted to God. Though they do not acknowledge Jesus as God, they revere Him as a prophet. They also honor Mary, His virgin Mother; at

times they even call on her with devotion. In addition, they await the Day of Judgment when God will render their deserts to all those who have been raised up from the dead. Finally, they value the moral life and worship God especially through prayer, almsgiving and fasting.

Since in the course of centuries not a few quarrels and hostilities have arisen between Christians and Moslems, this sacred synod urges all to forget the past and to work sincerely for mutual understanding and to preserve as well as to promote together for the benefit of all mankind social justice and moral welfare, as well as peace and freedom.[1]

This friendly statement on Islam was an important step forward in view of the long history of rivalry between the two religions. In my own estimate, although a big step forward, it was inadequate because, on purpose, it makes no reference to Prophet Muhammad and to the Qur'an, the two subjects at the heart of Islam, on which Christians have had problems with Islam. However this limitation has been rectified by the other statements and actions by Pope Paul VI, Pope John Paul II, and the statements from the PCID which have built significant bridges of relationships.

The World Council of Churches, which is a fellowship of most of the mainline Protestant Churches and Orthodox Churches around the world, has also been exploring, especially from the 1950s, new ways of relating to people of other religious traditions. Its deliberations led to the creation of the Sub-Unit on Dialogue with People of Living Faith and Ideologies in 1971, with a specialized position to foster Muslim-Christian relations. Like the Vatican, WCC's Dialogue program also produced documents such as 'Guidelines for Dialogue', 'Ecumenical Considerations on Muslim Christian Relations', etc. to promote a new approach to Christian-Muslim relations.

There have been numerous dialogue events between Christians and Muslims at the local, regional, and international levels. Dialogue centers, study centers, and research centers for the study of Islam and to promote Muslim-Christian relations have emerged in different parts of the world. Several academic institutions and universities specialize in Muslim-Christian relations. For instance, the Macdonald Center for the Study of Islam and Christian-Muslim Relations at the Hartford Seminary in Connecticut. This center is the country's oldest for such study, opened in 1973. It organizes programs to challenge scholars, students, the media and the general public to overcome

1. http://www.vatican.va/archive/hist_councils/ii_vatican_council/documents/vat-ii_decl_19651028_nostra-aetate_en.html.

stereotypes and to have an informed understanding of Islam and its teachings. Out of the center comes one of the much respected academic journals on the study of Islam, *The Muslim World.*

Muslims have also been engaged in promoting dialogues with the help of Islamic international organizations like World Muslim Congress. There is full participation of both Christians and Muslims in international interfaith organizations like Religions for Peace, Parliament of World's Religions, etc. Today there are enormous amount of material on Christian-Muslim relations, all pointing to an emerging new future to this relationship.

THE IMPACT OF THE CONCEPT OF DIALOGUE

Some of the foundational concepts of dialogue have been instrumental in enabling this new relationship. Dialogue does not require one to compromise or hide one's convictions; neither does it require one to accept the convictions of others. What is required is respect for one another's convictions. Further, dialogue insists that what is 'different' does not mean that it is 'wrong', and that the encounter of different perspectives may help in mutual enrichment and correction. It goes further to hold out the possibility that people who hold different convictions can indeed join together toward building a world of justice and peace for all.

Much more has been said on the concept and practice of dialogue, but what I have noted above are some ground rules of dialogue that met the initial suspicions and uncertainties that surrounded the concept of dialogue. The clarification of what dialogue is and what it is not served the purpose of moving forward the Muslim-Christian relations despite continuing groups within both traditions that look upon each other with mutual suspicion. There is every reason to hope, even in the midst of the current problems, that there awaits a new positive future for Christian-Muslim relations. This future, however, would not happen by itself but has to be created by both communities.

11.

Buddhist–Christian Dialogue: In Search of Common Grounds

It is difficult to have an overall view of Buddhist–Christian dialogue for a number of reasons. Most important among them is the enormous diversity of Buddhist traditions that are generally brought under the umbrella term, Buddhism. It is true that all religions have internal diversity, but the diversity within Buddhism is something peculiar to Buddhism because of the way it assimilated, or was assimilated into the local cultures as it spread through Asia.

Many would be aware of the three main branches of Buddhism, namely, Theravada, Mahayana and Vajrayana. But when one talks about Buddhism today, one is most likely to speak of Sri Lankan Buddhism, Tibetan Buddhism, Chinese Buddhism, Japanese Buddhism, Vietnamese Buddhism and so on. This is because the national expressions of Buddhism have emerged as the primary markers of its diversity than the three main branches of Buddhism. The enculturation of Buddhism into the local cultures was so deep that it would be difficult for an outsider to recognize anything in common between, for instance, Sri Lankan and Tibetan Buddhisms, except that they both relate to the figure of the Lord Buddha. But even the representations of the figure of the Buddha in Tibetan art and Sri Lankan sculptures are distinctly different from each other.

In the United States, for instance, almost all the national expressions of Buddhism are present, in addition to the other contemporary

Buddhist sects and lay Buddhist movements that have grown mostly in Japan and Korea. The question who within other religious traditions should be the dialogue partners with Christians has always been a problem. It becomes more pronounced in Buddhist-Christian dialogues.

The second major difficulty has to do with the different dimensions of Buddhism with which Christians interact, with or without any expressed intention of entering into dialogue as it is commonly understood. The most common expression of this mode of relationship has to do with Christians adopting Buddhist meditation practices, with little regard to the philosophical beliefs that lie behind them. From the time D. T. Suzuki, the celebrated Zen master in Japan, moved to the United States in 1897, Zen meditation practices have attracted Christians. Since then, other forms of Buddhist meditation like *Samatha* (tranquility) and *Vipasana* (insight) meditations have also become common among Christians, not only in the U.S. but also in much of the Western hemisphere.

What I hope to do in this chapter is to point out two rather different manifestations of Buddhist-Christian encounters that would fit more readily the rubric of dialogue, one from the Mahayana and the other from the Theravada traditions. These Buddhist-Christian dialogues happen at the philosophic, academic and theological levels.

THE PHILOSOPHIC–ACADEMIC DIALOGUE

The academic-philosophic interest in Buddhist-Christian encounter has a long history. Within this long history is the notable work of the Kyoto School, founded by Nishida Kitaro (1870–1945). His first book, *An Inquiry into the Good*, published in 1911, is often considered the most significant beginning of modern thinking within Buddhism under the influence of Western philosophy and Christianity.

Another significant player in Buddhist-Christian dialogue is the National Christian Conference Center for the Study of Buddhism and Dialogue, founded in 1959 and led by successive Christian professors from the universities of Japan. I had the opportunity to visit the Center during the leadership of Professor Musatoshi Doi, and Prof. Yuki Hideo, who followed him, to learn of the extensive contacts they had with Buddhist scholars in Kyoto. Of similar importance is the work of the Nanzan Institute for Religion and Culture in Nagoya.

In the United States the Society for Buddhist-Christian Studies, founded in 1987, and the regular East-West Religions in Encounter conferences, nurtured by David Chappel and based in the Department of Religion of the University of Hawaii, have made significant contribution to Buddhist-Christian dialogue at the academic level. Now, there are many centers for Buddhist-Christian studies in number of universities in the U.S. and other parts of the world.

My intention here is not to be exhaustive about the many activities that have been going on at this level but to give an indication of what is happening at the academic-philosophic level. A good example of this would be the encounters between the Japanese Zen scholar, Masao Abe, and the U.S. process theologian, John B. Cobb, on the interpretation of *sunyata* (emptiness) under the umbrella of the East-West Religions in Encounter project of the Department of Religion of the University of Hawaii.[1]

Another significant example would be the Christian-Buddhist encounter on the meaning of *dukka* (suffering), again held under the wings of the East-West Religions Project. In the first part of this encounter, Ryusei Takeda (Ryukoku University of Kyoto) and Gishin Tokiwa (Hanazono College, Kyoto) from the side of the Buddhists, and John Hick (University of Birmingham) and Langdon Gilkey (University of Chicago) from the Christian side, attempted to interpret the concept *dukka* (suffering) in ways the other side could understand.

They were then joined by a group of scholars, including Masso Abe, John Cobb, Rita Gross, Gordon Kaufman, David Chappell, David Kalpahana, Hans Kung, and a few others to explore how Christian and Buddhist understandings and approaches to suffering can enrich and inform each other's religious tradition.

A scholarly journal, *Buddhist-Christian Studies* by the University of Hawaii Press, carried the details of these encounters and is a good source, among others, to know what is happening in Buddhist-Christian dialogue at the academic level.

---

1. Muse, jhu.edu/article/176742/pdf.

BUDDHIST-CHRISTIAN MONASTIC DIALOGUE

Also of interest in looking at the variety of Buddhist–Christian relations is the Inter-Monastic Dialogue, in which Zen monasteries in Japan and Benedictine monasteries in Europe have regular exchanges to learn from the spirituality and spiritual practices of each other's tradition. This is replicated locally in some other parts of the world, as for example in Berkley, California, where Benedictine and Cistercian monks and nuns engage in Monastic Interreligious Dialogue to facilitate encounters of those in contemplative practice in their respective religions.

BUDDHIST-CHRISTIAN DIALOGUE WITHIN THE THERAVADA TRADITION

Having had a general overview of some developments in the Mahayana tradition, I now will move to the consideration of the dialogue within the Theravada tradition by taking the example of Sri Lanka, recognized worldwide as the most significant representative nation of the Theravada tradition. What I wish to do here is not to give a general overview but take two examples of persons who have made significant contribution to the rethinking of Buddhist–Christian relations at the local and national levels. What is significant in their contribution is that they have attempted to interpret both Christianity and Buddhism in the light of their encounter with each other.

THE BACKGROUND

The biggest theological challenge to Christian theology when Christianity was brought to Sri Lanka was to make sense of the gospel in the context of Buddhism. From 1505 the country had been under successive colonial rulers—Portuguese (from 1505), Dutch (from 1658), and British (from 1796)—until the island gained independence in 1948. Although over 70 percent of Sri Lankans are Buddhist, Buddhism had a difficult time during the colonial period because most of the missionaries would not even recognize Buddhism as a religious tradition; it was too difficult for them to even contemplate the possibility of a spiritual tradition that paid no attention to what

Christians called 'God'. It was further exacerbated by Buddhist doctrine of *annata,* which held that there is nothing abiding in human beings that can be called a 'soul'. With the advent of the successive colonial rulers, the significant place Buddhism had played in the social, cultural, and spiritual life of the nation was undermined. Grievances from this period of history simmer to this day.

This reality resulted in a number of confrontations and public disputes between the two religious traditions. One of the fascinating accounts of such confrontations is found in the record of the Pantura Vada (Panadura debate) between the Buddhists and Protestant Christians. In this public debate, the Buddhist side was represented by Ven. Migettuwatte Gunananda Thero (supported by about 200 priests), and the Protestant side was led by the Methodist minister, Rev. David Silva, (supported by priests, catechists, and others from many Protestant denominations).

Gunananda Thero had good knowledge of the Bible, and Rev. David Silva was considered a scholar of Buddhism. Each was to make presentations that would be refuted by the other, and the debate, held on a specially constructed, massive stage, was to last for two days. The Buddhist and Christian audiences were separated by a centre isle; mounted police on horseback were in position for 'crowd control' for the fear that the emotions created by the debate might spill over into an all out fist fight among the respective supporters.

It would be good to recall some of the details related to the debate (in the interest of those who are not aware of it):

- About five to six thousand people gathered to listen to the debate on the 26th and 27th August 1873.

- The emphasis was to prove which religion was right by pointing out the defects of the other religion.

- The Christians attacked the Buddhist doctrine of no-soul, its indifference to God.

- The Buddhists accused the Christians of deception in mission, and worshipping a warrior God.

At the end, both parties claimed victory.[2]

2. Cf. Abhayasunrara, *Controversy at Panadura or Pandura Vadaya* (Colombo: State Printing Corporation, 1990).

I have recalled this event to indicate the depth of alienation, misunderstanding, and enmity that had characterized one of the aspects of Christian-Buddhist relations in Sri Lanka during the colonial period. The debate in Panadura is only one of many debates, and similar controversy also happened between Hindus and Christians in the northern part of Sri Lanka, which had a concentration of Hindus.

Therefore, in the post-colonial context the church was challenged to rethink its relationship to other religious traditions, especially Buddhism, and to find ways of building bridges of mutual respect and understanding. Unfortunately the churches took little interest in the Buddhist insights on life, its predicament, and its goals.

It is in this context that I wish to highlight the contributions made by Sri Lankan theologians like Aloysius Pieris, Lynn A. de Silva, Anthony Fernando, and others who have earned the respect and admiration of Buddhist and Christian scholars in many parts of the world.

I would, in the interest of brevity, deal here only with two of the scholars—Lynn A. de Silva, and Aloysius Pieris. They are of special interest because the two of them take two different approaches that enrich the pool of theological resources for Buddhist-Christian dialogue that emanate from the island.

LYNN A. DE SILVA

Lynn de Silva, a Methodist minister, developed his dialogical theology on three basic principles[3]:

1. If Christianity has a universal message it must make sense within the Buddhist categories of thought.

2. Some of the basic Christian teachings are indeed close to the teachings of Buddhism, but they will have to be re-stated.

3. Both Buddhism and Christianity need to learn from each other and can benefit from each other's teachings.

At the Panadura debate, Rev. David Silva took Buddhism to task on its fundamental teachings of *anicca* (impermanence and

---

3. The discussion of Lynn de Silva's thought and theology, and brief quotes are all taken from his volume, *The Problem of Self in Buddhism and Christianity* (New York: Barnes and Noble, 1979).

change), *anatta* (no-soul), and *dhukka* (the existential angst or suffering). In this view, argued David Silva, existence is in a constant state of flux; there is nothing permanent in it but an enduring process of change. Therefore there is also nothing enduring or permanent in human beings (*anatta*). This results in meaninglessness hollowness of existence, which is suffering (*dhukka*). Therefore the search is to go beyond existence to the state of bliss (*nirvana*). This, in David Silva's view, was an extreme form of pessimism about human life and its destiny.

Interestingly, Lynn de Silva saw these teachings to be quite close to the Biblical approach to life:

> "O Lord, what are humans that you regard them, or mortals that you think of them? They are like a breath; their days are like passing shadows." (Ps 144:3–4)

> "The days of our life are seventy years, or perhaps eighty if we are strong. Even then their span is only toil and trouble; they are soon gone, and we fly away." (Psalm 90)

> "The whole creation is subjected to decay; groaning as it were in childbirth." (Romans 8)

> "By the sweat of your face you shall eat bread until you return to the ground, for out of it you were taken. You are dust and to dust you shall return." (Gen 3:19)

Based on these and other themes in the Bible, Lynn de Silva argued that the "polarity of the conflict between being and the possibility of non-being that lies at the core of human existence, the mood of anxiety, finitude, the precariousness of human life, is a familiar theme that runs through the Bible." And he saw Soren Kierkegaard and Paul Tillich capturing the sense of the Buddhist understanding of *dukka*: The existential anxiety (angst) that "I too must die;" the anxiety that comes from "the state in which a being is aware of its possible non-being."

In other words, Lynn de Silva argued that the existential understanding of life as *dukka* is not alien to the Bible. Building on this, he went further to show that Jews did not believe in the immortality of the soul or even of a soul in human beings. The idea of the immortality of the soul came into Judaism with their exile in Persia. Human being in the Hebrew tradition, argued de Silva, is a psycho-somatic unity. Modern science and psychology also denies that there is something called the 'soul' that gives identity to humans.

Having challenged the Christian presuppositions, Lynn de Siva called upon the Buddhists to also look more closely at some of their own understanding of the human predicament. If there is no soul (with which he agreed) what is the purpose of *karma samsara* (cycles of rebirth)? The Buddhist answer, 'the person who is born is neither the same nor is he another' does not satisfy de Silva. He tended to agree with some scholars who held that the doctrine of *anatta* (no-soul) is not consistent with the belief in rebirth. On this basis, some scholars hold that the concept of *karma samsara*, or cycle of births, must have been a later addition to Buddhist teachings. In de Silva's view, the *anatta* doctrine also presented problems in relation to the ultimate goal, *nirvana*. If in reality there is no self, who is it that attains *nirvana*, especially when it is argued that *nirvana* is not nihilism?

Therefore, while agreeing with the Buddhist doctrine of no-self, de Silva thinks that the Christian notion of 'spirit' (*pneuma*) may provide some answers. Spirit in Christian understanding is both God, who is Spirit, and human beings, who were enlivened by the Sprit. "Human being is spirit only in relation to God who is Spirit." God is eternal (*amata*) and humans share this deathless quality only in relationship with God. Thus the human spirit is the authentic 'self'. Humans find this participation in the unconditioned, the bliss, the nirvana, only in so far as they are able to overcome the false notion of the self. It is in self-denial that the human spirit relates to the Eternal Spirit.[4]

Therefore Lynn de Silva developed the concept of '*anatta-pneuma*'. Christians need to have a firm grasp of the concept of *anatta* (no-soul), and Buddhists need to develop something along the lines of *pneuma* to give more content to the concepts of *karma samsara* and *nirvana*.

It is not my intention here to fully expound or evaluate Lynn's dialogical theology. The primary emphasis in his approach is the mutual interpenetration of Buddhism and Christianity to correct and enrich each other. His disciplined study of Buddhism, his humility and openness, and the genuinely truth-seeking dialogue events he

---

4. These discussions are taken from Lynn A. deSilva, *The Problem of Self in Buddhism and Christianity* (New York: Barnes and Noble, 1979).

held at the Ecumenical Institute for Study and Dialogue won him many Buddhist friends in Sri Lanka and abroad.

ALOYSIUS PIERIS

As a theologian, scholar of Buddhism, and the director of Tulana Research Institute in Kelaniya, near Colombo, Aloysius Pieris is among the best known and most admired Asian theologians today.[5] His contribution to Christian theology in the context of Buddhism and the Asian social realities is considered a comprehensive and original approach to doing theology in the Asian context.

Pieris challenges the traditional Christian uneasiness with Buddhism because of its approach to the human predicament without such theological symbols as 'God', 'sin', 'salvation', etc. He points out five areas where Christians must rethink their approach in order for Christianity to relate to Buddhism.

The first is on the relationship between 'cosmic' and 'metacosmic' approaches to reality. In traditional religions the worldview is 'cosmic', where nature, human life, and the divine are seen in a continuum. But the Western apprehension of reality is 'metacosmic', where transcendence is imposed between the Divine on the one hand, and nature and human beings on the other. This metacosmic view has been fully synthesized into Western thought and Christian theology. This reality must be born in mind in our approach to the relationship between Eastern and Western religious/philosophic traditions.

The second relates to the primacy of language in Asia, especially in the form of stories, myths, legends, poems, etc. Religion arises out of experience and experience can be expressed in multiple forms. Language is not simply a tool of communication; it is also the medium of religious experience.

Third, we should recognize the interdependence and mutual support of philosophy and religion in the Asian religious experience. In the West, philosophy is an attempt to give a coherent rational explanation of reality; religion has to do with faith. Asians do not make this distinction. In Asia, "Philosophy is the religious vision; religion is the philosophy of life."[6]

---

5. Aloysius Pieris's thoughts and brief quotes are from his volumes, *An Asian Theology of Liberation* (Maryknoll, NY: Orbis, 1988), and *Love Meets Wisdom* (Maryknoll, NY: Orbis, 1988).
6. Pieris, *An Asian Theology of Liberation,* 25.

Fourth, in addressing theological concerns, we must take seriously the *soteriological nucleus* and the *liberative core* of Asian religions. Traditionally we have only dealt with the fringes of Asian religions.

Fifth, the Asian religious traditions should be understood in the light of two fundamental pervasive realities of Asia: the *crushing poverty*, and *profound spirituality*.

In looking at Buddhism, therefore, Christians must look at the doctrinal side (*darsana*) as well as the institutional-experiential-practice side (*pratipada*). It is both a teaching and a way of life.

On the basis of this analysis, Pieris holds that the East and the West, the Semitic and the Asian traditions, are not just two geographical realities, but two spiritual realms and two distinct ways of relating to reality. Buddhists emphasize 'liberative knowledge' (*gnosis*); Christians place their trust in 'redemptive love' (*agape*). Christians have gradually lost their familiarity with the Gnostic idiom; more importantly, they have inherited an anti-gnostic idiom.

Therefore Christianity, in Pieris's view, has rejected Buddhism as a world-denying asceticism whereas it is only a world-relativizing affirmation of the absolute. In reality, both are salvific: Self-transcending events that transform persons affected by it. The Bo tree under which the Buddha was enlightened is the Tree of Knowledge; the tree on which Jesus hangs is the Tree of Love. The first tree bears the fruit of wisdom, and the second bears the cost of love.[7]

At the heart of Pieris's thesis is the conviction that these two approaches are not contradictory but complementary to each other. They are, in fact, incomplete each in itself, and are, therefore, complementary and mutually corrective. He goes even further to insist that these two idioms are also psychological realities. They are instincts that arise dialectically from within the deepest zone of each individual irrespective of religious affiliation. Our religious encounter with God and humankind would be incomplete without this interaction.

To quote from his book *Love Meets Wisdom*:

A genuine Christian experience of God-in-Christ grows by maintaining a dialectical tension between the two poles:
between action and non-action,
between word and silence,

7. Pieris, *Love Meets Wisom*, 114–19.

between control of nature and harmony with nature,
between self-affirmation and self-negation,
between engagement and withdrawal,
between love and knowledge,
between karuna and prajna,
between agape and gnosis.[8]

But Pieris says that both traditions already have the two elements. In Christianity the importance of knowledge is emphasized, especially in John and Paul, but knowing is interpreted in terms of love. The Father 'knows' the Son and the Son 'knows' the disciples (John 17). Loving one's neighbor is the way to 'know' God (1 John 4:7–?). However, both in the early church and in the Middle Ages distinction was made between 'intellectual knowledge' and 'saving knowledge'.

In Buddhist teaching, liberative knowledge consists of removing three roots of evil: *raga*, *dosa*, and *moha*. *Raga* is the erotic, sensual, self-acquisitive 'love' that is the root of evil and is against agape; *dosa* represents hatred and ill-will, which is again a denial of agape. And *moha* is delusion, slowness of mind and ignorance. Thus *raga* and *dosa* are absence of what Christians call agapeic love; *moha* is the absence of gnosis, or liberative knowledge. On the basis of the in-depth analyses of the ultimate concerns of the respective emphases, Pieris concludes: Christians have an '*agapeic gnosis*' and Buddhist have a '*gnostic agape.*'

Pieris also points out that Buddhism speaks of *nirvana* as the non-existence of the three evils. In the Gnostic language these are evoked in the negative:

- *Arogya* – non-sickness

- *Araga* – absence of selfish love

- *Adosa* – absence of hatred

- *Amoha* – absence of ignorance

Positively, they would be non-selfish love, forgiving love, and liberative knowledge. Thus, even though *nirvana* cannot be 'conceived', it can be said to be 'love experienced within perfect knowledge.'

8. Ibid., 27.

Therefore Buddhism, in his view, does hold gnosis and agape together: salvific knowledge leads to compassionate love toward society for its redemption. Thus agape and gnosis are not alternatives but two poles that must find expression in every life and in religion.

Pieris also finds the need for an important dialogue between Christians and Buddhists on the question of the crushing poverty of Asia. Jesus was against only one religion: the religion of Mammon—the lure of wealth and power that leads to destruction of persons and societies. "You cannot serve two masters; you will hate the one and cling on to the other." (Matt 6:24)

However, the Christian civilization is under the grip of capitalism and the results are the prevalent secularism, consumerism, materialism, and the pollution of the earth. We may have been freed from the cosmic worldview, but have been enslaved by Mammon. Pieris says that Karl Barth, Karl Marx, and the Latin American Liberation Theologies have all not taken seriously the need for a spirituality that resists Mammon, which is the only antidote to the culture of Mammon.

But how does one reconcile the struggle against the lure of power and wealth and the need to fight the crushing poverty of the Asian masses? Here Pieris takes the Buddhist ideal of the monk to make a distinction between 'voluntary poverty' and 'enforced poverty', arguing that while we should struggle against enforced poverty, it should be accompanied by a spirituality that rejects greed and the lure of wealth. Christians and Buddhists should stand together to promote liberative knowledge and compassionate love in the face of the forces of wealth and power that enslave and crush human lives.

What is clear from the overall discussion is the variety of ways in which Christian-Buddhist encounters go on in different parts of the world. It ranges from the simple act of sitting in a Vipasana meditation session to the in-depth probing of two religions that at first sight appear to have little in common, but have much to contribute to each other's growth and enrichment.

12.

Hindu–Christian Dialogue: "Apples and Oranges"

Of the many relationships Christians have with other religious traditions the most elusive and indefinable relationship is that with the Hindus. There have, of course, been dialogue encounters between Christians and Hindus in the past. As Program Secretary for Hindu–Christian relations of the dialogue program of the WCC, I had, for instance, organized a Hindu–Christian dialogue for about thirty persons at a study center in Rajpur, India, in 1981. This encounter, on the theme, 'Religious Resources for a Just Society', proved to be a fruitful one, and the summary of the findings were published as a booklet in the same year.[1] However, unlike the other dialogues, organized Hindu–Christian encounters in India are sporadic, and when they happen, they take many forms depending on the interests of the individuals who initiate them.

From the middle of the twentieth century, however, there was growing interest in this relationship in Europe and North America, especially within sections of the academic community within religious studies. A significant development in the United States was the creation of a 'Society for Hindu–Christian Studies' and the periodic publication, *Journal of Hindu–Christian Studies*, which carries regular articles on the interaction between Christians and Hindus, mostly

1. *Religious Resources for a Just Society – A Hindu–Christian Dialogue* (Geneva: WCC Publications, 1981).

at the academic level. Many involved in this area of dialogue would look upon Prof. Harold Coward, professor of religious studies and the Director of the Humanities Institute at the University of Calgary, in Alberta, Canada, as someone who had tirelessly worked on promoting, monitoring, and reporting on Hindu-Christian studies and dialogue.

My intention in this presentation is not to give a history of Hindu-Christian relations, or of the many missionaries and groups that have attempted to enter into deep dialogue with Hinduism by encountering its spirituality and adopting many of the Hindu customs and spiritual practices, which is in itself a long and interesting story.[2] Rather what I hope to do is to examine the reasons why the Hindu-Christian relationships and dialogue have not been a robust one, and go on to explore some of the ways in which it can move forward in the future. Let me begin with an account of a Hindu-Christian encounter that would help us enter this discussion.

INVITATION TO DIALOGUE REFUSED

One of the earliest multi-faith encounters facilitated by the WCC took place in Ajaltoun, Lebanon, in March 1970. It was designed by Dr. Stanley Samartha, who was on the staff of the WCC, as a conversation between a group of Hindus, Buddhists, Muslims, and Christians on the meaning and practice of interfaith dialogue and the prospects it held out for the future. The Ajaltoun Memorandum, which came out of this meeting, was an important document that helped in the creation of the WCC sub-unit on dialogue in 1971, with Dr. Stanley Samartha as its first director.

I recall this meeting here because the publication that came out of the Ajaltoun meeting carries part of a fascinating exchange between one of its Christian participants, Fr. Murray Rogers, an Anglican priest who had a center for dialogue and spirituality in India (Jyoti Niketan), and Sivendra Prakash, a Hindu scholar, whom Murray Rogers looked upon as his dialogue partner. Rogers, along with some of his friends, had attempted to organize two dialogue events in Banaras with twelve Hindus and twelve Christians as part of his

---

2. Those interested in the detailed history of Hindu-Christian relations, especially in the context of the ecumenical movement, can find it in my book, *Hindus and Christians: A Century of Protestant Ecumenical Thought* (Grand Rapids, MI: Eerdmans, 1991).

preparation for the Ajaltoun meeting. However, both meetings had to be cancelled at the last moment because only one or two Hindus responded positively to the invitation.

Rogers had raised the issue of the lack of interest in dialogue on the part of the Hindus with his friend, Sivendra Prakash. Rogers's contribution at Ajaltoun carries parts of a letter Sivendra Prakash wrote him telling him why the Hindus did not turn up. Here are some extracts:

Dear Murray bhai,

You have told me last week how sorry you were that the Hindu-Christian meeting your friends had so carefully planned did not materialize. You even almost reproached me—very amicably of course—not to have worked myself in the scheme with the eagerness you have all shown. I think I owe you a few words of explanation.

Of course it would have been delightful for me also to meet such old and new friends in those wonderful surroundings and to share some at least of our best experiences in our common endeavour towards the divine goal. Yet to be quite frank with you, there is something that makes me uneasy in the way in which you Christians are trying so eagerly now to enter with us into official and formal dialogue.

Have you already forgotten that what you call the "inter-faith dialogue" is quite a new feature in your understanding and practice of Christianity? Until a few years ago—and often today still—your relations with us were confined either to the merely social plane or to preaching in order to convert us to your *dharma*– except of course for a very few like you, bhai-ji, and you know better than me that those very few were not seen with great favour by the majority of their colleagues!

For all matters concerning *dharma* you were deadly against us, violently or stealthily according to cases. It was plain to see from your preaching to old Christians or prospective converts, or from your at best condescending attitude towards us in your pamphlets and magazines. And the pity was that your attacks and derogatory remarks were founded in sheer ignorance of what we really are, or what we believe and worship.

Now you want to dialogue with us. You tell us very nicely that you have to learn from us. You begin to speak a great deal about our Scriptures, our traditions, the religious experiences of our mystics. . . . Is it not true that all Semitic religions, be they Judaism, Islam or Christianity, are founded on the notion of a chosen people which has received from God directly the mission to convert the whole world to their particular tenets? Do you not realize then that such an approach to religious sphere affects immediately all attempts at real dialogue? You should not be surprised therefore when not a few among us suspect your "stretched out hand" and your so sweet invitation to dialogue. . . .[3]

Sivenra Prakash continues to say that one of the real problems for the Hindus is the way Christians make exclusive claims for Christ, and that by doing so they have only minimized the real significance of Christ. He holds that only when Christians had found the 'inner light' that comes from true spiritual discipleship to Christ would the Hindus find in them real partners for dialogue—not so much on doctrinal and social issues but in the area of spirituality.

I have quoted a substantial part of Sivendra Prakash's letter because it illustrates a number of issues in Hindu-Christian relations. To begin with, it shows that only one or two Hindus were willing to turn up for two well-organized attempts to hold Hindu-Christian dialogue in Banaras. Sivenda Prakash gives a few reasons why this was the case. The first is the lack of trust in Christian intentions. Hindus had been led to believe that the only reason why Christians show interest in them is to convert them. Therefore they are not sure of the motives of a dialogue encounter.

Second, they see in Christians what Sivenrda Prakash calls a 'condescending attitude' arising from the belief that Christian religion and culture are superior to what Hinduism offered. It is in fact the case that often, Christian missions presented a very negative picture of Hindus as polytheists, idol-worshippers, and people who live by superstitions. Hindus are simply shocked by Christians' ignorance of Hinduism and their unwillingness to delve deeper into the Hindu religion to discover the spiritual riches and the long and truly fascinating story of their attempts to explore the mystery of the divine and the meaning of the human existence. Although there have been individual missionaries attracted to the Hindu scriptures and Hindu spiritual practices, average Christians and most missionaries believed that Hindus needed to move to the Christian faith for their own good.

The third issue is the disappointment they had with the way Christian faith was actually practiced by those who claimed to follow Christ and to have experienced the salvation/liberation he offered. While they saw in Jesus a teacher with teachings and a spirituality that deeply resonated with Hinduism, they found in the church a group that was exclusive, judgmental, and dogmatic, presenting a

---

3. S. J. Samartha, ed., *Dialogue between Men of Living Faiths*, Papers Presented at a Consultation held at Ajaltoun, Lebanon, March 1970 (Geneva: WCC Publications, 1971), 22–28.

Christ that had little to do with the historical Jesus. Hindus have never been able to figure out why Christianity moved so far from the teachings and the spirituality of Jesus. This is why Sivendra Prakash tells Rogers that Hindus will be ready for dialogue when Christians have found the 'inner light' that comes from true discipleship to Christ.

STAGES OF HINDU-CHRISTIAN ENCOUNTER

Broadly speaking, there had been at least four different types of Christianity that have encountered Hinduism in the Indian subcontinent. The attitude and approach to Hinduism of the early Syrian tradition, commonly associated with Apostle St. Thomas, are different from the Roman Catholic and Protestant traditions that encountered Hinduism during the Western Colonial era. Again, the post-colonial relationships of both the Roman Catholic and mainline Protestant churches with the Hindus differ from the contemporary free-church evangelical movements that still follow an aggressive missionary policy, which is responsible for some of the tensions we face in Hindu-Christian relationships today.

Even though these Christian groups have significant differences among them on many issues, including on their attitude to other religions, most Hindus do not readily recognize the internal diversity within Christian tradition. Much of the discussions on Hindu-Christian dialogue relate to the Roman Catholic and Protestant forms of Christianity, which is the most widespread expression of Christianity in India and has struck deep roots into Indian life in general through the many educational, health and other social institutions created during the colonial era.

The mostly positive story of the encounter of the Syrian tradition with Hinduism is quite fascinating but in the interest brevity here I would deal mainly with the issues pertaining to the relationships during the missionary era and the legacy it has left for Hindu-Christian relationships in our day.

CHRISTIAN BEWILDERMENT ABOUT HINDUISM

The missionaries who encountered Hinduism must have been totally bewildered by the reality before them. They knew what Judaism and Islam were, but what was Hinduism? The problem was Hinduism is not a religion like any other. In fact, Hinduism is not a religion at all, but a coalition of all the spiritual impulses, thinking, movements, and teachings that evolved in India from about 2500 BCE. It is a traditional religion in the sense that it has no known founder; it is an 'ethnic' religion in the sense that it is the religion identified with the Indian land mass; and yet within it, it accommodated numerous founded religions by teachers and gurus, like Ramakrishna Parama-hamsa, who began a movement that has become the Ramakrishna Mission with centers in many parts of the world.

Equally baffling were the number of gods, scriptures, practices, rituals and ceremonies related to gods and the cycle of human life—none of which appears to be monitored or directed by any vis-ible religious authority. Hinduism, as a religion, was different from everything that Christianity was. Even the name 'Hinduism' was dubbed on it by the Westerners in the eighteenth century simply to distinguish all that went on in the name of religion in India from Christianity and Islam. What surprised the missionaries was that Indi-ans themselves were not troubled by this complexity and went on with their normal life in what appeared to be the practice of choosing what they wished in order to cater to their spiritual needs. It appears that while some religions acted as if one size should fit all, Hinduism appears to say, "pick the size that fits you."

Equally baffling for the missionaries is the apparent stability of the social structure of Hinduism, which was based on one of the worst forms of hierarchical social stratification, the caste system, which even kept out millions of people outside that stratification as 'outcastes' and 'untouchables,' and were considered ritually polluting. The stability based on such a rigid hierarchy went against everything that Chris-tianity stood for. Hinduism and Christianity were apples and oranges; it appeared that there was nothing common between them except the name religion. While there were many issues Christians might have wanted to talk about with the Hindus, they did not know *who* the dialogue partner was.

Christian-Hindu relations have, of course, moved forward since the missionary era and even further since the exchange between Sivendra Prakash and Murray Rogers in the 1970s. Over this period of time Christians and Hindus have begun to understand the different nature of their religious traditions and found ways to talk to each other and to collaborate on many issues. Although organized

Hindu-Christian dialogues (except in the academic area) are few and far between, it is not a sign that Hindus did not believe in dialogue or the many benefits that come from interreligious cooperation. In fact, Hindus are very actively involved in local, regional, and international interfaith organizations and readily participate in multi-lateral dialogues involving a number of religious traditions.

But we are still left with the question of the asymmetry between Christianity and Hinduism, and the need to reflect on issues one should attend to in order to move forward. Here are some of the areas that need attention:

ATTITUDE TOWARD PLURALITY

I have described Christianity and Hinduism as apples and oranges to highlight the asymmetry between them. I have also noted that this asymmetry is the result of Hinduism being predominantly a traditional religion, whereas Christianity is a founded religion with the self-understanding that it should take its message to the ends of the earth. The first area where this divergence in character shows up is in their respective attitude toward plurality. On the whole, Hinduism is based on the Vedic dictum, "Truth is one, but sages call it by many names." The word 'names' here means more than what the word suggests; it refers to systems of theological and philosophical thoughts about the Truth. Since Hinduism holds that the Truth or the Ultimate Reality is beyond all human comprehension, it allows for many ways to understand it and speak about it, and proposes many paths to reach it.

This attitude has led to the emergence of many theological streams and philosophical systems that co-exist as part of Hinduism, and Hindus on the whole see this as normal and acceptable. This does not mean that there have not been active debates and disagreements over ultimate questions or that persons belonging to one or other of the philosophical systems claiming that their system was closer to the truth. There are also classifications of the systems into orthodox and heterodox systems; at one period of history Buddhists and Jains were persecuted for their heterodoxy. However, there is no firm teaching authority within Hinduism to dictate what everyone should believe in. On the whole, the emphasis is not on unity (the one truth) but on harmony (holding plurality of thoughts in tension).

Christianity is just the opposite in this respect. "There is only one Lord, one faith, one baptism and one God and Father of as all . . . "[4] is a biblical, not creedal, statement. But it indicates the ethos of Christianity. This approach is manifested more obviously in the claim that Christ is the *only* savior of all humankind. Both Islam and Christianity, with their claim to be religions based on divine revelations, have had enormous difficulty in dealing with plurality. It took centuries for Christians to tolerate internal plurality in the form of denominations, but they are yet to be at home with the wider plurality of religions.

The Hindus have had a very difficult time trying to understand why Christians want all the people of the world to accept their way as the only way; they have had problems in digesting the idea that God, whom Christians themselves declare to be the creator and provider of all creation, would reveal Godself only in the history of Israel and in a man from Nazareth. Even if they accept Jesus as an incarnation of God, or that God was present in him, they find it difficult to see why this has to be the only place where God's saving relationship to humanity should be expressed.[5]

The Christian self-understanding that militates against plurality is one of the biggest disconnects between Christians and Hindus. Faced with the global phenomenon of religious pluralism and challenges presented by interfaith dialogue, a number of Christian theologians have begun to explore new and non-exclusive ways to speak about the significance of Christ for their faith. But this reality is yet to adequately inform the Christian approach to other religious traditions.

Hindus, for their part, need to recognize that all religions do not necessarily share their experience of being a religion within which limitless diversity is taken for granted, and that this tolerant approach is not a conscious choice but one necessitated by the process of how religious life emerged in India. Recognizing and understanding the different starting points of Christianity and Islam, and the specific values they stand for, would help the Hindus to be more ready for a dialogical encounter.

4. Eph 4:5–6.
5. Abraham Oommen and A. Pushparajan, *Issues in Hindu Christian Relations* (Nagpur: NCCI, 1996).

MISSION, CONVERSION, AND RELIGIOUS FREEDOM

The second area, related to the first, is on the understanding of what constitute mission and how it might be carried out. The concept of mission is not unfamiliar to Hinduism. Anyone who has had a spiritual awakening, or had found an answer to the mystery of existence, or the way of liberation earns the right to teach it to others and to have a following. Many religious movements have arisen within Hinduism. However, these movements are not experienced as a threat at the level of theological and philosophical differences they embrace. The opposition to Buddhism, Jainism, and Sikhism, at the time they emerged, had more to do with their challenge to the social structure (the caste system) than with their teachings as such. In Hindu thinking, all such new teachings, even when they are offered with the intention of gaining followers, must be given as parallel to the other teachings. In other words, they should not violate the concept of pluralism.

Most Christians, however, have an understanding of mission which, if taken to its logical end, is interested in displacing all other religious teachings and communities with its own. It claims that it had the only way to salvation. Further, accepting Christianity meant one had to abandon Hinduism and the cultural heritage that went with it. The fundamentalist Christians go further to denigrate Hinduism and speak of it as a superstition and of Hindus as polytheists and idol worshippers. The pressure on Christian missionaries and their agents in India to show the results of their missionary activities is so intense that some of them resort to unethical methods of conversion by exploiting the poverty of the masses.

There is no agreement among Christians today on what constitutes mission, how it must be done, and when it is accomplished. Even in India, the Orthodox, Protestant, Roman Catholic, and Evangelical Churches have different approaches to mission. Early Syrian Christianity, as mentioned above, took a dialogical stance to the point of being considered Christian in faith, Hindu in culture, and Oriental (Syrian) in worship. But after the colonization of India, and today with the influx of evangelical missions from Western countries, the Hindu–Christian relationship has reached a new low over the mission issue. Mission rhetoric like 'India for Christ by 2020' irritates the Hindus.

CHRISTIAN AND HINDU UNDERSTANDINGS
ON SOCIAL ISSUES

As a religion not 'founded' at any particular time with any particular teachings, Hindu social organization, as indicated above, had evolved over a long period of history, eventually resulting in a hierarchical social stratification that is based on castes, sub-castes, and thousands of *jatis*. In fact, for a majority of Hindus, their self-understanding and identity are almost exclusively based on the caste into which they were born.

The suppression, depravation, humiliation, and the economic and social injustices that were suffered by the Dalit, who were considered untouchables and kept outside the caste classification, induced them to convert to Christianity. The conversions were sometimes based on conviction but more often as a way to attempt to free themselves from the clutch of the rigid social structure.

Christians believe that all human beings are created in the image of God. It was reinforced by Jesus's affirmation of the dignity of every human being and of God's impartial love for all. In fact, both the Hebrew and Christian scriptures go further to speak of God's 'preferential option for the poor' with the unequivocal demand for justice in all the spheres of human relationships.

The Hindu social stratification, which must have originally been based on occupations, was distorted and abused by the priestly Brahmin caste that had the power. They introduced three elements that worsened the situation. First, the caste system was given religious legitimacy by writing it into the scriptures (*Rig Veda*) and by giving scriptural status to the Laws of Manu (*Manavadharmasastra*) that spell out in great detail the oppressive laws that govern inter-caste and extra-caste relationships. Second, by defining the caste of the person by birth, rather than by occupation, the Brahmin caste excluded any possible social mobility. And third, by introducing the concept of graded ritual purity and impurity within the caste system they, sought to prevent any meaningful inter-caste relationships that might change the system over a period of time.

The Christian-Hindu encounter with such deep divergence in their anthropology was bound to be explosive, and continues to be so to this day. The Christian understanding of what it means to be human and its challenge to the caste system worked out in three ways in the Indian context. The first and foremost was that the Dalit, who had been suppressed for centuries, recognized and embraced the liberative dimensions of the gospel message and the opportunity it gave to escape the iron-clad system that denied them any possibility of social and occupational mobility. To the Dalit, as it was to the marginalized in Jesus's time, the gospel was indeed 'Good News'. Despite the imperfections of the church and its mission, and its own limitations in overcoming the entrenched caste mentality and practice within its own life, there is no denying that the Christian missions and urbanization were the two most significant forces that began to make a dent on the centuries old caste system.

Second, the gospel message, and the Western liberal education that went with it, inspired a number of modern reform movements within Hinduism itself and the framing of laws against caste discrimination.

And third, there was new and more intensified opposition to Christian missions and to conversions which, although often disguised in other arguments, was actually resistance to the impact the Christian message was making on the caste system. Thus, even though some of the opposition to Christian missions is well justified and needed, there is also opposition from parts of Hinduism that attempt to protect the oppressive caste structure from the impact of the gospel message.

One of the advantages we have had in Hindu-Christian dialogue was to be able to raise this questions in the context of dialogue, which has, in a number of instances, enabled Hindu participants to re-examine their caste based self-understanding and to even begin to rethink and re-interpret their scriptures.[6]

In the meantime, the whole 'conversion debate' has fallen into the trap of the nationalist Hinduthva movement and has necessitated further debates on other related issues like religious freedom, human and religious rights of individuals and communities, the definition of who an Indian is, and ethical and unethical practices in mission. This needs no elaboration here, but is one of the most pressing issues today in defining Christian engagement with Hinduism.[7]

In this area, Hinduism needs to show greater humility in its meeting with Christianity. The Hindu caste structure, and especially the

6. *Religious Resources for a Just Society – A Hindu–Christian Dialogue* (Geneva: WCC, 1981).

7. The WCC Dialogue Program held a series of meeting with the participation of Hindus on the issues of Conversion, Religious Freedom and related issues which is in the process of publication.

way the Dalit community is treated, are described by some as India's apartheid. Many Hindus would readily acknowledge that it is a blot on the otherwise rich spiritual heritage of India. Christian teachings did bring into the Indian Sub-continent a more egalitarian approach to life in community and the importance of justice in all human dealings. It should recognize that the number of Hindu reform movements that arose within Hinduism and the steps taken to give children and women their rightful place in family and society were also influenced by the entry of Christianity into the Hindu ethos. There also was much that Hinduism could learn from Christianity. Dialogues are important because they have a way of calling all partners in dialogue to account, resulting in mutual enrichment, mutual correction and healthy self-criticism.

'BELIEF' AND 'SPIRITUALITY'

I have attempted to identify above only a few of what I consider to be important structural issues that play an important role in the Christian and Hindu self-understandings that one should take note of. It is of course possible to list a number of other issues, but I want to conclude with an issue that pertains to the inner life of Christians and Hindus as individual persons and how they understand their spiritual lives. At the heart of Christian anthropology lies the doctrine of sin. Ever since St. Augustine elaborated and solidified the doctrine of sin in ontological categories and posited the doctrine of original sin, the Christian tradition has had a very low view of human beings as fallen creatures in need of salvation from sin. This anthropology is at the heart of much of the rest of the Christian doctrines.

Even though Jesus himself insisted on discipleship, and on bearing fruits, over a period of time the church has taught us to believe in Jesus Christ and what God has done for us through his life, death, and resurrection. This belief was further expanded into creeds to which Christians have to give intellectual assent. Even though spiritual dimension of religious life such as prayer, worship, and the ritual of Eucharist are part of the Christian practice, any Protestant Christian would readily answer that his or her Christian identity is that of a person who had been redeemed from his or her sins by what Jesus did on the cross. The starting point of Christian self-understanding is that of a sinner in need of redemption.

Swami Vivekananda insisted that "it is a sin to call a human being a sinner"[8] in this sense. Behind this assertion lies the Hindu rejection of an ontological concept of sin. In fact, most of the religious strands within Hinduism speak of the essential identity of the human soul with the Divine, which is hidden from human beings because of their ignorance or *avidya*. There is, of course, a plurality of views within Hinduism on the nature of the human condition, but none of them would hold human beings as sinners in the Christian sense, who can be redeemed only through Divine intervention to pay the price of sin.

What is also troubling is that, even in the area of redemption, Christianity puts more emphasis on 'belief' and on propositional statements of faith. Hinduism, for the most part, puts its emphasis on an inner 'spirituality' that would eventually lead to liberation. Many Hindus who reject Christianity are attracted to Jesus and his teachings, because he speaks to their inner spiritual life.

It is of interest to note that the letter to Murray Rogers by his Hindu friend, Sivendra Prakash, ends with the appeal to Christians to move away from absolutist claims for Christ to an inner spirituality rooted in his teachings. The Hindu complaint about the absence of inner spirituality among Christians must draw Christian attention more than it has done in the past.

Dealing with these dimensions of relationship has been the focus of the ecumenical movement. Both religious traditions need to allow themselves to be challenged by one another even as they gradually begin to form new self-understandings in the context of a global community in the making.

8. C. S. Shah, "Swami Vivekananda at the Parliament of Religions." http://www.boloji.com/index.cfm?md=Content&sd=Articles&ArticleID=1646.

PART VI

Three Relevant Issues to Interfaith Relations

13.

Conversion and Religious Freedom

The issues related to religious freedom are as old as religion itself. Human history is marked by many conflicts based on tribal, ethnic, and religious differences. It also shows that different nations and cultural groups adopted a variety of traditional customs to protect the rights of individuals and communities. Recent centuries, however, have seen much violence based on religious intolerance. In response, the international community, especially in the post Second World War period, worked toward generating agreements among nations that would protect the basic human rights, including the rights related to religious beliefs.

The conventions, covenants, and declarations drawn up by the international community seek to safeguard different dimensions of individual and community rights through commonly held agreements. The earliest among them was the *Universal Declaration of Human Rights* of 1948, which says:

> Everyone has the right to freedom of thought, conscience and religion; this right includes freedom to change his [sic] religion or belief, and freedom, either alone or in community with others and in public or private, to manifest his religion or belief in teaching, practice, worship and observance.

Explication and expansion of this provision, especially in relation to religious freedom, was done in the Article 18 of the *UN International Covenant on Civil and Political Rights*, drawn up in 1966:

Everyone shall have the right to freedom of thought, conscience and religion. This right shall include freedom to have or adopt a religion or belief of his choice, and freedom, either individually or in community with others and in public or private, to manifest his religion or belief in worship, observance, practice, and learning.

The articles from 1966 also had an additional provision that says: "No one shall be subject to coercion, which would impair his freedom to have or to adopt a religion or belief of his choice." In some of the national constitutions, as in the case of India, Sri Lanka, etc. the rights includes the word 'propagate': "the right to believe, practice, and to propagate one's religion."

INTERNAL AND EXTERNAL MANIFESTATIONS OF RELIGIOUS BELIEFS

Commentators of the religious rights enshrined in these articles point out that these provisions speak about both the 'freedom of thought and conscience' and the 'freedom of religion'. This formulation is based on the reality that there are two dimensions to religious belief: internal and external. The freedom of thought and conscience relates to convictions and beliefs that one holds both on religious and other matters that may or may not find external expression, and the freedom of religion points to the external expression of those beliefs.

Thus, on the matter of religion, conventions attempt to protect not only the right of persons to hold any belief but also to manifest those beliefs in public through worship, observances, practices, and learning, both individually and collectively. The attempt here is to insist that it is not sufficient to allow people to 'believe what they want to' or to reduce religion into 'a private affair' or 'a matter of the heart.' Religious freedom includes the right to manifest what one believes, also in public.

RELIGIOUS FREEDOM AND TOLERANCE

In this respect one needs to pay attention to the distinction between 'religious freedom' and 'religious tolerance'. In several countries, where one or other religion is a predominant majority, the word 'tolerance' is often used to indicate the status of other religious traditions. In some countries, like Saudi Arabia, the religious tradition of the majority is declared the religion of the state; while people of other religious traditions are tolerated, in the sense that they could live in the country and practice their faith in private, but they cannot seek citizenship and no other religion is officially recognized.

In Sri Lanka, while all religions are recognized and allowed to practice their faith in public, Buddhism as the religion of the majority is given a special place and is under the protection of the state. In England, while there is full and equal recognition of all religious traditions, in practice, the Church of England maintains a special status and place in relation to the state. The predominantly Hindu India, despite the creation of the Islamic nation of Pakistan (East and West) at the time of its independence, chose to remain a secular state, in the sense of giving constitutional guarantee of equality to all religious traditions within its borders. Indonesia, despite its overwhelming Islamic population, officially recognizes five of the religious traditions prevalent in the nation for equal treatment within *panchaseela*, a fivefold principle of peaceful coexistence.

In some of the Islamic countries, like Malaysia, while all religions are allowed to manifest themselves in public, it is permissible for a person to convert from one of the minority religions to the religion of the majority, but it is illegal to convert from the religion of the majority to that of the minorities.

Thus, the status of religions within the nations varies enormously. Tolerance is the word commonly used to indicate the levels of freedom that other religions enjoy in relation to the religion of the majority. However, tolerance is conducive to but does not constitute religious freedom. The conventions move away from the word 'tolerance' and place religious rights within universal human rights. Even as basic human rights are universal, cannot be overly qualified or set to degrees of observance, religious rights must also be seen as equal rights shared by all citizens of a nation. In this view, privileging any one religion over others or granting only limited rights to minority religious communities would amount to violation of religious freedom.

THE STATE AND RELIGIOUS FREEDOM

This brings us to the very important issue of the relationship between the state and the concept of religious freedom. At the superficial level, the state is important in so far as it is often responsible for the enactment of laws and practices that determine the levels of freedom offered to different religious communities within a nation. Often, it also enacts laws and provisions that limit the activities of religious communities, their participation in the welfare of the people, their place within the state, their relationship to believers in other parts of the world, and the flow and use of financial resources etc. Especially in countries where one religion is a predominant majority, it is not uncommon for the state to limit the activities and external relationships of other religious communities.

However, there is also a deeper dimension to the relationship between state and religious freedom that has to do with the understanding of the nature and purpose of the state itself in the different religious traditions of the world. In a study on the relationship between religious liberty and the state, Ninan Koshy speaks of four models:

Theocracy, where the state is under the control of religious leaders or institutions for religious purposes,

Erastianism, where the church (or religion) is under the control of the state (termed after the sixteenth-century Swiss German theologian Thomas Erastes),

Separation of religion and state, where there is a friendly separation of religious and political institutions that are not hostile to each other,

Separation of religion and state that is unfriendly, where the separated religious and political institutions are antagonistic to each other.[1]

Koshy also records a 1986 study where Elizabeth Odio Benito, the Special Rapporteur of the UN Commission on Human Rights, listed eight arrangements between religion and state, in order to distinguish some of the more subtle distinctions in the way the relationships are conceived and expressed:

1. Ninan Koshy, *Religious Freedom in a Changing World* (Geneva: WCC Publications, 1992), 36.

- State religions
- Established Churches (Religion officially recognized by state laws)
- Neutral or secular as regards religion
- No official religion
- Separation of religion and state
- Special arrangements with a particular religious tradition
- Protection (only) of legally recognized religious groups
- Millet system, were a number of religious communities are officially recognized.[2]

The United Kingdom is a good example of the ambiguities that mark the state-religion relationship. It doesn't have a written constitution and its approach to issues of religious freedom have evolved over the centuries. Although it doesn't have any statutes that prescribe freedom of all religious beliefs and practices, it is a signatory of all international conventions on human rights and those that protect civil and religious rights; all religions in its territory are free to exercise their religious beliefs in public.

And yet, the Church of England is the established religion of the UK. Peter Cumper says that the Church of England's established status means that it enjoys certain privileges denied to other faiths. The Church is uniquely entitled to organize national events such as coronations and war remembrance services. Twenty-six senior Anglican Bishops sit in the House of Lords (Parliament's Upper Chamber) and participate in decision making processes.[3] The relationship between religion and state in the United Kingdom is an example of a nation that holds on to its ancient tradition, and yet does not use it to deny the equality of all citizens and their legitimate right to practice their religions in public.

In much of Europe Christianity had been the official religion of the states, and constitutional steps had to be taken in countries like France, Germany, Sweden, etc. to officially separate the two, even

2. Ibid., 37.
3. Peter Cumper, "Religious Human Rights in The United Kingdom," in *Emory International Law Review* 10, no. 1 (Spring 1996).

though centuries of Christian influence still dominate the ethos of the state.

Traditionally, Islam does not make a separation between religious, social, and political life and Islamic nations did not have the custom of drawing up a constitution to regulate the affairs of the nation. Donna Arzt says that in the post-colonial era all Islamic countries, with the exception of Saudi Arabia and Oman, have promulgated written constitutions. Today, thirty-four states with majority Muslim populations have written constitutions. Of these, twenty-three, in addition to Saudi Arabia and Oman, have officially proclaimed Islam as the state religion and Shari'a as the principal source of law. Arzt notes that there is diversity even within this reality. A few, such as Turkey, the Gambia, and Senegal are avowedly secular; Iran explicitly Islamic, and all others attempt to fuse the Shari'a and other perspectives, some of them limiting the application of the Shari'a only to family law.[4]

Level of religious freedom that should be offered to non-Muslim religious minorities within an Islamic state is an unsettled question within Islamic states. *The Universal Islamic Declaration of Human Rights*, adopted by the Islamic Council in 1981, Arzt points out, does contain references to the discourse found in international law. Article X, titled "Rights of Minorities" states: "The Quranic principle that 'there is no compulsion in Religion' shall govern the religious rights of non-Muslim countries."

"In a Muslim country, religious minorities shall have the choice to be governed by Islamic Law or by their own laws." Article XIII provides every person with the right to freedom of conscience and worship in accordance with one's religious beliefs, while article XII (e) forbids "ridiculing, holding in contempt, or inciting hostility against the religious beliefs of others."[5] There were other declarations like the *Cairo Declaration on Human Rights in Islam* (1990) that also seek to hold a balance between affirmation of the Shari'a and the need to deal with religious plurality, with varying degrees of success.

It is important to recognize that some of the religious traditions have a theological/philosophical understanding of life in community that holds religion, culture, the state, and the legal system in a continuum and do not see them as aspects that must be separated or seen in isolation from one another. A full discussion of the different

---

4. Donna E. Arzt, "Religious Human Rights in Muslim States of the Middle East and North Africa," in *Emory International Law Review* 10, no. 1 (Spring 1996), 140.

5. Ibid., 142.

models of this reality, the history of the ways in which it plays out in our day, and its implications in pluralistic situations, is beyond the scope of this discussion. It is important, however, to emphasize that a discussion on religious freedom should pay attention to this reality.

Historically, different religious traditions have moved through many phases of this reality and can shed light on the discussion from their varied experiences. Globalization, population movements, and the evolution of religiously and culturally pluralistic societies call for a fresh discussion of this issue.

In many ways the state has become the main actor on issues of religious freedom in the modern period, and throughout history both the state and religious traditions have used and abused each other toward exercise of power and influence in society.

RELIGIONS AND RELIGIOUS FREEDOM

On the basis of the above, we should also pay particular attention to the role religions themselves play in the question of religious freedom. As noted above, throughout history many religious traditions have used their alliances with political power to deny the religious freedom of others. But the problem goes even deeper. Many religious traditions have also developed religious self-understandings and theological assumptions about other religious traditions that militate against religious freedom of those different from them.

Exclusive claims to truth or special revelation, claims to divine authority, claims to land based on divine promise, militant and aggressive understandings of mission, denigration of other religious traditions as pagan, heathen, superstition, etc., have often justified callous disregard of the religious rights of others. Most religious traditions are yet to develop sufficient theological and pastoral practices that would give equal respect and authenticity to a plurality of religious traditions.

CONVERSION AND RELIGIOUS FREEDOM

The word conversion has many meanings. At a basic level it can point to a transformation or change of heart and mind of a person on the basis of new experiences, convictions, or beliefs. Conversion can also have external manifestations like one changing one's religious affiliation publicly or moving from one community to another. Involved in the issue are one's right to convert others into one's faith or engage in activities that seek to gain converts to one's religious tradition. Also involved in the issue is the right of a person 'to become a convert' and join a new religious community.

It is clear that the intention of the covenants and declarations of religious freedom is that each individual has the right to his or her religion by birth or by choice, and to practice it privately or with others. Most of the nation-states and religious communities appear to accept this right in principle. However, as mentioned earlier, in many countries (especially where there is a special relationship between religion and state or where the state is theocratic) the tendency has been not to deny but to limit the exercise of religious life in public and in community. This also includes limiting any attempt to propagate one's faith. The extent and degree to which these limitations are placed overtly or covertly vary from nation to nation.

The more relevant aspect of the covenants and declarations, especially in relation to the debate on conversion, has to do with the provisions in the agreements to 'change to' or 'adopt' a religion of one's choice. This was understood as a right that needs to be protected both to uphold one's freedom of conscience, and as a matter of basic human right. Some of the religious traditions and states, however, challenge this right, and have instituted provisions within the state or religious laws to prohibit the option to change to or adopt a religion of one's choice, and to punish those who do so. In some countries like Pakistan and Egypt there have been highly published cases of persons put on trial for choosing to change their religious identity.

The main argument for this course of action has to do, as mentioned earlier, with different understandings of the location of the religious rights. While some see religious rights as belonging to the individual, others see religious rights as something the community holds, and as the identity-marker of the community. In this context an individual adopting a new religion as matter of conscience is seen as a betrayer of the community of which she or he is a part.

There are a number of unresolved issues here on the nature of the rights as they relate to individuals and community. It would appear that the provision in the conventions of the right to 'have' a religion or to remain in one's religious tradition was intended not only to protect one's religious rights but also to curtail any attempts by the state or non-state actors to force, induce, or in other ways pressure individuals and communities to move from one community to another.

Within Islam there are other significant issues of religious rights, especially in relation to religious dissent, movements of reform, apostasy, blasphemy, and the role of women in religious leadership, etc., that are at different stages of discussion in different Islamic countries. In a recent volume Clement John documents several concrete cases where blasphemy laws are abused in Pakistan to act against minorities or to punish a Muslim that had changed his or her religious allegiance.[6]

MISSIONS AND RELIGIOUS FREEDOM

This brings us to the heart of the conversion debate which has to do with missions to propagate one's faith among other believers. The conventions and constitutions argue for the right to manifest, to teach, and in some instances to propagate one's religious tradition. Most religious traditions, with the exception of traditional religions like those of Native Americans and those of African tribal groups, have, to different extents and in different periods of time, propagated their faiths. However, some of the major world religions, like Christianity, Islam and Buddhism have missionary mandates as part of their belief systems. Here one can broadly identify five different positions that have relevance to the discussion on religious freedom:

- Those religious traditions that do not engage in propagation of their faith and are opposed to missions aimed at them.

- Those who propagate their faith but are intolerant toward missions aimed at their own community.

- Those who propagate their faith and are also open for others to propagate their faith, also aimed at their own community, thus claiming that propagation of one's faith as a basic right.

- Those who accept the rights of all communities to propagate their faith but insist on ethical and non-coercive methods of propagation.

- Those who support the rights of all individuals to adopt, remain,

6. Clement John, *Religion, State and Intolerance* (Geneva: WCC Publications, 2009), 42–59.

and to change their religious affiliation as a personal right but are opposed to organized missionary activity to gain converts.

Four basic issues that arise from the above need special consideration:

1. Reciprocity

First relates to reciprocity. As religious traditions begin to relate closely with one another, the position that holds that a particular community has the right to convert others but would not allow conversion of their own believers has come under increasing pressure. This has been a matter of tension especially between some of the Islamic countries and Western nations with Christian majorities. Many Christians in the USA and in some of the European countries, for instance, are troubled by the fact that while there are heavily funded Islamic missions from Saudi Arabia in Western countries, there is no possibility for Christian minorities living in Saudi Arabia to build a church even for their own worship in community.

2. The right to remain in one's faith

The second is the much more complex issue of the rights of individuals and their relationships to the rights of the community as a whole. This issue relates to missionary methods, political or economic pressures, and demographic realities that overtly or covertly violate a person's religious right to remain in his or her religious tradition. This is also related to current discussions on cultural imperialism, the use of mass media, economic disparities, etc. as they relate to conversion.

Some religious communities hold that many of the international conventions on human and religious rights arise out of Western humanistic tradition and put all the emphases on the rights of individuals. They claim that these conventions do not take sufficient note of the large sections of human community where the primary focus is on the interest of the community within which the rights of the individuals are enshrined.

In some of these traditions, it is claimed, that of necessity the rights of the community take precedence over the rights of the individual in order to protect the integrity, identity, coherence and unity of the community. It is argued that even though it is important to protect the rights of the individuals from the possible oppressive dimensions of community pressures, there is reason to look more carefully at the balance between these two rights especially where religion is understood primarily as a manifestation of life in community. In other words, today some argue that the right to remain in one's faith is in need of greater protection than the right to adopt or change one's faith, or that the right to remain must be seen as a more fundamental right than that to change.

Others, coming from other experiences, disagree, and say that there are inalienable rights of individual that needs to be protected, precisely because of the ways in which basic rights of individuals have been and are being denied or violated in the name of community, tradition, or religious teachings. This matter needs greater exploration and perhaps the religious communities with different views on this subject should engage in developing new guidelines that defines the borders of individual and community rights and the ways in which they can be held in tension so that one is not used to exploit the other.

This is also important because of the increasing instances of violations of basic human and religious rights, including the right to life, which is defended in the name of community rights. While some of the accusations in the Western mass media of violation of human and religious rights in Islamic countries are, in fact, based on cultural insensitivity and the expectation that everyone must agree with the definition of rights framed by the West, there is increasing unease within all religious communities when some of the basic rights of women, children, immigrants, minority communities, etc., are denied and defended on the basis of religious, cultural and community rights. Here again it is not easy for any community to determine when religious beliefs are abused in another community. We need to find ways to engage in dialogue on this question to find commonly agreed criteria to evaluate specific cases.

3. Alliance between Religion and State

Third, one of the intensions of the conventions is to free individuals and religious communities from the oppressive control of the state, and to prevent religious communities using the state as an instrument to suppress the religious rights of other communities. Historically, the abuses in this area have been so massive that many insist that the only way to overcome this danger is through the separation of religion and the state.

However, as seen earlier, there are religions that see personal, family, social, economic, and political dimensions of life in a continuum and see the benefit of maintaining it. Further, they claim it as part of their religious self-understanding. Others are quick to point to the difficulties such an understanding presents to the rights of religious minorities on matters of religious practice, and to their civic right to be equal citizens of a nation state. We have shown earlier that there are many different ways in which religion and state relationship can be fashioned and that it is indeed possible to build models that can overcome possible abuse. This is another area that needs careful consideration and common agreements.

4. The right to propagate one's faith and unethical missionary practices

Last has to do with the complex issues related to the right of individuals to share their faith, the right of persons to remain in their faith, the right to adopt a new faith, and the accusations of unethical methods of winning converts. This has been a difficult problem to resolve mainly because of the ambiguities involved in making judgments about people's intentions and motives; competing claims are made about motives and ultimate goals of missionary activities and of those who choose to adopt a new religion.

On the one hand, there are, in fact, communities that engage in unethical missionary practices by using coercive methods, by misrepresenting the faiths of others, or by the use of inducements. Some have also rightly been accused of exploiting the poverty of the people toward the numerical growth of their faith community. There is no doubt that some of the Christian missionary activities in the 'third world', emanating especially from some evangelical groups from the USA, are conducted in a culturally insensitive manner toward simply increasing the numbers of their religious community. There are also good reasons to believe that often material inducements are used to gain converts. These, no doubt, need to be condemned and one should plainly maintain that shutting them down would not involve a violation of the religious freedom to share one's faith.

However, genuine desire to share one's faith with others, humanitarian assistance programs to those in desperate needs, and attempts to help people liberate themselves from oppressive situations have also been prevented under the guise of rejecting unethical means of conversion. This is a pressing problem today in counties like India and Sri Lanka and has been the cause of active violence against one community by another. In India, there are many clear instances of unethical missions from Western countries conducted by those who come from outside or by their agents within the country.

In responding to these unethical missions some of the regional Indian states have promulgated laws banning conversion under certain circumstances, which unfortunately are open to a wide variety of interpretations. Since the applications of these laws can easily become indiscriminate, the nation may be in breach of some of the provisions of religious freedom of its regular citizens, namely, to propagate one's faith and to adopt a faith of one's choice. For instance, many of the Christians who lost their lives or homes, or had to flee their homes in the anti-Christian violence in Gujarat, India, were innocent victims of indiscriminate response to Christian missionary activities—both ethical and unethical.

Recognizing the complex issues involved in this question, religious communities have come up with codes of conduct that are appropriate for sharing one's faith with others. The implementation of these codes will help to ease some of the tensions and conflicts that have risen over this issue.

IS RELIGIOUS FREEDOM AN ABSOLUTE RIGHT?

One of the issues that needs some consideration here is whether religious freedom is an absolute right. In drawing up its statement on religious liberty in the aftermath of the Second World War, the World Council of Churches for instance held that "the freedom of religion is fundamental to all other freedoms." The document of the Second Vatican Council dealing with this issue, *Dignitaries Humane*, declared that ". . . the right to religious freedom has its foundation in the very dignity of the human person, as this dignity is known through the Revealed Word of God, and by reason itself."[7] Yet, there is general recognition that like all other rights, religious freedom also

---

7. The Vatican II document "Dignitatis Humanae," in *The Documents of Vatican II*, ed. Walter H. Abbot (Piscataway: New Century Publishers, 1966). Quoted in Ninan Koshy, *Religious Freedom*, 42.

has its limits, and that a claim that it is absolute in all its dimensions would lead to the abuse of these rights. At the same time, there is also concern that religious rights could be suppressed under the pretext of law and order, well being of the community, or national interest.

As soon as 1948, the Amsterdam Assembly of the WCC felt the need to address this issue. It affirmed parts of the right as inalienable and others as subjected to limits:

1. The liberty of conscience or right to determine one's belief is practically subject to no legal limitation at all.

2. The liberty of religious expression is subject to such limitations prescribed by law as are necessary to protect order and welfare, morals and the rights and freedoms of others.

3. The liberty of religious association is subject to the same limits imposed on all associations by non-discriminatory laws.

4. Similarly, the corporate religious freedom is limited by the provisions of non-discriminatory laws passed in the interest of public order and well-being.

What the Amsterdam Assembly sought to do was to reiterate that all rights are, of necessity, limited by other equally important concerns of society. But at the same time, it insisted that there are elements within religious freedom, as the freedom of conscience and belief, which are absolute and non-negotiable. One should also note that the Assembly is careful to maintain that the limitations on the rights, when necessary, have to be non-discriminatory so that the limiting clauses are not used to deny the rights of only sections of the population.

Unfortunately, the limitation clauses intended for extraordinary situations are often abused, and states use the pretext of national security, public order etc. to interfere with legitimate exercise of religious freedom. This is one of the accusations against the United States in the way it used the Homeland Security Act in the period following 9/11. Because of possible abuses, today there are calls to declare more dimensions of religious freedom as absolute rights.

SPIRITUALITY AND RELIGIOUS FREEDOM

The discussion above shows that in the last analysis religious freedom is not only a legal issue but also a spiritual issue. Religious communities need to find ways in which explication of their beliefs, their understandings of sharing their faiths, the methods used to do so, and their approach to other religious traditions respect the dignity and humanity of all their neighbors. Love, respect, compassion, justice, and peace are affirmed by all traditions. There is a universal belief that one should not do to others what one would not want others to do to oneself. The way a religious tradition looks at the rights of others is a sign of its own spiritual maturity.

Religious traditions also need to engage in in-depth dialogue of the issues mentioned above, and should together stand up against violations of religious freedom, wherever it comes from, and whoever is affected by it. The drawing up of codes of conduct is one step, but a greater goal is the elimination of the need for such codes. No religious community will be able to address this question to the satisfaction of all. This is one issue that cries out for interfaith dialogue, mutual understanding and collaboration in the interest of the whole human community.

14.

Religion and Violence

In early 2000, the Interfaith Dialogue Program of the WCC decided to bring together a group of scholars who would meet regularly for a sustained period of time to discuss some of the crucial and complex issues facing all religious traditions in our day. The group of 12–15 theologians and thinkers who came from Buddhism, Christianity, Hinduism, Islam and Judaism were named the "Thinking Together" group, pointing to the need that some of the difficult issues facing us need collaborative and sustained thinking across religious traditions. One of the topics taken up was 'religion and violence' in which I, as one of the Christian members of the group, was requested to set out the Protestant perspectives on the question. Those interested in the perspectives of other religions on this issue can read them in *Current Dialogue* no. 39, June 2002, which can be accessed on the Internet.

A PROTESTANT CHRISTIAN PERSPECTIVE

It is common knowledge that much violence that goes on in the name of religion has little to do with religion. Often religion is used, misused, and abused in conflicts that have social, economic, and political motivations, and many of the persons that actively perpetrate violence have little or no knowledge of the tenants of the faith in the name of which they join the battle. In most of these cases it is religious identity and fervor that play the important role than the motivations provided by the faith itself.

Our purpose here, however, is not to deal with this broader issue but to ask ourselves whether our respective religious traditions do, in fact, contribute to violence in its many forms and manifestations. "It is too easy in an apologetic concern," says Francois Houtart, "to claim that the content of the religion is essentially non-violent and that it is the human beings who, whether individually or collectively, divert them from their meaning," adding that "in fact the roots of violence can be found right back in the religions, and that is why the religions can also easily serve as vehicles for violent tendencies."[1]

One needs to heed this warning when one speaks of religion and violence from a Christian perspective. Beyond doubt, Christianity has had a violent history and today many trace this history to the Bible itself, and to the way it has been interpreted and applied in the development and spread of Christianity as a religion. Speaking about the Bible in an interfaith context, however, is a difficult matter because what Christians call the Old Testament is also, and primarily so, the Hebrew Scriptures. There are considerable differences between Christians and Jews in the understanding and interpretation of scriptures, and therefore what I say here must be seen as a Christian perspective on some parts of the scriptures shared by Jews and Christians.

VIOLENCE IN THE BIBLE

The Bible begins with the affirmation that God saw the universe that had been created as 'very good'. But soon, it moves to outlines the human predicament, through the myth of Adam and Eve in the garden, as a state of alienation between God and human beings, and between human beings and nature (Genesis 3). This chapter is immediately followed by the story of the brutal murder of Abel by his brother Cain. The story is said to reflect on the early struggle between the pastoral and agricultural ways of life. However, even though the story says that God held Cain accountable for his brother's murder, in fact, it depicts Cain, the murderer, as the one who begins human civilization under the protection of God. In response to Cain's fear that he might himself be killed as a fugitive, God said, "Not so!

---

1. Francois Houtart, "The Cult of Violence in the Name of Religion: A Panorama," in *Religion as Source of Violence?*, ed. Wim Beuken and Karl-Josef Kuschel (Maryknoll, NY: Orbis, 1997), 1.

Whoever kills Cain will suffer a sevenfold vengeance." And the Lord "put a mark on Cain, so that no one who came upon him will kill him" (Gen 4:15).

Soon violence is also to be attributed to God: "Then the Lord saw that the wickedness of humankind was great in the earth, and that every inclination of the thoughts of their hearts was only evil continually. And the Lord was sorry that he had made the earth, and it grieved him to his heart. So the Lord said, 'I will blot out from the earth the human beings I have created—people together with the animals and creeping things and the birds of the air, for I am sorry that I have made them'" (Gen 6:5-7).

This attribution of violence to God is to continue in much of the rest of the Bible. The devastation brought on Egypt, including the death of the first born of Egypt, the destruction of the Egyptian army in the Red Sea, the conquest of Canaan, including the genocidal acts of wiping out whole tribes are all depicted as acts done by or supported by God. The conquest of Jericho, for instance, ends in this note: "As soon as the people heard the trumpets, they raised a great shout, and the wall fell down flat; so the people charged straight ahead into the city and captured it. Then they devoted to destruction by the edge of the sword all in the city, both men and women, young and old, oxen, sheep, and donkeys" (Josh 6:20-21). All the wars that are won are presented as the Lord himself leading the people into battle, and all wars lost are God's punishment for the sins of the people.

There is considerable dispute among biblical scholars and theologians on how to interpret these events and the attribution of violence to God, especially in view of an entirely opposite view of God as loving, kind, forgiving and merciful in other parts of the same Bible. There is no agreement, even among Christians, on how to read and interpret the Bible.

WHAT IS VIOLENCE?

Within the first few books of the Bible we come across the many dimensions of what is generally covered by the word 'violence':

1. Violence as a human response arising from jealousy, fear, or hatred (Story of Cain and Abel).

2. Violence as judgment or punishment (The flood and the destruction of Sodom and Gomorrah).

3. Violence as structured oppression (The Hebrews under the Egyptians).

4. Violence as part of a liberation struggle (Events connected with freeing the Hebrews from the Egyptian bondage).

5. Violence in war and conquest (The occupation of Canaan).

6. Violence as part of maintaining law and order (punishments related to the breaking of the social laws).

7. Violence as part of religious duty or practice (The sacrificial system).

The stories of violent warfare in the Bible should of course be read in their historical context. They are part of the prevalent practice of tribes in the deserts of the Middle East constantly waging war against each other to control the few, scattered fertile portions of the land on which the survival of the tribes depended. Thus, it was not only the Hebrews but all tribes at that time engaged in warfare and violence to control, protect, or expand their territories.

It should also come as no surprise that the gods of such tribes are represented as ones that give them victory in the conquest of fertile lands. It is also to be understood that the biblical stories and historiography are theological readings and interpretations of events by a particular people, with all the promises and problems such readings entail. But what is important for our present concern is that one of the prominent dimensions of the Biblical image of God gets closely associated with domination, conquest, and violence.

Contemporary Christian thinking is also delving deeply into the impact of the concept of 'sacrifice', which is at the heart of both the Old and New Testaments, on the psychology of violence. The requirement to shed animal blood as the symbol of reconciliation between God and a person who had sinned, it is claimed, justifies the shedding of blood as a religious duty. This basic principle is worked out in Christian theology in the theory of Atonement, which claims that Jesus had to die a violent death in order to placate God's anger over the sins of humankind. Jesus's 'sacrificial death', 'shedding of blood for our sins', and 'paying the price of sin', etc., are common themes in Christian hymnody, piety, and theology.

The second area where such violence plays a major role lies in the way some biblical imagery and theology depict the problem of evil in terms of violent and ongoing battles between good and evil, light and darkness, God and Satan. Hence, the eschatological vision in the Book of Revelation presents a cosmic battle between the powers of evil and good in which the powers of evil, after a violent struggle, are conquered, overcome, subdued, and eventually abolished by God and God's angels. Power, conquest, and domination take the center stage in these images.

Violence is also clearly present in Christian images of mission and evangelization of the world. Military language like 'conquering the world for Christ', 'deployment of missionaries', 'mission strategy', 'soldiers of Christ', and 'evangelistic crusades' are still very much in use in some sections of the church. It is little wonder then that parts of the history of the church are also closely associated with violence. The burning of heretics, the Inquisitions, Crusades, Holocaust, slavery, and the ruthless violence that accompanied the establishment of Christianity in Latin America, Africa, and Australia are all part of the history of Christianity.

Christians, therefore, can approach this subject only with humility and repentance.

THE OTHER SIDE OF THE BIBLE

While the Bible has many such violent episodes, there is also another stream within the Bible that resists war and violence as against God's will and purpose. God is also presented as loving, forgiving, and compassionate (Psalm 103), who demands righteousness and justice in human affairs. Clear and unambiguous prohibition of killing is part of the Ten Commandments, and there are detailed provisions against social and economic violence in the form of relentless advocacy for justice, especially in favor of the poor and the oppressed. The prophet Amos recalls God's displeasure with the violence perpetrated not only by Israel and Judah but also by the neighboring nations (Amos 1–2).

Significantly, all the eschatological visions in the Old Testament deal with cessation of violence and a state of reconciliation between nations, between God and human beings, as well as in the natural world. In Isaiah's vision, "The wolf shall live with the lamb, the leopard shall lie down with the kid. . . . The cow and the bear shall graze, and their young shall lie down together; and the lion shall eat straw like an ox. . . . They will not hurt or destroy on all my holy mountain; for the earth will be full of the knowledge of the Lord as the waters cover the sea" (Isa 11:6–9). Micah sees a vision of an absolute reversal of the way nations relate to one another: "He shall judge between many peoples, and arbitrate between strong nations far away; they shall beat their swords into plowshares, and their spears into pruning hooks; nation shall not lift up sword against nation, and neither shall they learn war any more" (Mic 4:3).

JESUS'S TEACHING ON VIOLENCE
AND NONVIOLENCE

Christians are, of course, specifically interested in the teachings of Jesus on violence and non-violence. There is considerable discussion among New Testament scholars on Jesus's attitude to the Roman Empire and his relationship to the zealots who advocated a violent overthrow of the Roman power. At one point Jesus is presented as saying that he has come "not to bring peace but a sword" (Matt 10:34), and in chapter 13, Matthew again presents Jesus as reproaching the unrepentant cities in harsh language (Matt 11:20–24).

But the bulk of New Testament witness, including that of Matthew, presents Jesus as one who advocated radical non-violence. "You have heard that it was said, 'An eye for an eye and a tooth for a tooth.' But I say to you do not resist an evildoer. But if anyone strikes you on the right cheek, turn the other also. . . . You have heard that it was said, 'You shall love your neighbor and hate your enemy.' But I say to you, love your enemies and pray for those who persecute you, so that you may be children of your Father in Heaven; for he makes his sun to rise on the evil and on the good, and sends rain on the righteous and the unrighteous." . . . "Be perfect, therefore, as your heavenly Father is perfect" (Matt 5:38–45, 48).

Matthew also presents Jesus as espousing total nonviolence in his account of Jesus's arrest and trial. When one of the persons with Jesus drew a sword to defend him, Jesus is reported to have said, "Put your sword back into its place; for all who will take up the sword will perish by the sword" (Matt 26:52).

The study of the life of the early church also shows that the church, as it emerged into a new religious tradition separated from its Jewish moorings, basically espoused a nonviolent stance in its relationship to the Roman Empire. Even though the Empire had begun an active persecution of the church for the fear that those who followed 'the Way' were disloyal to Rome, the church's stance on nonviolence appears to have held until its whole ethos changed with the conversion of Emperor Constantine. When Christianity became the official religion of the Roman Empire, political power and material wealth that came with the status completely changed its attitude to violence and nonviolence.

CHRISTIAN APPROACHES TO WAR AND VIOLENCE

Even though Christianity eventually developed into a religion that in principle rejected violence, Christian discussions on violence have centered mainly on the issue of whether there are situations in which some measure of violence is justified. Some are very clear that, in accordance with Jesus's own teachings, violence is not justified under any circumstance. Within the mainstream of the church, the historic Peace Churches (mainly the Mennonites and the Quakers) have adopted the pacifist position of rejecting war and violence for any reason.

'JUST' WAR

But after the Roman Empire adopted Christianity as the religion of the state, the church was faced with the problem of having to respond to the acts of war undertaken by the Empire, often as offensive wars, but also in self-defense when attacked by outside forces. The initial response of the church was not to bless wars, but soon Cicero, in response to pressure from the rulers, started the idea of a 'just war'. This concept was later developed and perfected by Ambrose and Augustine in the fourth century, when the church would support wars under certain conditions. Six criteria were developed by which a war might be declared 'just':

1. The war must be declared by a legitimate authority;

2. It must be undertaken with a right intention, namely, to promote peace;

3. It must be used only as the last resort, namely, when all other ways of resolving the conflict have been exhausted;

4. It must be waged on the principle of proportionality, which means that the evil and destruction perpetrated should not outweigh the good that comes of it;

5. It must have a reasonable chance of success, so that no wonton destruction is done when it is clear that the intention cannot be achieved;

6. It must be waged with all the moderation possible, which means that violence unrelated to the battle (and to persons unrelated to the war) must be avoided.[2]

These principles were of course subject to interpretation, and were constantly abused to undertake military adventures and to persecute minorities and those who challenged the state for any reason. These led Thomas Aquinas, in the thirteenth century, to take the position that war is always sinful, even though it may have to be waged at times for a just cause.

The popularity of the theory of 'just war' declined in the twentieth century. But its principles have constantly reemerged and have influenced the discussions and jurisprudence on the conduct of modern wars. In recent times the Gulf War reopened the question of just war, polarizing Christians toward both sides of the argument.

Within the ecumenical movement, however, there is hesitation to call any war 'just' because modern weaponry and methods of warfare make it difficult to maintain proportionality and to separate civilians from combatants. The advent of nuclear weapons has pushed more and more churches to take a stand against war as a method of resolving conflicts. What we need, the ecumenical movement says, is 'Not Just War, but Just Peace'.

---

2. Cf. Robert McAfee Brown, *Religion and Violence* (Philadelphia: Westminster, 1973), 19–20.

RESISTING EVIL

The second area of intense Christian discussion is on the use of violence to resist evil. The Nazi regime in Germany produced the classical case in which Christians had to take sides either to support evil (also by remaining silent) or to resist it actively. For Dietrich Bonhoeffer, resisting the Nazi regime became a matter of Christian faith and discipleship. Therefore he terminated his privileged research position at the Union Theological Seminary in New York and returned to his native Germany to participate in a clandestine plot to assassinate Hitler. The plot was discovered, and the Nazis hanged Bonheoffer.

Today Bonheoffer is considered a modern martyr, and his actions are cited by moral theorists as an example of "how Christians could undertake violent actions for just cause and how occasionally they are constrained to break the law for a higher purpose."[3] Reinhold Niebuhr, who was the colleague of Bonhoeffer at Union Seminary and who began his career as a pacifist, also began to admit that there may be situations in which limited violence might be necessary for a just cause.

The issue has resurfaced in our day with regard to the 'positive' use of violence, for example, by an armed contingent of the United Nations, to prevent massacre of innocent peoples. The tragedies in Rwanda and Bosnia, for example, are cited as instances where limited and well-directed violence or armed intervention would have saved the lives of tens of thousands of innocent victims.

There are, however, many Christians who believe that any use of violence would only breed more violence, and maintain that we should work harder on developing measures to predict, prevent, manage, and transform conflicts and on finding peaceful ways of resolving conflicts. Many groups have arisen within the Christian fold that put greater emphasis on conflict resolution, conflict transformation, peace making, and prevention of conflicts.

LIBERATION STRUGGLES

The third area where Christians disagree on the legitimate use of violence has to do with liberation struggles. The struggle against the

3. Mark Juergensmeyer, *Terror in the Mind of God – The Global Rise of Religious Violence* (Los Angeles: University of California Press, 2000), 24.

apartheid regime in South Africa and against the brutal dictatorships in Latin America (where thousands of dissidents simply 'disappeared') provided the stage for much discussion within the ecumenical movement on the right of peoples to take arms to liberate themselves from oppressive regimes. While some still opt for nonviolent resistance, as advocated by Gandhi in the Indian liberation struggle and by Martin Luther King Jr. in the struggle against racism in the USA, others insist on allowing the oppressed to decide on the nature of the struggle that is appropriate in a given situation.

YES AND NO

The World Council of Churches has struggled with this question from its inception in 1948. Through several stages of debate within its program on church and society an important statement was made in 1973 under the title, "Violence, Non-violence and the Struggle for Social Justice." Without itself taking a stance on the issue, it summarized the state of the debate for the study of the churches in the following affirmations:

1. Nonviolent action is the only way that is consistent with our obedience to Jesus Christ;

2. However, there may be extreme situations where violent resistance may become a Christian duty, and in such circumstances Christians must follow principles like those enunciated for 'just wars';

3. This is being considered because violence seems to be unavoidable in some situations where nonviolence does not appear to be a viable option.

The report also identified kinds of violence that Christians must vehemently resist:

1. Violent causes like conquest of a people, race, or class by another;

2. Unjustified violence such as holding hostages, torture, deliberate and indiscriminate killing of non-combatants, etc.

Again, much of the emphasis was on ways of avoiding conflicts by building a culture of peace and dialogue.

FORMS OF VIOLENCE

One of the results of the long history of Christian discussions on violence and nonviolence has been the emergence of the awareness that violence is a complex reality and manifests itself in many forms. Thus, in addition to overt acts of violence, like killing a person or engaging in warfare, there are other forms of violence that also need to be addressed. Some of these include:

1. Physical violence, which expresses itself in killings, massacres, genocides, and other forms of bloodletting.

2. Structural violence, where the very social, political, and cultural structures oppress, discriminate, exclude, or marginalize groups of people.

3. Economic violence, where the economic life is organized in a way that denies even the very basic needs of people to live in dignity.

4. Social violence, where forces like racism and sexism exclude peoples on the basis of color, gender, caste, ethnicity, etc.

5. Domestic violence, where women and children are abused or treated brutally within established relationships.

6. Psychological violence, where persons or groups of persons in an institution, or in a society in general, are kept intimidated and live in fear.

7. Moral violence, where the brutal force of the state or a dominant group denies peoples' human rights or their right to peoplehood.

Within the ecumenical movement, therefore, there is a general concern about a 'culture of violence' that is expressed in many forms and in many places. The Council declared a Decade to Overcome Violence, so that Christians and churches would become more aware of the violence that has seeped into all dimensions of contemporary life at all levels, and seeks ways and means to overcome it. Violence in and in the name of religion is included in these discussions.

TERRORISM AND STATE TERRORISM

The September 11th incident in New York has brought into greater focus the question of 'terrorism' as a form of violence, and the religious and moral issues involved in suicide attacks as ways of perpetrating violence to achieve what the perpetrators consider to be just causes. On the one hand, Christians distance themselves from terrorist and suicide attacks because of the indiscriminate way in which violence is directed on innocent peoples. By and large, churches and Christians also reject terrorism as a way of attracting attention to causes that may well be just.

But, even here, Christians disagree. While there are some acts of terrorism that arise out of hatred and malice (and should be resisted and stopped), there are others that are part of the cry for attention in desperate situations. Some Christians have, therefore, begun to also say that indiscriminate violence in the name of 'anti-terrorism', without consideration and alleviation of the causes that produce terrorist attacks, would only deepen the problem of violence, not resolve it. This division among Christians has become very pronounced, for example, over the Israeli–Palestinian conflict in the Middle East. There is very little conviction left that attempts to quell what is considered terrorist violence without resolving the underlying socio-economic–political–land issues and would lead to peace and justice.

In the same manner, deep economic disparities that keep peoples in abject poverty or oppression, in any part of the world, is a breeding ground for violence. It is difficult to expect those who have been disenfranchised of power, pushed against the wall, and left with no hope for the future not to resort to desperate methods to call the attention of the world. The concepts of 'social violence' and 'economic violence', therefore, have been receiving greater attention of the churches today.

In relation to this, there is also greater awareness of 'state terrorism', where the state, which is expected to protect the people, becomes the perpetrator of violence over sections of the population, resulting in alienation and counter-violence against the state.

THE NEED FOR NEW THINKING

Part of the discussion on Religion and Violence, therefore, has to do with the need to become more aware of the complexity of the concept of violence and its manifold expressions in personal, social, and religious life. The thirst for power that goes with violence has been an abiding temptation to religious traditions, and Christianity for its part has succumbed to the lure of power in its theological expression, ecclesial structures, and its mission practice. It should, therefore, engage in an honest self-examination to understand how it has imbibed, consciously or unconsciously, structures of domination, power, exclusion, and discrimination in its teachings, practices, and structures. Thanks partly to theological insights from the 'third-world' churches, the rise of feminism, and some dimensions of post-modern criticism, Christianity has begun to look more closely at itself in relation to religion and violence. There is a long way ahead.

CHRISTIAN AWARENESS OF THE NEED
FOR COLLABORATION

In the meantime there is increasing recognition among Christians that struggling against the culture of violence needs collaboration beyond all religious boundaries, and there are some religious traditions like Hinduism, Buddhism, and especially Jainism that have enormous teaching resources and practical guidelines on the issue of violence and nonviolence. There are also significant numbers of people and groups that are not part of any religious tradition but that are deeply committed to overcoming the culture of violence. Christians therefore see collaboration across boundaries as an important step forward in the search for peace and nonviolence.

An in-depth dialogue among religious traditions on violence would not only help in lifting up the teaching on non-violence but would also serve the purpose of helping all religious traditions to recognize the way their scriptures, teachings and social organizations, often unintentionally, contribute to the perpetuation of violence in society.

Interfaith dialogue, it has been said, has the function of holding up a mirror in front of the religious traditions involved so that they might see themselves also as others see them. Self-knowledge that comes from it leads to self-criticism that can lead to real reform and renewal within all religious traditions. Such renewal is one of the important components in our search for justice and peace in a world so deeply mired in violence.

15.

Religion and Reconciliation

There are two distinct and mutually opposing views about religions among people. Some look upon religions as those that uphold high spiritual values such as love, forgiveness, justice, peace and harmony. The purpose of religions, they would argue, is to tame the evil instincts in human beings and help them espouse values that help us live in communities. Others hold just the opposite view and see religions as one of the main the problem of the world, in so far as they divide the human community into sectarian groups with exclusive claims. They point to the past and present conflicts and wars where religious beliefs or sentiment or its abuse has played a significant role. Even today, they would argue, one of the major factors that separate communities from each other is religious identity.

Although neither of these views tells the whole truth about religions traditions and the role they play in the life of individuals and communities, as historical and social manifestations, they have indeed been deeply implicated in many conflicts in the world in the past and even today.

At the Centennial of the Parliament of World's Religions in Chicago (1993) Hans Kung came up with a three-fold thesis, the first of which was: "There will be no peace in the world until there is peace among religions." This statement points to two dimensions when one speaks about Religion and Reconciliation. The first is the role of religions in the search for reconciliation in conflict situations, and the second is the need for reconciliation between religions themselves that have historically been in a state of alienation or even in conflict and war with each other.

The purpose of beginning this discussion with the observations above is to face one of the important questions in our day: Can religions play a role in bringing about peace and reconciliation in the world? The remarks with which we began shows that there would always be two responses to this question, each with convincing arguments and examples of the positive and negative roles religions have played in concrete situations.

Happily, I have not been asked to answer this particular question. Rather what I have been asked is to make a presentation on what are the Christian motivations to struggle for justice, peace and reconciliation in the world, and what have we learned about the ministry of reconciliation in the process.

FOUR BASIC THEOLOGICAL CONVICTIONS

The belief that Christians hold that they have a ministry of reconciliation is based on some theological convictions that can be summarized as follows:

1. God loves the world and all its peoples. All forms of violence and warfare are against God's will; God is at work to heal the world and to establish God's peace on the earth. This is not only a promise about life beyond our earthly existence, but also about the here and now.

2. For Christians, this promise of reconciliation and peace has been made manifest in the life, death and resurrection of Jesus Christ. Jesus calls us to work with God in making the world whole. Jesus' intention is made clear in his teaching on loving one's neighbor as oneself, and by his declaration, "Blessed are the peace makers, for they shall be called the children of God." Our right to be the children of God is linked with our willingness to be peace makers.

3. In the ministry of reconciliation and peace-making we are engaged in a struggle that may be beyond our own capacity and of which we may not see the results. But Christian peace-making is rooted in faith and hope. Since peace and jus-

tice in the world is what God wills for the world, we struggle with the knowledge that what is required of us is faithfulness. In other words, we should never lose hope even in what appears to be hopeless situations.

4. Since peace and reconciliation are part of the *mission Dei* or the mission of God, we recognize that God uses many others and other movements for God's purposes. We should therefore work along with all others who are also struggling toward peace and reconciliation.

5. What we seek to build in human life are values of the Reign of God, which have to do with reconciled communities that uphold peace and justice in the world. The church is only a witness and an instrument in the service of God's mission.

The overall theological conviction is summarized in the following words of Paul in his Second Letter to the Corinthians 5:18: "All this is from God, who reconciled us to himself through Christ, and has given us the ministry of reconciliation."

The church's involvement in peace and reconciliation has a long history. Here I would highlight only some of the major efforts since the end of the Second World War for the purpose of drawing some of the lessons learnt in the areas of peace and reconciliation and building communities of reconciliation.

ECUMENICAL INVOLVEMENT IN RECONCILIATION

The negotiations for the creation of the World Council of Churches (WCC) had already begun in the 1920s, but it actual formation was hastened by the Second World War. The desperate need to serve the millions of refugees at the end of the war, and the urgency to bring about peace and reconciliation between the nations that had been in war are said to be the factors that precipitated the birth of the WCC in its founding assembly at Amsterdam in 1948. Ever since, peace-making and building communities of reconciliation have been at the heart of the work of the ecumenical movement in general and of the WCC in particular.

The legacy of building peace and reconciliation between the people of Germany and those of the Allied Nations became an abiding feature of the ministry of the WCC. Almost every conflict in the world since then has had the involvement of the WCC and its member churches, openly or behind the scenes, in attempts at peace making and reconciliation. Further, numerous studies were done to analyze specific conflict situations and on the issues related to peace and reconciliation in each of them.

The churches have thus been deeply involved in peace making in some of difficult and prolonged conflicts like those in Northern Island and in the Middle East. They have also been active in many of the more recent conflicts like those in Fiji, Sudan, Nigeria, and Sri Lanka. The role of the churches, and especially of Archbishop Desmond Tutu, in the Truth and Reconciliation Commission in the post-apartheid South Africa has been recognized in all parts of the world. Building communities of reconciliation in post-genocide contexts, like that in Rwanda, is also a challenge in which churches are involved. Individuals and churches in Korea have also been deeply engaged in efforts to prepare the ground for possible peaceful reunification of the divided Peninsula.

Since most of us are aware of the nature of these conflicts and the work Christians and churches are doing to bring about peace, I wish to devote the rest of the discussion to the lessons we have learned in the areas of peace and reconciliation, particularly on building communities of reconciliation. Among many others I would highlight seven areas that need attention:

SEVEN DIMENSIONS IN THE MINISTRY
OF RECONCILIATION

The first most important dimension in the work toward reconciliation of communities that have been alienated from each other for prolonged period of time is the firm faith and conviction that *peace is possible* and *can be achieved*. This is the bedrock on which all work on reconciliation is done. It is important because there are many conflict situations that are mired in so much historical grievances, territorial disputes and irreconcilable claims that, at first sight, it would appear that there are no possible solutions to the problem. Northern Ireland, for instance, appeared to be a conflict to which no satisfactory solutions could be found. Yet, with faith, perseverance, and long, hard work, and numerous frustrations on the way, it was possible to achieve peace. Even in an intractable problem like that of Middle East, one is aware that in one way or another the Israelis and Palestinians have to come to a solution that would enable them to live side by side. Therefore is it not sufficient to be for peace, or simply to call for peace. Peace needs to be made, and at the heart of this endeavor lies the conviction that it is possible.

This leads to the second learning that peace making and building communities of reconciliation *is a process*. No one can be a peace maker unless he or she is willing to be in it for the long haul. This is mainly because reconciliation cannot be delivered from the outside to communities that have been in prolonged conflicts. There are hatreds and animosities to overcome, genuine grievances to be resolved, memories to be healed, and bridges to be built. Reconciliation cannot be built unless those who need to be reconciled are led to believe in it, to consider it to be desirable, and want to have it.

The effort has to begin with building trust and confidence, and in creating small communities of conversation, united in heart and mind across barriers erected sometimes over decades and even centuries. One needs to find and develop allies for peace. All these are processes that take time, energy and perseverance.

The considerations on just grievances and unhealed memories lead us to the third requirement that a reconciled community cannot be built without paying attention to the *concern for justice*. It is all too tempting to attempt at reconciliation without taking account of the inalienable link between peace and justice. Any peace that is built without resolving the issues of justice would not last long. What constitutes justice, in protracted conflict situations and where there are conflicting claims, is hard to determine or to implement. However, all the hard work on this question needs to be done, so that all parties involved are led to see that whatever measure of justice possible in the circumstances has been done. Just solutions prevent new fissures opening within a reconciled community.

Fourth, building communities of reconciliation also calls for the awareness of some of the *spiritual dimensions* that are inalienable to this effort. Many attempts at building communities fail because those involved approach the question primarily as political, social, tribal, ethnic, economic or territorial issues that can be addressed at those levels. There is no doubt that one or many of these issues are at the heart of many conflicts, and must be addressed. Rebuilding communities, however, cannot be done only by addressing these concerns.

Once alienation sets in, overcoming it needs acts of repentance, conversion, forgiveness, mutual acceptance, reconciliation, etc., and even the willingness where necessary to suffer wrong. These are subtle spiritual qualities to which people should be challenged to rise for the sake of the greater good. As witnessed in public hearings of the South African Truth and Reconciliation Commission, these acts of confession, repentance, forgiveness and facing truth are hard and often heart-wrenching experiences for all sides. But these play an important role in the healing process that is required to building reconciled communities.

The fifth area is that communities that have been brought together after a period of conflict and alienation *have to be glued together*. Otherwise, they can easily fall apart over the very same old issues or new ones that arise. This means that the reconciled communities must be enabled to create a new story about who they are now, which is commonly owned by them. This does not mean that the identity and specificity of the partners in a new community should lose their identity or sacrifice their language, culture, or other elements that are essential to them. And yet, establishing a shared identity is crucial for the building of a new community. People need to be helped to move from the 'us' and 'them' to a new 'we'. This would happen only as new commonly-held practices, customs, stories, celebrations, and institutions arise that gradually help the community to develop the common 'we'.

The sixth, related to the above, is the need of *peace education* and development of skills in conflict resolution. It is said that as long as human beings have freedom to think, to will, and to act, there will always be disagreements among them on policies, priorities, and on what is right or wrong in given situations. Further, one cannot ignore the reality of human weaknesses such as greed, pride, craving for power, etc., that leads to dissentions. In other words, conflicts cannot be avoided and perhaps should be expected within human communities.

Avoiding open conflicts can lead to other problems like bitterness, hatred, frustration, and prejudices that would silently eat into the health of the community. This means that while conflicts cannot be avoided, they have to be managed so that they do not lead to violence and alienation. Peace education and learning the skills to manage conflicts are essential parts of building a reconciled community. It is important that conflicts are anticipated and prevented, and when they do break out they are dealt with early to the satisfaction of all the parties. A community needs to know the informal centers within its life that can come to their help to resolve conflicts peacefully. The problem in most conflict situations is that they had not been dealt with in the early stages; the wounds that begin to fester are difficult to heal.

For this reason yet another field has been developed within the ministry of reconciliation that is called *conflict transformation*. Here attempts are made to help people to have new perceptions of the conflict, to help them understand the intractable problems that have led to the conflict, to enable them to view the conflict with the eyes of the other group, and above all to be able to perceive the benefits that would arise from seeking reconciliation and peace. Conflict transformation attempts to help people look at the same problem with new eyes.

In the end, an enormous amount of energy needs to be spent on examining the religious, cultural, and social ethos in which *children and young adults* are nurtured in our day. All the basic formations that would inform and affect a person's attitude and behavior as an adult are shaped during this period. Grievances, unhealed memories, and prejudices against each other, in many of the conflicts around the world, have been handed down from generation to generation. Much of the exclusivist and judgmental attitudes on the part of religious communities toward other religious traditions is part of the way the religious traditions have been taught to the children. Much of the games, especially since the advent of the computer games, and many contemporary movies foster a culture of violence, and the mentality that resorting to violence and destroying the other is the only way to resolve conflicts and to survive.

We often forget that children are the greatest assets we have for building communities of peace and reconciliation. Peace-making and peaceful ways of resolving conflicts must be fed into the school system not only at the curricular level but also (perhaps more so) at the levels in which conflicts emerge among children in the playground and in course of their life together.

It is important to note that even though these seven learnings are drawn from Christian involvement in reconciliation, they are applicable to the efforts of any religious or secular group. They are also a useful guide to those who seek to bring about peace and reconciliation among religions themselves.

FAITH, HOPE, AND VISION

No one can read the Bible without being impressed by the persistence of faith, hope, and vision about what God intends to do in the world. In many passages the reconciled community does not relate to the Jewish, Christian, or even only to the human community but to the entire creation; a reconciliation where all forms of enmity is ended and war is no more. The prophet Isaiah holds up such a vision in chapter 11:

> The wolf shall live with the lamb, the leopard shall lie down with the kid, the calf and the lion and the fatling together, and a little child shall lead them. The cow and the bear shall graze, their young shall lie down together; and the lion shall eat straw like the ox. The nursing child shall play over the hole of the asp, and the weaned child shall put its hand on the adder's den. They will not hurt or destroy on all my holy mountain; for the earth will be full of the knowledge of the Lord as the waters cover the sea (vv. 6–9).

What is impressive about this vision is the courage to hope for what appear by all human standards to be the totally impossible. If one wants to talk about false utopias, it appears that we have one here. But the prophet would not dare to hope for anything less, because he was convinced that justice and peace and communities of reconciliation are what God wills for the world, indeed for the whole creation, and God will bring it to pass. Nothing less can be the hope and inspiration for those who attempt to build communities of reconciliation.

Index

Abe, Masao, 185

Barth, Karl, ix, 70, 98, 109, 135
Bassham, Rodger C., 132, 132n1, 134
Bonheoffer, Dietrich, 135, 235
Bosch, David, 129–30, 133–34, 134n2, 142n4
Bible, x, xi, xiv, 28, 36, 45, 47, 49, 59, 61–64, 69–70, 75–76, 80n4, 82, 82n5, 83, 85–86, 88, 93, 98–99, 108, 119, 122, 158, 159, 165, 175, 187, 189, 194, 228–29, 230–31, 248
Buddha / Buddhist / Buddhism, viii, ix, x, 20, 25, 29, 49, 53–54, 57, 58, 83, 97, 125, 164–65, 183, 192
Buddhist-Christian Dialogue, x, 97, 183–86, 188

Cobb, John, 185
conflict, 33, 37, 48, 51, 62, 97, 120–21, 126, 138, 156, 189, 211, 234, 238, 234, 244–47
conversion / convert, xi, 37, 80, 82, 119–21, 124–26, 136, 139–46, 157, 160, 197–98, 203–4, 211, 213, 217–23, 246
Constantine (emperor), 157, 233

De Silva, Lynn, x, 97, 97n5, 188–90

ecumenical / ecumenism, ix, x, xiv, 46, 95, 105–13, 119, 121, 129, 134–35, 153, 161, 169, 180, 191, 196n2, 207, 234, 237, 243

Gandhi, M. K., 27, 64, 64n10, 66, 236
globalization, 34, 39, 177, 217

Hick, John, 101, 101n8, 106n1, 185
Hindu / Hinduism, vii–x, 20, 23–25, 37–38, 49, 51, 54, 55–56, 60, 61, 64–65, 77, 87, 94, 96, 97–98, 98n6, 99, 111, 199, 123, 138–41, 147–48, 148n7, 149, 153, 164–66, 171, 188, 195, 195n1, 196, 196n2, 197–207, 227, 239
Hindu-Christian Dialogue, viii, 139, 195, 198, 199, 201, 205, 205n6
human rights, 37, 62, 177, 211, 213–17, 237

identity, 41, 60, 110, 149, 171, 190, 204, 206–7, 218, 220, 227, 241, 246